THE OBAMAS

THE OBAMAS

The Untold Story of an African Family

PETER FIRSTBROOK

preface
publishing

Published by Preface Publishing 2010

10 9 8 7 6 5 4 3 2 1

Copyright © Peter Firstbrook 2010

Peter Firstbrook has asserted his right to be identified as the author of this work under
the Copyright, Designs and Patents Act 1988

First published in Great Britain in 2010 by Preface Publishing
20 Vauxhall Bridge Road
London SW1V 2SA

An imprint of The Random House Group Limited

www.rbooks.co.uk
www.prefacepublishing.co.uk

Addresses for companies within The Random House Group Limited
can be found at www.randomhouse.co.uk

The Random House Group Limited Reg. No. 954009

A CIP catalogue record for this book is available from the British Library

Hardback ISBN 978 1 84809 272 3
Trade paperback ISBN 978 1 84809 214 3

The Random House Group Limited supports The Forest Stewardship Council (FSC),
the leading international forest certification organisation. All our titles that are
printed on Greenpeace approved FSC certified paper carry the FSC logo.
Our paper procurement policy can be found at
www.rbooks.co.uk/environment

Typeset in Electra LH by Palimpsest Book Production Limited, Falkirk, Stirlingshire
Printed and bound in Great Britain by Clays Ltd, St Ives PLC

For Roy Samo

May your dream of a better
Kenya one day be realised

CONTENTS

The African ancestry of Barack Obama c. 1250 to present

SIN-KURU aka KUKU LUBANGA b. uncertain

[12 wives]

LIOLEITUK DYANG
The Plains Nilotes
including the Maasai, Langi,
Turkana, Samburu & Teso

ODONGO POK BONI
The Highland Nilotes
including the Nandi, Kipsigis,
Pokot, Tugen & Elgeyo

OPIYO PODHO KOMA
The River-Lake Nilotes
including the Shilluk, Dinka,
Nuer, Acholi, Alur, Padhola & Luo

. . . .

RINGRUOK b.1245?

OWAT b.1274?

TWAIFO b.1303?

JOK I b.1332?

NAYO b.1361?   OMOLO   OWINY

JOK II b.1390?

RAMOGI I b.1419?

PODHO II b.1450

LANG'INI   OKOMBO   OMIA   DIDANG'   MUWIRU b.1479?   OLAK b.1481?

RAMOGI II b.1469?   NYANDGUOGI b.1508?

ARUWA b.1448?   RAMOGI AJWANG' b.1500?   ORIAMBWA b.1537?   GOMA   WIRI   ADHOLA

NYALUO b.1498?   MONGRA b.1502?   OWINY b.1566?   NYALA   ADHOLA

OMOLO I b.1529?   OCHIELO b.1531?   KISODHI b.1595?

RAGAM b.1560?   GEM b.1562?   Naika

UGENYA b.1564?   Jong'a

[2 wives]

OGELO b.1624? NYABONG'O AGER WAMERAA OYO OMENYA ABURA OWINY SIGOMA

OKWIRI b.1655? NYAKWAR b.1657?

OKOTH b.1684?

NYOGORO b.1653?

ONYANGO MOBAM b.1713? (born with a curved back) NYANYODHI b.1715?

OGOLA b.1742?

OCHUO b.1771? OTONDI b.1773?

OBONG'O b.1802?

OGOLA b.1800?

OPIYO b.1833? Kendu Bay AGUK b.1835?

OBAMA b.1831?

OBAMA b.1864? Kendu Bay, d.1935? Kendu Bay AGINGA b.1864?

OBILO b.1862?

Nyaoke Auma Mwanda Odero Augo

[5 wives]

NDALO RABURU b.1893? Kendu Bay

HUSSEIN ONYANGO OBAMA b.1895 Kendu Bay, d.1975 K'ogelo SALMON OGUTA b.1897? Kendu Bay

m.Habiba Akumu b. ?
Kendu Bay d. Kendu Bay 2006

m.Sarah b.1922 Kendu Bay

[5 wives] Unknown name b. ? m.Halima b. ? Sophia Odera b. ?

BARACK OBAMA Snr b.1936 Kendu Bay, d.1982 Nairobi Hawa Auma b.1942 Kendu Bay

Ruth Nidesand, m.Nairobi 1965 Jael, m.Nairobi 1981?

Sarah Nyaoke b.1934 Kendu Bay, d. ? Nairobi

Kezia Nyandega, Kendu Bay m.1957

Stanley Ann Dunham m.2 Feb. 1961, d.29 Nov. 1995

[4 wives]

BARACK HUSSEIN OBAMA b.Honolulu 4 Aug. 1961

Michelle LaVaughn Robinson b.Chicago 17 Jan. 1964 m.3 Oct. 1992

Natasha b. Chicago 2001

[Wife]

Malia Ann b. Chicago 1998

Based on: Weere, Melik Ogutta, *Mel Dhoudi moko mag Luo* loosely translated as 'Other Sub-Tribes of the Luo Community', Edition, Earstar, 2007, original research, personal communication with Professor Ogutu and oral history from Obama elders. Ogot (1967 & 2009), Cohen (1968), For further details of methodology; see page 244.

MAPS

LIST OF
ILLUSTRATIONS

ACKNOWLEDGEMENTS

Ling' chicko it en ohala
The good listener learns many new things

Over the course of several months from November 2008 and throughout 2009, I criss-crossed Kenya as part of my research for this book. It is impossible to spend this amount of time in a foreign country without relying on the wisdom and support of many people. First, my gratitude has to go to the many members of the Obama family who opened their doors and welcomed me into their homes. In K'ogelo, I watched 'Mama' Sarah, step-grandmother to President Obama, greet literally coachloads of people who came to pay their respects to her; I would wait my turn to see her, and she always greeted me with kindness, patience and good humour. In Ouygis, Hawa Auma, President Obama's aunt, was always ready to stop her work to spend time with me – and she was always ready to kill a chicken and cook me a meal. Kendu Bay is home to most of the Obama family, and Charles Olouch, Elly Yonga Adhiambo, John Ndalo Aguk and Laban Opiyo were all very generous with both their time and their insight into the history of the Obamas; my thanks also go to Imam Saidi Aghmani, who introduced me to the Islamic community in Kendu Bay. In Kisumu, Wilson Obama and his wife Karen were always generous with their support, as were Aloyce Achayo and Leo Omolo Odera. Sam Dhillou from Nairobi was also very helpful and supportive during my early research. This list cannot do justice to the many other

Kenyans I interviewed for the book, but their contribution is recognised within the body of the text.

In the USA my old friend Thom Beers was very supportive at a crucial early stage of my research, and in Oxford Professor David Anderson gave me valuable counsel about the early history of Kenyan independence. In London I have special thanks for my agent, Sheila Ableman, who encouraged me to write a book rather than make a film. At Preface my editor Trevor Dolby has offered his constant encouragement and support during both gestation and delivery, and has gently nudged me at the right times to tease the most from my material.

In Kenya Roy Samo acted as my researcher and translator; he was always on hand, and without his unceasing help it would not have been possible to write this book. At home my wife Paula has balanced being both my fiercest critic and at the same time my strongest supporter.

I thank them all.

Wuothi eka ine
To travel is to see plenty

Barack Obama's election in November 2008 resulted in a demonstration of wide-spread public support on the streets of Kisumu, the heartland of the Luo tribe.

PROLOGUE

Wat en wat
Kinship is kinship

When the American people elect a president, they choose, de facto, a new leader of the free world. Overnight this individual becomes the single most powerful person in the world. The election of a young senator from Illinois in November 2008 caused more of a stir around the world than usual. It was not primarily because of his lack of experience in executive decision-making, but because he was black – or to be strictly correct, half-black. Although Barack Obama was brought up in Hawaii and Indonesia by a single mother for most of his early years, his absent father was African, from a tribe called the Luo who live around the shores of Lake Victoria in western Kenya. President Obama never really knew his father, and he recalls meeting him only once during a brief visit that he made to Hawaii just before Christmas 1971, when the young Barack was just ten years old. The president never saw his father again, because Barack Obama Snr died eleven years later, when he crashed his car into a tree one night in Nairobi.

It is clear from his two books, *Dreams from My Father*, and *The Audacity of Hope*, that President Obama is very conscious of his mixed heritage, unsure of where he belonged as a young man, in a multi-cultural world. In his self-deprecatory style, he referred to himself as a 'mutt' in his first speech after his election, when he spoke about getting a dog for his children:

'Our preference is to get a shelter dog, but most shelter dogs are mutts like me.'

In *Dreams*, he talks about his struggle as a young man to come to terms with his mixed racial heritage; later, he recalls his first visit to Kenya in 1987 to meet his father's family, and to learn more about his African birthright. It is clear from *Dreams* that his African 'roots' became important to him; his relatives asked him: 'Barry, what made you finally come home?' He felt welcomed in Kenya, and he came to understand the importance that Africans place on family. Obama was taken to see his step-grandmother, Sarah Obama, who still lives in her husband's compound which the family call 'Home Squared'. It is here that Barack Obama Snr is buried, and he wrote movingly about the father he never knew:

> I dropped to the ground and swept my hand across the smooth yellow tile. Oh, Father, I cried ... When my tears were finally spent, I felt a calmness wash over me. I felt the circle finally close. I realised that who I was, what I cared about, was no longer just a matter of intellect or obligation, no longer a construct of words. I saw that my life in America – the black life, the white life, the sense of abandonment I'd felt as a boy, the frustration and hope I'd witnessed in Chicago – all of it was connected with this small plot of earth an ocean away, connected by more than the accident of name or the colour of my skin.[1]

Even the title of this first book hints at his lost opportunity in life – of never really knowing his father: 'I had been forced to look inside myself,' he wrote in *Dreams from My Father*, 'and had found only a great emptiness there.'[2] In his second book, *The Audacity of Hope*, he again hints at the influence his multi-racial background has on his character. When talking about growing older, he notes that 'each successive year will make you more intimately acquainted with all your flaws – the blind spots, recurring habits of thought that may be genetic or may be environmental, but that will almost certainly worsen with time, as surely as the hitch in your walk turns to pain in your hip.'[3]

When talking of his political beliefs in *Audacity*, Barack Obama acknowledges that he is a prisoner of his own biography: 'I can't help but view the American experience through the lens of a black man of mixed heritage, forever mindful of how generations of people who looked like me were subjugated and stigmatized, and the subtle and not so subtle ways that race and class continue to shape our lives.'[4]

Perhaps the most telling part of Obama's prologue to *Audacity* is where he makes a direct reference to his own father. He wrote: 'Someone once said that every man is trying to either live up to his father's expectations or make up for his father's mistakes, and I suppose that may explain my particular malady as well as anything else.'[5]

It was because of what he called 'a chronic restlessness' that had pursued him throughout his adult life that Obama decided to run for the US Senate in 2000. That year he was unsuccessful, but he tried again in November 2004 and won with 70 per cent of the vote. Obama then made headlines around the world when he announced, in February 2007, his candidacy for the 2008 Democratic presidential nomination. He was locked in a tight battle with the former first lady, and later the New York senator, Hillary Clinton, until he became the presumptive nominee on 3 June 2008. Five months later, on 4 November 2008, Barack Obama defeated the Republican presidential nominee, John McCain, to become the 44th president of the United States and the first African-American to hold the office.

Like many Americans, President Obama can trace the ancestral background on his mother's side to a broad mix of European blood; he is, apparently, about 37 per cent English, with additional contributions from German, Irish, Scottish, Welsh and even Swiss forebears. In many ways, this is a mixture which is not uncommon among white Americans descended from European stock. On his father's side, however, the mix is much simpler; he is 50 per cent African, descended from a long line of Luo tribal warriors who originally lived in the Sudan; over the centuries they migrated across 1,000km of desert, swamp and jungle before eventually settling around the shores of Lake Victoria in Kenya.

This book has grown out of my long interest in Africa as a documentary filmmaker. Over the years I have made dozens of visits to Africa, but I had not actually worked in Kenya since 1987. Within just a couple of weeks of Obama's election as the new president, I was out again in Kenya with the intention of researching a film about the village where his family originated. I met many members of the Obama family; some had been in the media spotlight in the run-up to the election, but there were many more whose voices had never been heard. Even though I only scratched the surface of the history of the Obamas and the annals of the Luo people on this first visit, I realised that there was a fascinating story to be told. So the documentary was put on hold, and I decided that the story of Obama's family – and the extraordinary history of the Luo people – needed to be told in a different way.

This book, then, is the fruit of several more visits to the shores of Lake Victoria, to that part of western Kenya that is called Luoland. Barack Obama's upbringing and education in America, and then in Indonesia, has been well covered elsewhere, both by the President himself and by other writers. I hope, therefore, that this book will offer some insight into the little-known half of President Barack Obama – that half of him which is Luo and which has its genetic roots in a long line of formidable African warriors. It is a family lineage of which the President himself is only vaguely aware. In 2006 he made his third visit to Kenya, but this time it was in an official capacity as an African-American member of the US Senate. He upset many senior Kenyan politicians on that trip with his outspokenness, but the ordinary people loved him. His visit was brief and he had only a short time to visit the village where his father grew up. His relatives told me that he had less than forty-five minutes to meet his extended family, who lined up in the hot equatorial sun in their dozens outside Mama Sarah's hut, waiting for their brief few seconds with their most favoured son. Barack Obama's aunt and closest living relative showed me, with obvious pride, the set of drinking glasses which she had been given on that visit; sadly, in the few seconds that she spent with her nephew, Hawa Auma did not have time to tell him the extraordinary story of how his grandfather fell in love with his grandmother, nor the tragic circumstances of their separation; Charles Olouch did not tell the Senator about his suspicions as to how Barack Obama Snr *really* died in 1982; nor have his father's friends ever had the chance to tell Barack Obama about the parties they had together at Harvard as students in the mid-sixties.

Despite his American upbringing, President Obama has taken on the position of a near demi-god in Kenya. Like all African tribes, the Luo have a rich chronicle of proverbs and sayings, and there is one which strikes me as particularly poignant: *Wat en wat* – 'Kinship is kinship', which loosely translated means 'blood is thicker than water'. The Luo will never consider Obama to be a white man. Regardless of where he was raised, or what he might say or do, they will always see him as an African – a true Luo with an ancestry that can be traced back two dozen generations.

Writing *The Obamas* has really been a process of assembling a large pile of jigsaw pieces. Without the patient support, help and generosity of dozens of local people – eminent historians, members of the Obama family and Luo elders alike – this book would not have been possible.

These people unstintingly supplied me with all the individual pieces to the jigsaw; all I have tried to do is to arrange them into a coherent picture of the past.

Peter Firstbrook,
Kisumu,
Western Kenya

·The 44th President of the United States takes the oath of office from US Supreme Chief Justice John Roberts Jnr, 20 January 2009. Michelle Obama holds the Bible used by President Abraham Lincoln at his inauguration in 1861.

1

TWO ELECTIONS, TWO PRESIDENTS

Ber telo en telo
The benefit of power is power

**The elections of Barack Obama of the USA, and of Mwai Kibaki of
Kenya; the cultural, social and political issues in Kenya today**

The evening was drawing in, dark clouds rolled overhead and ominous
specks of rain were making themselves felt in the hot, sticky, tropical twilight.
It was not the ideal start to the evening; five hundred relatives and friends
had gathered in the Obama ancestral home to watch on television the
presidential inauguration of their most famous son. We were all sitting
outside in the family compound in a remote village in western Kenya, just
a stone's throw from Lake Victoria, and the heavens looked as if they were
about to open. Some of the people had already walked several miles to get
here, and many of them were related to the president-elect either through
birth or by marriage. We had less than two hours to go before Barack
Obama took his historic oath of office, but the inclement weather and
encroaching darkness were not the worst of our problems. We still had no
television available, the only generator to be found had no fuel or oil, and
there was no aerial set up to receive the broadcast.

It had seemed so simple and straightforward the previous day, when I
sat down with the village committee to discuss their preparations for the
celebrations – the Kenyans love their committees. Yes, there would be three

televisions for people to watch, and three generators to power them. The trees around the compound would be strung with electric bulbs, and all of them 100 watts, so that we would have plenty of light. They would slaughter a cow and several goats, and they welcomed my offer to bring a dozen crates of soft drinks, but definitely no beer as they were all Seventh Day Adventists.

I was in K'obama, a small village just outside of Kendu Bay, itself a small township on the shores of Lake Victoria. K'obama is home to dozens of families, all of them related in one way or another to the recently elected president. Like many small villages in this part of Kenya, the ancestral name takes the prefix 'K' to denote the family homestead. I had found that K'obama had been largely ignored by the international press since the election of Barack Obama. Journalists and television crews had all headed to K'ogelo, a small village on the northern side of Winam Gulf and home to 'Mama Sarah', step-grandmother to the president-elect. Yet when I visited K'ogelo a couple of months previously just after the election, I found a sleepy, quiet village, and the only 'Obama' living there permanently was Sarah herself. K'obama, however, was very different and a hive of activity, with literally hundreds of Obama relatives in residence. Yet here I was, on the eve of the presidential inauguration and not a journalist in sight, or even another *mzungu* (a white man in Swahili). I had my suspicions why K'ogelo had attracted all the attention of the world's press, but I did not get confirmation of the real reason until sometime later.

Meanwhile, although the party in K'obama was in full swing, there was still no sign of a television set. I had tracked down a couple of empty fuel cans and I sent our van off to buy some petrol for the generator, but that had not materialised either. It had been a few years since I had last worked in Africa. It is one of my favourite places to visit, but it is not without its challenges. I knew that the Luo, Obama's African tribe, were known for being easy-going and generous, and I had received nothing but help and support from them. But they also had a reputation for, among other things, talking big and doing very little.

With little more than an hour to go before darkness fell over K'obama, my luck began to change; not one, but two televisions suddenly arrived. The first made its entrance balanced precariously on a wheelbarrow. Then the second turned up – this was one that I had previously negotiated to hire for the evening from a neighbour. The van came back with fuel for the generators, and within minutes I breathed a sigh of relief as the little Honda spluttered into life and the televisions lit up into a grainy image.

Perhaps we would, at least, be able to watch the historic inauguration after all. It was, however, not all going my way; we could not get both televisions to tune to the same station at first, and a TV aerial had to be lashed to a long wooden pole and hoisted high above rooftop level in order to get reasonable reception.

Meanwhile the Obama family members began to drag their cheap plastic garden chairs in front of the two screens. Darkness falls quickly in the tropics, and soon everybody was settling down for the evening, apparently oblivious to the gathering storm clouds. It was a wonderfully diverse mix of people, from six-year-old school children to great-grandmothers in their eighties. Dozens of people came and thanked me for helping to get the TVs working, some of them smelling as if they had been drinking more than fizzy soda. I had not actually seen any beer around, but illicit alcohol is commonly available in Kenya, and I suspect that some of the revellers were not conforming to the strict lifestyle expected of Seventh Day Adventists.

Local brew has always been fermented in Kenya, but traditionally it was only as strong as beer. However, stronger and more potent brews have become more popular in recent years, encouraged no doubt by the high taxes imposed on alcohol by the government. The police often turn a blind eye to the brewing in return for a cut of the profits. Sometimes these drinks are 'fortified' with methanol, a toxic wood alcohol, which can have disastrous consequences. They call the drink *chang'aa*, but it is also given other popular names such as 'Power Drink', which gives a hint to the strength of the industrial additive, and 'Kill-Me-Quick', which frankly is a more honest description. It has been known for people in illegal drinking dens to complain that the lights had been switched off in the bar, when in practice the lethal concoction they were drinking had turned them blind in an instant. One of the most severe drinking accidents happened in 2000, when 130 people died and over 400 were hospitalised after drinking a toxic batch of the brew.

As darkness began to fall, we managed to tune the televisions to gain a reasonable reception on the same channel, and the audience became transfixed by the events unfolding before their eyes, 12,000km away in Washington DC. Unknown to us at the time, some of the Obamas who had travelled to the USA had arrived at the White House late for the inauguration, only to be turned away because they could not take their seats in time before the president-elect arrived on stage. Apparently there had been a mix-up with the arrangements, and they were picked up late

from their hotel; despite producing their Kenyan passports and their
official invitations which showed the most famous surname in the world
on that day, their pleas went unheeded, and they returned to their hotel
where they watched the very same CNN coverage that we were watching
in K'obama.

There was little interest in much of the early proceedings of the
inauguration ceremony and people chatted among themselves. After all,
these people lived in huts with tin roofs, with neither running water nor
electricity. What interest did they have in the finer details of the president's
new limousine, with its eight-inch armour plating and tear-gas cannons?
Most of these people do not even own a bicycle, and they would have no
idea whether Obama's new Cadillac, which gets eight miles to the gallon,
was a good thing or not. The long list of guests arriving on the podium
meant nothing to the five hundred-strong Obama family. As the assembled
dignitaries shivered in the bitter Washington winter, where the air temper-
ature had fallen several degrees below freezing, the Kenyans were glancing
nervously upward and wondering if the tropical rainstorm was going to stay
away.

One by one, past presidents assembled in front of the podium: Jimmy
Carter, George Bush Snr, Bill Clinton, and finally the outgoing George
W. Bush. Then the president-elect appeared, and the imminent downpour
over Kendu Bay was instantly forgotten as the crowd roared his name, and
stood up to applaud 'their' man. As the proceedings moved at a glacial
speed in Washington, the raindrops over Kendu Bay dried up in the tropical heat, only to be replaced by mosquitoes and flying ants. Personally, I
preferred the rain – at least it didn't bite.

Finally, the big moment arrived. Supreme Court Justice John Roberts
moved to the podium to be joined by the president-elect. (Cue more
exuberant cheering from the Kenyans.) Obama was about to make history
by becoming the first African-American US president in history. Before
him, over a million people were gathered in the National Mall, with the
vast crowd stretching as far back as the Washington Monument in the
distance. Justice Roberts led with the oath, 'I, Barack Hussein Obama, do
solemnly swear [pause] that I will execute the Office of the President faithfully.' Like the majority of television viewers around the world, nobody in
Kendu Bay was aware at the time that Justice Roberts had made an error
in the order of the words. No doubt the two men had practised this moment
several times, and a faint smile seemed to cross Obama's face as he realised
that Roberts, a fellow Harvard Law School graduate, had misplaced the

word 'faithfully' during the oath. Barack Obama continued, '... and will to the best of my ability, preserve, protect and defend the Constitution of the United States.'

With the President now secure in the highest office in the world, the Kendu Bay Obamas went wild, chanting 'Obama! Obama! Obama!', echoing the exuberant crowd in front of the White House. It was a night that united Kenya. At no other time since Nelson Mandela became president of South Africa has the continent been filled with such hope for the future and, not surprisingly, it took several minutes before everybody in K'obama settled down to listen to Obama's inauguration speech.

Rarely has an American president taken office with so many profound challenges facing him, both at home and abroad: 'My fellow citizens; I stand here today humbled by the task before us, grateful for the trust you have bestowed, mindful of the sacrifices borne by our ancestors.'

In Washington, as in Kendu Bay, the crowds were transfixed by both the mesmerising rhythm of his elegant delivery and the content. Obama continued: 'Yet every so often the oath is taken amidst gathering clouds and raging storms . . . On this day, we gather because we have chosen hope over fear, unity of purpose over conflict and discord.'

Obama was laying out his priorities for the next four years: 'We will build the roads and bridges, the electric grids and digital lines that feed our commerce and bind us together.'

As I looked around at the people watching his speech, their faces beaming with pride, it struck me that Kendu Bay could do with a few roads, bridges and electric grids. Obama continued to lay out his manifesto for the world: 'And so, to all other peoples and governments who are watching today, from the grandest capitals to the small village where my father was born . . .'

This was too much for the Obamas in Kendu Bay, who were sitting less than a hundred metres from that very spot. The party dissolved into a riotous cheer, which surely must have been heard 12,000km away in Washington.

Three months earlier, in November 2008, I had sat up in London into the early hours of the morning to watch the drama of the US election unfold around the world, live on global television. This presidential election, perhaps more so than any other in recent memory, had galvanised the whole world. As Barack Obama walked out onto the stage in Grant Park,

Chicago, on the evening of 4 November 2008, he made his acceptance speech to a devoted audience, some of whom had been standing for over four hours in the chill Illinois evening. 'It's been a long time coming,' announced the president-elect, 'but tonight, because of what we did on this day, in this election, at this defining moment, change has come to America.' It was a momentous occasion: the first 'person of colour' had been elected to be president of the United States of America. It had been a remarkable road for a nation to follow and came just forty-five years after the landmark Civil Rights Act of 1964, which outlawed racial segregation in schools, public places, and employment.

When Barack Obama was born in August 1961, much of the American South remained segregated, and black and white American citizens were separated from cradle to grave. Black Americans were born in segregated hospitals, they were educated in segregated schools and they were buried in segregated graveyards. In 1961, the year that Obama's father married Ann Dunham in Honolulu, a racially mixed marriage was not even legal in seventeen states of the Union. Forty-seven years on, their son stood in front of an international television audience measured in billions, to accept the mantle of leader of the free world.

As Barack Obama noted in his acceptance speech that evening: 'The road ahead will be long. Our climb will be steep. We may not get there in one year or even one term, but America – I have never been more hopeful than I am tonight that we will get there. I promise you – we, as a people, will get there.'

It was rousing oration and it appealed to what is arguably the greatest single historic achievement of the USA as a society – the ability over a period of three centuries to absorb a disparate group of immigrants and bind them into a single nation, a people with a common purpose and with a strong sense of national identity. In 2004 Obama spoke about this accomplishment at the Democratic National Convention in what was then the FleetCenter in Boston, Massachusetts: 'There is not a black America and white America and Latino America and Asian America – there's the United States of America.'

It is a very different scenario in the homeland of the president's father, Barack Obama Snr. Even today, if you stop any Kenyan at random, even in Nairobi where traditional customs are weakest, and ask them where their main allegiance lies, they will almost certainly reply that their tribe is much more important to them than their country. This is certainly the case with the Luo, the tribe of the president's African family. Even though Kenya has been an independent nation since 1963, ethnic groups in the country go back for centuries, and there is still much to keep tribal identity strong. This is especially true in the rural areas, and particularly among the biggest five tribes in Kenya. This has, inevitably, led to a fractious history, both before British colonial rule and after Kenyan independence. The problem with tribal conflict is particularly acute between the Kikuyu (the largest and most dominant tribe in Kenya) and the Luo (the tribe of the Obamas).

I first worked in Kenya in 1987, five years after Barack Obama's father died in a car accident in Nairobi and the same year Barack Obama Jnr first visited his African relatives. Inevitably, Kenya was a very different country back then, but in some ways, I also found very little had changed. Back in 1987, Daniel arap Moi had been president for nearly ten years, and he would remain so for another fifteen. He came to power promising an end to corruption, smuggling, tribalism and the detention of political opponents, and he enjoyed popular support throughout the country. By the time I made my first visit to Kenya, his good intentions had not stood the test of time, and his government increasingly relied on the use of secret police, torture, human rights abuses and political assassination to stay in power.[1] He changed the nation's Constitution to make Kenya a single-party state, suppressed political opponents, and cleverly manipulated Kenya's mix of ethnic and tribal tensions to weaken and divide the opposition.

In 1999 Amnesty International and the United Nations compiled reports which accused Moi of serious human rights abuses.[2] Moi was barred for running for another presidential term in 2002, and the following year news of even more human rights abuses began to surface, including the use of torture. Throughout his time in power, corruption was rife in Kenya, and in October 2006 Moi was found guilty of taking a US$2 million bribe from a Pakistani businessman in return for a monopoly of duty-free shops in the country's international airports.[3] Although people told me that in many ways life was better in 2009 than it was back in 1987, I was soon to find out that political assassination, corruption and tribalism were still a routine part of political life in Kenya.

As soon as I stepped off the aircraft at Jomo Kenyatta International Airport in November 2008, it was obvious that other big changes had happened since my first visit. Nairobi is no longer the gentle colonial city that it had been in 1987; traffic now clogs the streets and air pollution has become a serious problem. The number of vehicles on the road has doubled in ten years and Kenya now has one of the worst road safety records in the world. Yet despite the large numbers of Mercedes and Land Cruisers on the streets, the majority of people still earn less than $2 (£1.20) a day. When I first came to Kenya in 1987, the population was 22.4 million; today, it is 39 million people (2009 estimate).[4] In Nairobi, 60 per cent of the population live in shanty towns and the city's largest, Kibera, is said to be Africa's biggest slum, and home to over one million people.

Kenya has always been a nation with strong tribal divisions, and this had not changed in twenty years. There are over forty separate tribal groups in the country, with the Kikuyu the biggest group by far with 22 per cent of the population, followed by the Luhya with 14 per cent, the Luo with 13, the Kalenjin with 12 and the Kamba 11 per cent; other smaller tribes make up a further 27 per cent of the population, and non-African (Asian, European and Arab) just 1 per cent. Religious beliefs are equally divided: 45 per cent of Kenyans are Protestant, 33 per cent are Roman Catholic, with Muslims and traditional religions making up about 10 per cent each.

As the most populous tribe, the Kikuyu have dominated Kenyan politics ever since the country gained its independence from Britain in 1963. In that year Jomo Kenyatta, a Kikuyu, became the country's first president. (The similarity of his name to his country's is coincidental.) The Kikuyu also have a reputation for being very successful in trade and commerce. The traditional Kikuyu lands are in central Kenya, in the fertile highlands to the south and west of Mount Kenya. It was this region which attracted the white colonists in the early part of the twentieth century. As a consequence, the Kikuyu (along with the Kalenjin and the Maasai), suffered extensive displacement as the whites took over their traditional lands and turned their farms into large plantations growing coffee, tea and cotton.

The Luhya are the second largest tribe with a population of over 5 million, but they are widely spread around the country and much more diverse than any other ethnic group in Kenya, with around sixteen or eighteen sub-groups. Many of these sub-groups speak their own Luhya dialect, and several are so different from one another that some linguists consider them to be separate languages altogether. Because of their diversification, the Luhya have a much smaller political voice in the country than might be expected from their numbers.

The Luo, Kenya's third largest tribe, has a population of just under 5 million (2008 estimate). This is the tribe of Barack Obama's ancestors.

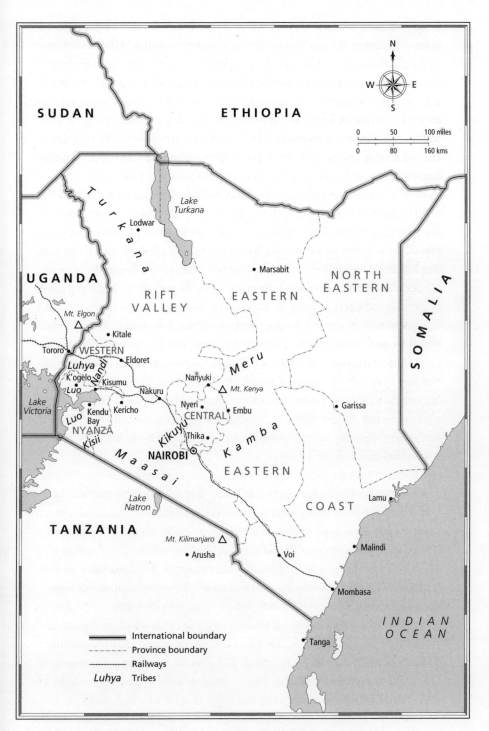

Provinces, major towns and main tribal areas in Kenya.

They traditionally place much emphasis on education, and have produced many scholars in Kenya, some of whom have graduated from prestigious colleges around the world (including Barack Obama Snr, who graduated from the University of Hawaii in 1962, and later took a master's degree in economics at Harvard). As a result, Luo professionals dominate almost every part of Kenyan society, and frequently serve as university professors, doctors, engineers and lawyers.

One such Luo professional is Leo Odera Omolo, a respected journalist based in Kisumu. Leo has spent all of his life reporting from around Africa, and was on first-name terms with practically every African president who has ruled since their country became independent. He once told me that Idi Amin of Uganda challenged him to a wrestling match – not once, but three times. He was very proud to have beaten him on each occasion; I told him that I thought accepting a match with Amin was a very brave thing to do, but actually beating him was probably reckless. (During Amin's brutal regime in Uganda, between 100,000 and 500,000 people are thought to have died.)

I asked Leo to explain to me what made the Luo different from other Kenyans. He pulled down his lower lip to reveal six missing front teeth. Most African tribes traditionally circumcise boys to mark the onset of manhood. But the Luo (and some other Nilotic tribes whose ancestors migrated south from Sudan), mark the end of childhood of both sexes in a different, but still painful way, by removing the six bottom front teeth. 'I am a Luo,' he said with a cheeky grin and a twinkle in his eyes, which belied his seventy-three years:

'I have twenty-three children by five wives, and another three children by women who were not quite my wives. We are tall, very black and very intelligent because we eat lots of protein, lots of fish. We like to party, and we are generous with our friends.

'The Luo are fair and they are democratic people. They want to discuss issues. They don't want secrecy. They don't have "night meetings". If they call a meeting, they will reveal it outside when they've done.

'They also squabble and fight, but the fight can be resolved very quickly. The next day, if nobody is killed, you are friends again. That is a trait of the Luo. Some of them are hot-tempered – they come up and down quickly – but they don't hold a grudge after a disagreement.

'There are also so many parties with the Luo. At a funeral – a lot of it; marriage – a lot of it. Everything in Luo society is a party. They spend a lot of their energy and resources in parties. A funeral will deplete a family and leave them poor, like the one we went to yesterday. They will clear everything in the home and leave them poor, because they slaughter all the cows they have, goats, everything. They will even clear their grain store.'

When Kenya became independent in 1963, it was the Kikuyu and the Luo who primarily inherited political power. This has led to inevitable tension between the two tribal groups, which most recently led to vicious and barbaric inter-tribal conflict in January 2008, when the fighting degenerated into riots against President Mwai Kibaki, a Kikuyu. The opposition leader, Raila Odinga, a Luo, accused Kibaki of vote rigging. Kibaki went ahead and unilaterally declared that he had won the election, but local and foreign observers claimed it had been 'fixed'. It was this manipulation of power which led to the eruption of violence. However, the simple fact is that inter-tribal tension lies perpetually just below the surface of Kenyan politics, and this has been the case for many decades.

Although the worst atrocities during the post-election violence took place in the Rift Valley, there was also carnage in Kisumu, Kenya's third largest city and the centre of the Luo homeland. Roy Samo is a local councillor in Kisumu, and he experienced the post-election violence at close quarters:

'I saw everything because I was a political leader. They were counting the figures and Raila Odinga [the Luo political leader] was leading the president by more than a million votes. Then there was [an electrical] blackout and the next minute, [President] Kibaki was leading Raila by one million votes. Nobody could believe it! All these were disputed figures. We have a town with an 80,000 maximum electorate, so how can the President get 150,000 out of a possible 80,000 votes?

'So when people were watching all this on their TVs, and they announced that Kibaki had won, then violence erupted. I remember when they announced it – I was here in my house watching the result. People from all their houses and in the bars, they started screaming and shouting and a cloud of death could be seen hanging around Kisumu. It was a big voice all over Kisumu. It was around 6 p.m. I was there, and I was seeing this. People were watching their TVs and they started seeing how people in Nairobi were reacting. Like in Kibera [Nairobi's biggest slum], they started burning tyres, uprooting the railway. So that is what sparked off the violence in Kisumu, 'cos they saw that their cousins, their brothers and other Luos in Nairobi were doing this. And not only Luos – they were hearing what was happening in the Rift Valley, where they all started burning houses.

'Around 8 p.m., Kisumu also started going up in flames. In Kisumu it was about looting and the burning of property. The Luo never killed, because they are afraid of blood. In Kisumu, I can confidently say this, they never killed anybody. [But] so many people rushed into supermarkets to loot. In that place, sixteen people were burned [to death] and fifteen people were shot dead. In my area, ten people were shot dead, because by now the police were shooting people. The violence in Kisumu was between the Luos and any Kikuyu or anyone with Kikuyu interests. They burned properties and looted. For example, if you're a Luo but married to a Kikuyu, then they'll burn your house. They started on the 29th of December 2007, up to February the 28th when Raila [Odinga] and Kibaki signed an agreement.

'The government figures say that 1,500 were killed, which we dispute. It's ten times more than that, and 500,000 people were displaced. But now, as we are talking [in May 2009], 220,000 people are still living in tented camps. We call them IDPs – internally displaced persons. Fifteen hundred [Kenyan] people are still living in Uganda.'

Tribalism remains strong in Kenya for several reasons. Primary school children usually learn their tribal language first, before moving on to Swahili and then English. Even today, young people usually marry within their own tribe, especially if they stay living within their tribal area. Religion and traditional customs also strengthen the tribal bond of Kenyans. Teeth extraction is now mostly a thing of the past, and circumcision is encouraged for all Kenyan males as a way of reducing HIV/AIDS, which has reached epidemic proportions of 1 in 5 of young Luo males. (Recent research has shown that circumcised men are 60 per cent less likely to contract the disease).[5]

Not surprisingly, many of the younger, sexually active men support the idea of circumcision, but it has caused a storm of protest from the more traditional Luos. I went down to Dunga beach, a small fishing village on the shores of Lake Victoria near Kisumu, and talked to some of the fishermen there. Dunga is the only working fishing village left in the Kisumu area, and women walk up to 15km every morning to buy fish to carry back and sell in their village. The women earn less than 100 Kenyan shillings (80 pence) a day, but the fishermen are traditionally some of the best paid workers in the region, often earning Ksh500–1000 (£4–8) a day or more. With a steady daily income, the fishermen have money to burn. I spoke to Charles Otieno, a local fisherman and a community leader in the Dunga cooperative:

'HIV is a very big problem along the beaches. For example this beach. If I told you most of these women here are widows and most of their husbands have died of HIV. So they come and interact with the fishermen. The men have many girlfriends, they never have one girlfriend. For example, I'm a fisherman. I can fish at Dunga beach one week, another week I go to another beach and I fish there, and then I go to another beach and I have to obtain another girlfriend there. So every time I do that, most of the fishermen do that.'

I asked Charles if many of his friends had been circumcised to help prevent catching the HIV virus: 'According to our customs and beliefs – it started from earliest times – our people were not being circumcised. So most of the people don't believe in that. Some of the people have gone for circumcision, but most of the people, they are not going.'

'The kind of money they are making makes them lead these careless lives,' claims Pamela Akinyi, a clinical administrator in a Centre for Disease Control nearby: 'We did some mobile HIV testing and we went down to the beach, and we found about six out of ten were HIV positive. We refer them to the patient's support centre for more [medical] intervention and more information. We refer them and tell them, "Please go to this place!" But most of them don't go to the patients' support centre.'

About 80km west of the main city of Kisumu is the tiny village of Nyang'oma K'ogelo, where President Obama's father, Barack Obama Snr, and his grandfather Hussein Onyango Obama, are buried. Even during the primary elections in the USA, media attention on the Obama family in K'ogelo was intense, and it became positively frenzied once Obama won the election. Within a couple of weeks of the election, I found myself driving along a newly repaired red-dirt road into K'ogelo, where President Obama's step-grandmother Sarah Obama still lives. The road was in much better condition than I expected, and I mentioned this to Roy Samo, my researcher and translator: 'Ber telo en telo – the benefit of power is power,' he chuckled as he recalled a Luo proverb. The road had obviously been upgraded very recently, and workers were still putting in culverts to deal with the flooding during the rainy season. Alongside the dirt track, more workers were installing wooden electricity poles. For the first time in their history, some of the residents of K'ogelo would have light after dark, at the flick of a switch, but only if they could afford it. The first person to benefit from the electricity was 'Mama Sarah' as she is universally known, step-grandmother to the new president and the youngest wife of Hussein Onyango Obama, the president's grandfather.

K'ogelo is in Nyanza province in western Kenya, virtually on the equator and about 25km from the shores of Lake Victoria and 40km from the Kenya/Uganda border. The area is almost as far west as you can go in Kenya without ending up in Uganda, or getting your feet wet in Lake Victoria. The village is part of the Siaya district, one of a dozen sub-divisions of Nyanza. (Nyanza is the Bantu word for a large body of water.) Nyanza is one of seven regional administrative provinces in the country, with Kenya's third largest city, Kisumu, the provincial capital.

K'ogelo turned out to be a very ordinary, very sleepy Kenyan community, with no running water and a population of just 3,648.[6] Most of the huts are spread across the rolling hillsides, separated by fields of maize. The village centre has a handful of shops scattered round an area of hard-baked earth, which serves as the market place on Tuesdays and Fridays. In the local shops you can buy a leg of goat from the butcher, a bottle of local beer from the bar, or a simple meal in one of several small 'hotels' – tiny drinking and eating establishments with not a bed in sight. There are even two barber shops, which are usually good places to hang out to get the latest gossip. But in all the time that I spent in K'ogelo, I never actually saw anybody having their hair cut, and the two barbers seemed to earn their living from renting out their battery-powered disco equipment for parties. The busiest workers in the village were the two old men who repair punctures; they both seemed to have a never-ending row of bicycles lined up against the trees, all in need of some tender loving care. However, the real action in K'ogelo seems to take place under the shade of a large Acacia tree. Here, the young men of the village spend most of the day sitting around smoking and putting the world to rights.

In this part of Kenya, most rural people live modestly, working as small-scale farmers growing subsistence crops such as maize, millet and sorghum, supplemented with the occasional cow and a few chickens. The region around K'ogelo is one of gently undulating hillsides, where farming is modestly productive, but not especially fertile. Nyanza, often referred to as Luoland, does not have the rich farming land of the central highlands, and therefore this area was less attractive to the white colonists when they settled in the region a century ago. The close proximity to Lake Victoria also means that this region is one of the worst places in Kenya for mosquitoes, and malaria is a common killer, especially among young children. In sub-

Saharan Africa, almost 3,000 children die *every day* from malaria, and it is the biggest killer of children under the age of five. However, the recent introduction of free mosquito nets in Kenya has resulted in a dramatic fall in child mortality from the disease, down by over 40 per cent.[7]

Like the more fortunate villages in Kenya, K'ogelo also has two schools. The land for these two schools was donated by President Obama's grandfather, and they were named the Senator Obama Primary School and the Senator Obama Secondary School, after the senator (as he then was) visited the village in 2006. These two schools are typically Kenyan; simple, brick structures with no window frames and few facilities. Outside, the neighbour's cattle graze in the school grounds; inside, the classrooms are packed with eager young faces. Everywhere in Africa, you will find school children with an enthusiasm to learn and improve themselves, a commitment which somehow eludes many pupils in the Western world. But here in K'ogelo, the children have a clear pride in their village school for a very obvious reason. As their local hero repeated throughout his election campaign, 'Change can happen' and 'Yes we can', and the pupils in the Senator Obama schools of K'ogelo believe the message just as devoutly as Obama's most fervent campaigners in America.

For Sarah Obama, change was certainly happening and this genial 87-year-old woman had hosted the world's media for the previous two years with all the regal patience and good humour of an African version of the late British Queen Mother. Sarah still lives in her husband's compound, which he established when his family moved there in 1945. But within a few months of moving to K'ogelo, Onyango's other wife, Habiba Akumu, who was the paternal grandmother of President Obama, left home and returned to live with her parents. It was only many months later that I learned about the extraordinary circumstances behind this acrimonious family squabble. This left Sarah to care not only for her own four children, but also Habiba Akumu's three children as well – the young Sarah, Barack Obama Snr, and his younger sister Hawa Auma. Although Mama Sarah is related to the president only by marriage, she raised Barack Obama Snr from a young boy. It is for this reason that President Obama often refers to her as 'Granny Sarah'. Sarah has only a few words of English and prefers to speak either Dholuo (the traditional Luo language), or Swahili. Nevertheless, on most days when she is in K'ogelo, she sits patiently in her front garden under the shade of a large mango tree planted by her husband and holds court, welcoming the dozens of visitors who come to pay their respects, literally by the bus load.

Being the oldest surviving relative of the US President has been a mixed blessing for Sarah Obama. She certainly welcomes the new borehole which was drilled just outside her front door, which relieves her of the daily chore shared by practically every woman in Africa – that of collecting water from the nearest well. But Sarah was less enthusiastic about the three-metre wire fence which now encircles her compound, or the constant presence of a dozen members of the Kenya police force, who are now permanently camped outside her compound in a makeshift security post: 'It is God's will. The electricity and the water are good. But now I cannot go anywhere without being mobbed by all the people. I am like a prisoner in my own house. I cannot go anywhere.'

Mama Sarah's compound is also the final resting place of her late husband, Hussein Onyango, who died in 1975 (although he is sometimes incorrectly reported as having died in 1979), and also of Barack Obama Snr (the President's father), who died in a motor accident in Nairobi in 1982, in what I later discovered were very suspicious circumstances. Their graves lie adjacent to each other to the left of Sarah's house, a cheerless reminder of a different life, now long past.

Sarah is not the only member of the Obama family to live in K'ogelo. Her son Malik still looks on the village as his natural home, even though he travels regularly to Europe and the USA; today he lives mostly in the nearby town of Siaya. Kezia Obama, Barack Obama Snr's first wife, also keeps a hut next to Sarah, although she now lives in southern England. Being a large and extended family, other members periodically pass by to give Sarah their support – they affectionately call the house 'Home Squared'. Yet on most days, the visitors and journalists coming to Mama Sarah's house vastly outnumber the tiny number of Obama family members in the village, and I was constantly puzzled why the media seemed to show so much interest in such a small, sleepy village like K'ogelo.

After just a few days in K'ogelo I had seen everything that there was to see: the Obama compound, the Catholic church, the two schools, the clinic and the market. I had come to the end of the road. Yes, there was grand talk of building a conference centre and a modern hotel in the village, but Luos have a reputation for talking big and I doubted whether anything would change very quickly in this sleepy African outpost.

On more than one occasion whilst I was talking to people in K'ogelo, they had mentioned that there were more Obamas living in another place called Kendu Bay. Barack Obama wrote about this township in his book *Dreams from My Father*, when he made his first visit to Kenya in 1987; but he said little about the town, preferring instead to write more about his visit to Nairobi and K'ogelo. Now, with only one day left of my visit to Nyanza, I decided to try my luck elsewhere.

Kendu Bay lies on the opposite side of Winam Gulf from K'ogelo, and it involves a 160km drive around the bay, passing through Kisumu, the provincial capital. I had been warned that the road from Kisumu to Kendu Bay was very poor, so we made an early start. However, like many of the major roads in this part of Kenya, it had recently been resurfaced and driving was really not a problem – except for the appalling driving standards of most Kenyan drivers. Nor was it really that difficult to find the Obama homestead. By now, Obama was easily the most famous name in Africa, and after a few enquiries we were directed off the main road from Kendu Bay and up a dirt track.

It never ceases to amaze me how relaxed and welcoming Africans can be to total strangers. In the West, our lives are tightly scheduled and we consult our diaries a dozen times a day; we make prior arrangements to see even our own closest friends, often many days ahead. In Kenya, a complete stranger can arrive unannounced – and a *mzungu* at that – and they treat your visit as the most normal thing in the world.

Even so, I was feeling a little uncomfortable arriving at the Obama homestead without making any arrangements. I had not been able to phone ahead and I did not even know who I should talk to about the family. Yet within five minutes I was walking though the family homestead with Charles Oluoch, a cousin to President Obama. Charles is a tall, thin, handsome man, just past his sixtieth year. As such, he is one of the family elders and, as he explained to me in excellent English, he is also chairman of the Barack H. Obama Foundation.

With obvious pride and with grand sweeping gestures, he took me around part of the Obama homestead, known locally as K'obama, a large area of sprawling compounds with scores of small brick huts stretching out into the distance among the trees: 'Here is the entrance to the Obama home. There are several homes here. It is a big home because the children are many. This one is Joshua Aginga's home. He was the third son of Obama Opiyo. This is his first wife's house, and this is his second wife's house . . .'

Charles continued telling me an extraordinary history of the Obama family as he guided me through what was only a small part of the homestead. My mind reeled as he recited, in extraordinary detail, a fascinating but complex family history – husbands with four or five wives, a dozen children, brothers, cousins and uncles ... The family complexity was mind-boggling.

I soon learned that it is a Luo tradition that the husband and each of his wives have separate huts, with the first wife having a bigger dwelling than the second wife, whose house is slightly larger than that of the third wife, and so on down the pecking order. Every building here was very modest by any standards, and typical of this part of Africa. Traditionally, Luo huts had round walls made of wattle and daub, and were thatched with a straw roof. But in recent years the Luo have begun to accumulate pieces of furniture and the round huts have mostly been replaced with a square design which allows the cupboards and dressers and sofas to be pushed back against a flat wall. Today the huts are also built more permanently of brick or stone, and sometimes daubed with mud; sadly, the traditional straw thatch has now given way to corrugated iron roofs.

Charles took me by the arm and walked me in a new direction: 'I want to show you something special.' We arrived at a tiny hut, with wooden shutters in place of the windows: 'This house is where the President slept in 1987. He came visiting – he wanted to know his roots. So he came up to Kendu Bay, and this is where he slept.'

We pushed open the simple wooden door with faded, peeling paint and noisy, doubtful hinges. Inside, the room was dark and cool, in contrast to the oppressive tropical heat and light outside. On the hard earth floor was a thin straw mat, which I soon learned had taken on almost mythical status within the family: 'This is the mattress he was given to sleep on. We could not afford the big mattresses from the supermarket.' Charles lit up the dark room with a broad grin: 'He must have been very uncomfortable for the whole night, because he is not used to such things.'

I asked Charles how many journalists had come to Kendu Bay, and I was immediately aware that he tensed at the question. 'Very few. Very, very few. They all go to K'ogelo. They don't come here.' I was interested to know more. 'But there is very little to see in K'ogelo, and so many more Obamas are living here,' I said. 'So why do all the journalists go to K'ogelo?' Charles looked rueful and said nothing. I sensed that there was something he was not telling me; perhaps there was some family rivalry involved – there was certainly some resentment. But today, I decided, was not the time to pursue the matter.

It was a couple of months later, during my next visit in January 2009, when I joined the family to watch the presidential inauguration on television, that I discovered the real reason for the press's interest in K'ogelo above Kendu Bay. When Barack Obama came to Kenya in 1987, he was guided through his huge, diverse family by his half-sister, Auma. She is the second child of Barack Obama Snr and his first wife, Kezia. Auma was brought up in K'ogelo, even though most of the Obama family lived elsewhere. So it was inevitable that Barack would be taken to the village where she grew up.

I also discovered that Raila Odinga, the Kenyan Prime Minister and a Luo, is from Bondo, a small town less than 40km from K'ogelo. His family still has very strong ties to the area, and his brother is the local MP. I was told that when President Obama visited in 2006 as a US senator, it had been the Prime Minster's Office which had been channelling press interest in the Obama family to K'ogelo, and not to Kendu Bay. After all, any politician would want international or regional investment to come into his own patch, rather than anywhere else in the region. And should the President of the USA ever decide to pay another visit to Kenya, then the Prime Minister would be only too happy to entertain him in his own area . . .

Time was beginning to run out for me with Charles Oluoch in Kendu Bay. Driving in Kenya is hazardous even in daylight, and I was keen to return to Kisumu before it got dark. But Charles had one more thing to show me. He led me around a hedge of small trees to a clearing to one side of the huts. There was a simple grave, not dissimilar to the two I had seen in Mama Sarah's compound in K'ogelo. Here, on a brass plaque screwed to the concrete headstone, were the words:

HERE LIES OBAMA K'OPIYO OF ALEGO K'OGELO
FROM WHOM ALL OF US JOK'OBAMA COME.
DEDICATED BY THE BARACK H. OBAMA FOUNDATION,
ABONG'O MALIK OBAMA.

I was intrigued and a little confused. Obama Opiyo? Charles explained: 'The man who is lying here is Obama Opiyo, our great-grandfather. Obama had four wives, and between them there were eight sons and nine girls, and one of his sons was Hussein Onyango, who is the grandfather to the President now of America.'

I did some quick mental arithmetic. If Charles was 60 and Opiyo was his great-grandfather, then Opiyo must have been born around 1830. 'But Charles, if the family came from K'ogelo more than 150 years ago, but Opiyo is buried here in K'obama, how did he get here?'

'That,' said Charles, with another of his big smiles beginning to break out, 'is a very long story, and it will have to wait until you come back to visit us next time!'

A Luo man heavily adorned with a necklace of cowrie shells (gaagi) and other ornaments on his arms, legs and ankles; he is described as Ukeri, a professional buffoon from the Ugenya clan in Nyanza, c. 1902.

2

MEET THE
ANCESTORS

Oyik biecha kaluo kae
My placenta is buried here in Luoland

**The migration of the Luo-speaking people from Sudan
and the early Obama ancestors from the early 1200s to the late 1800s**

Flight JO 831 leaves Jomo Kenyatta International Airport in Nairobi for
Juba, in southern Sudan, every morning at 7.30 sharp. It is a short flight
of only 900km, and it usually takes less than ninety minutes. Yet the cheapest
return ticket costs $738.75 (about £450), which is more than the price of
a return ticket on the nine-hour flight to London. Mile for mile, the Nairobi–
Juba route must be one of the most expensive flights anywhere in the world.
I asked the ticket assistant at Nairobi airport why the price was so high. He
shrugged his shoulders: 'No other airline really flies there so often,' he said
with a smile, 'and all the aid agencies must go there now.' It still seemed
to me to be a lot to pay for such a short flight. 'Is it *so* nice that it's worth
nearly $800 to get there?' I teased. 'You go only if you have to,' he said,
and he shrugged his shoulders and smiled awkwardly again.

Between 1983 and 2005 southern Sudan was embroiled in a vicious,
bloody conflict between the Muslim government in the north and the
Sudanese People's Liberation Army in the mainly Christian south. It was
Africa's longest-running civil war; nearly 2 million civilians were killed and
another 4 million were forced to flee their homes. Since January 2005 a

UN-sponsored settlement has brought an uneasy peace to the area, and a
chance to rebuild a region which has been devastated by twenty-two years
of fighting. Within a few months of the peace agreement, the Nairobi-
based airline JetLink opened a lucrative daily schedule into Juba, the historic
capital of the south, giving access to hundreds of humanitarian aid workers
from the United Nations and other international agencies.

After flying over Kisumu, which lies at the eastern end of Winam Gulf,
the aircraft passes over some of the most remote regions of East Africa. To
the right is Mount Elgon, straddling the Kenya–Uganda border; it is Kenya's
second highest mountain and it is named after the Elgeyo tribe which once
lived in the huge caves on its southern side. Soon, you are over Lake Kyoga,
a vast, shallow lake and swamp area in eastern Uganda, and home to large
numbers of crocodiles. Another thirty minutes into the flight and the aircraft
passes over the White Nile; at 6,670km long, the longest river in the world.
Providing there are no delays, the aircraft begins its approach into Juba
international airport before ten in the morning. The aircraft loses altitude
over the foothills of the Imatong Mountains which straddle the border
between Sudan and Uganda. To the north is the Sudd, which stretches as
far as the eye can see. This is the world's biggest swamp, a vast and formidable expanse of waterlogged lowland the size of Belgium. In the dry season,
the region is rocky and sandy and the smaller rivers frequently run dry;
during the wet season in late summer, the waters of the Bahr-al-Jabal (White
Nile), and its western tributary the Ghazāl (meaning River of Gazelles in
Arabic), burst their banks and flood the region. It is an annual pattern of
flooding which has lasted for thousands of years.

The southern part of the Sudd, which stretches from Juba through
Rumbek and Wau, is also called the Bahr-al-Ghazāl; historians and anthropologists believe this to be the 'cradleland' of Barack Obama's ancestors.
The area is a series of ironstone plateaus incised by the tributaries of the
big rivers which flow north towards Egypt and the Mediterranean. These
early people were called the River-Lake Nilotes, or sometimes the Western
Nilotes, and they lived a hand-to-mouth Iron Age existence in this part of
Sudan more than a thousand years ago. These people were mainly pastoralists and fishermen, and thought to be part of the Jii-speaking people, which
include the Jiaang (or Dinka) and the Naath (or Nuer).[1] During the wet
season when the waters were high, these people gathered on the ridges
and plateaus which formed low islands surrounded by flood water; during
the dry season, they moved out to the lower land and allowed their cattle
to take full advantage of the flourishing grazing lands below. When

Migration of the Luo ancestors from southern Sudan from c.1300 to 1750.

they moved away from their villages during the dry season, they lived in temporary huts made from branches and leaves called *kiru*.

It is often the case in Africa that geography and climate shape its history, and this is certainly what happened with the River-Lake Nilotes. Between six and eight hundred years ago, these people left the Bahr-al-Ghazāl and started on a perilous migration south into Uganda and eventually Kenya. Historians and anthropologists have long questioned why these people took such a huge gamble to move into unknown territory, populated with wild animals and hostile tribes. It took the River-Lake Nilotes more than a dozen generations to complete this almost biblical movement of people; it proved to be a long and painful process, but in time it laid the foundation of the Luo of Kenya. It is a journey which started with a local chief living in a mud hut overlooking the White Nile, and ended seven centuries later with the leader of the most powerful nation on earth, living in the White House.

Nobody can be absolutely sure what triggered the migration of the Luo from southern Sudan, but historians and archaeologists are confident that it began during the late fourteenth and early fifteenth centuries, and about a hundred years before Columbus sailed for the New World. One likely possibility is that climatic change gradually forced the pastoralists to move on to find a better environment in which to live. There are certainly plenty of examples of rock painting throughout the Sahara which show that the climate across the region has changed dramatically over time. These rock paintings portray elephant, rhino, hippo, buffalo, crocodile and giraffe – animals associated with much wetter, savannah conditions than exist today – and this suggests that conditions have become progressively drier over thousands of years.

In southern Sudan too, the climatic conditions are thought to have been much wetter than at present.[2] We know from detailed records kept in Egypt, for example, that there were great variations in the flooding of the Nile, which suggests that rainfall was irregular, and this would have had potentially catastrophic consequences in southern Sudan, where the water floods over a much bigger area and is therefore more prone to evaporation.[3] This is quite possibly what triggered the great Luo migration, perhaps combined with other pressures such as overpopulation, famine or epidemic diseases. One elder from Alego, Lando Rarondo, told me that he thought the Luo moved from Sudan because of an anthrax epidemic. His suggestion is entirely plausible; anthrax is one of the oldest recorded diseases, and it is believed to be the sixth plague recorded in the Book of Exodus. It is an acute, lethal bacterial disease which affects grazing animals, including sheep and cattle, and it can also be passed on to humans, either through direct contact or through eating the flesh of an infected animal.

Whatever initiated the migration of the Luo, whether it was climate change, overcrowding, disease, drought, or conflict, historians are confident that from around AD 1400 onwards (or perhaps even earlier),[4] the River-Lake Nilotes began their diaspora, which was to become one of the greatest migrations in the history of the African continent. This was not a grand, organised movement of people, but rather a gradual dispersal, as extended families began to migrate south and east from their cradleland in southern Sudan. Over the next 400 years part of this disparate group of migrants slowly moved towards what is now Kenya; over a dozen generations, their language changed and they adopted traditions which made them distinct from other peoples, and in doing so they forged a clear tribal identity and became known as the Luo.

Historians have broken down the Luo diaspora into three distinct phases. The first involved leaving the Bahr-al-Ghazāl and the start of their dispersal. According to the rich oral history of the Luo, this period involved disputes and leadership challenges, something which I have come to find is common throughout the fascinating history of the Luo. Some of the migrants are thought to have moved north from the Bahr-al-Ghazāl region to Shilluk in southern Sudan, a region on the White Nile around the town of Malakal; another group went east to Anuku, or into the highlands of Ethiopia; and still others went west into central Africa and towards Nigeria.[5] However, under the leadership of Obama's ancestors, a large group of River-Lake Nilotes began their long trek southwards towards Uganda, following the course of the Upper Nile.

For any people on the move, there are three essentials for survival; water, food and shelter. For this reason, the Luo never strayed far from the river, as this was the easiest and safest way to travel; the river also provided fish to eat, and water for their cattle. It seems likely that it was this movement up the White Nile which gave the Luo their name, which is derived from the vernacular saying, *Oluwo Aora*, which means 'The People Who Follow the River'.

In many ways the transhumance lifestyle of these people was the perfect preparation for their migration. These people were used to moving their cattle every year up to higher ground as the Nile flooded, and then taking them back down during the dry season; in doing so they set up temporary camps *en route*, and it is thought that these migration encampments were probably organised in a very similar way to the dry-season camps in Bahr-al-Ghazāl.[6]

Whatever it was that started the Luo off on their long migration, it seems to have created a bellicose and belligerent period in their history, and they developed a reputation for being aggressive and dangerous. Their success in battles might have been aided by the expertise they had developed in iron-making in their cradleland, and so they were probably better armed and more practised in warfare than the tribes to the south who they were about to displace.[7] For a period of two or three generations, the Luo effectively became riverine pirates, plundering villages along the length of the Upper Nile; they operated rather as the Viking marauders had along the European coastline some 500 years previously. Although the Luo canoes were flimsy craft, they were light, fast and manoeuvrable, and this allowed small bands of young Luo warriors to make daring raids up and down the banks of the Nile, stealing cattle, crops and women.

The Luo became adept at incorporating captives into their societies, so their numbers increased at an astonishing rate. And as their numbers increased, so their military strength grew; but this also put greater demands on their food supply, and that in turn increased the rate of their territorial expansion. Father Joseph Pasquale Crazzolara was a Catholic missionary who worked for much of his life in East Africa. Crazzolara did some of the very earliest research into the migration of the Luo (or, as he chooses to call them, the Lwoo), and in his epic history of the traditions of the tribe he wrote:

> On the march, as still in big hunts, the tribal, clan and family groups kept closely united . . . Female prisoners were absorbed and became completely submerged . . . For male captives the case was different in theory, but scarcely in practice. Prisoner slaves were allocated to a family or clan-group, and treated as blood-relations, and even given wives, or cattle as dowry. But with their children and descendants they started their own sub-clans and social life, as a clan-segment, related and hence exogamous, to the main Lwoo clan.[8]

In these early days of the migration south, the various communities on the move were based around patrilineal clans, which recognised an aristocratic or 'dominant' clan; this was usually the largest clan in the region, or the first to establish in a particular area. This marked an important stage of the development of the Luo as a discrete tribe, and the people began to attach greater significance to ancestral land, shrines and rituals. With this hierarchical identity also came an acknowledgement of power in the form of a *ker* or king, a *ruoth* or chief, and *jago* or sub-chief. The rest of the people were called *lwak* or *luak*. Associated with the leaders were the regalia of power, the most important of which was the royal spear or *tong ker*, the sacred drum or *bul ker*, and the royal three-legged stool, or *kom ker*.[9]

As the early Luo society developed, so some fundamental beliefs began to emerge which helped to consolidate their union as a people, and which helped them invade and dominate a significant part of central and eastern Africa in the centuries to come. Firstly, the Luo believed that only the son of a king or chief could legitimately succeed to the leadership, and that the descendants of sons who did not succeed would eventually lose their aristocratic status. Secondly, there was a recognition that the strength and power of the group grew from their allegiance to the leader, and from the cooperation among the people; this strengthened the political union both among the Luo clans and between Luo and non-Luo groups. Finally, the leaders believed that their royal lineage and ritual powers gave them the right to rule over others who did not have these special attributes – in other words, this was the beginning of a conceit and arrogance among these people which many Kenyans would claim is a characteristic of the Luo today.

As the Luo moved south along the length of the Upper Nile during the fifteenth and early sixteenth century, so they left southern Sudan and entered what is now northern Uganda. It is about 350km from Juba to Lake Albert on the River Nile, and it took several generations for the Luos to reach this destination. Here at a site called Pubungu (now called Pakwach), they built a great military encampment beside the river, about 16km downstream from where the Nile exits the lake,[10] and this period is seen as the second major stage in the migration of the Luo.

The historian David Cohen believes that the Luo first established themselves in Pubungu by the middle part of the fifteenth century,[11] and this coincides with the lives of Jok I and Nayo, early ancestors of Barack Obama. Today, Pubungu-Pakwash is a forlorn little town with a single main street and a stout but simple bridge over the White Nile made from steel girders. Five hundred years ago, the early Luo chose their spot well, for this bridging point is still an important strategic position on the river, and even today the Ugandan military will try to stop people taking photographs of the bridge. For the Luo, Pubungu became an important staging post for the conquest of the region, and it marked a dramatic change in their lifestyle, from nomadic pastoralists to a ruling elite. As the Luo established themselves in the region, so they adopted new ways in which to incorporate their captives into their clans, making only the distinction between the *jo-kal* – the true Luo of the chief's enclosure, and the *lwak* – the incoming subjugated people.[12]

According to Luo oral history, it was Podho II (11),* great-grandfather to President Obama, who was at least partly responsible for building Pubungu up to become an impressive war-camp, and the citadel became a springboard for the Luo to radiate outwards and dominate the region for several generations. It is said that Olum was an influential figure in the Luo community in Pubungu in the late fifteenth century, and his family are a good example of the restlessness and enterprise shown by the Luo during this period. One son called Labong'o (or Nyabong'o) is said to have led a small group in the early 1500s called the Babito-Luo into western Uganda, where they settled with a Bantu group and displaced the ruling Bachwezi dynasty. This remains an historic triumph for the Luo people. Olum's other two sons, Gipiir (or Nyipiir) and Tifool moved further west into what is now the Congo, and they established themselves as rulers over the people there, who today call themselves the Alur.[13]

Little remains today of this imposing fortress, but there are many old villages and archaeological sites in western Kenya which display similar dry-stone walling, which can give us an idea of what Pubungu was like at its peak. These stone settlements are called *ohinga* in Dholuo, a name that implies a refuge or fortress. There are still several hundred such stone fortified settlements in the region in varying states of decay, but there is one particularly fine example in south Nyanza called Thimlich Ohinga (*thimlich* means 'frightening dense forest'). Archaeological evidence suggests the site was occupied by the Bantu more than 500 years ago, but it was the Luo who started to build in stone when they occupied the region circa 1700.[14]

The fortified town is built on a hill in a very isolated part of south Nyanza. The approach to the site crosses a large area of swampland which becomes virtually impassable during the rainy season. Today, Thimlich Ohinga is preserved as a national museum, but its remote position means that it gets very few visitors. When the curator, Silas Nyagwth, asked me

---

* Bracketed numbers are used throughout as shorthand where there are large generational gaps; (3) great-grandfather signifies great-great-great-grandfather and so on.

to sign the visitors' book, I noticed he had not had a guest for over a week. It is a pity, because the fortress is built on a low hill which gives a magnificent view across the region. Silas took me round the site, which covers over ten acres and includes six large stone enclosures which nestle among the trees and shrubs on a gentle slope, and with *Euphorbia candelabrum* – that great, spiky succulent which is traditionally found in many Luo homesteads – towering above all the other vegetation.

> 'This is the original wall, roughly five hundred years old,' he told me. 'The wall is what we called the ohinga, a Dholuo word meaning a barrier. It is like a ring, a circular wall, which is the main defensive wall. There is only one main entrance and at the back there is an exit. So when these people were attacked through the main entrance, they could escape out the back.'

Inside the stone compound the wall was reinforced with stone towers where the guards could keep watch over the flat plain below. Silas explained that in the early days the main tribe here was the Maasai, who had a formidable reputation for fighting. As we walked round Thimlich Ohinga it became clear that it was really quite a substantial size for a settlement of this period. The stone walls were thick, between one and three metres, and up to four metres high. The walls were well constructed from loose stones and large blocks, without mortar. This gave the inhabitants very effective protection from both hostile neighbours and wild animals. Inside the stone enclosures the original huts have long since gone, but the outlines of house pits and cattle enclosures can still be seen.

It is likely that, in its day, Pubungu resembled Thimlich Ohinga, and was probably substantially larger. This suggests that the Luo made a conscious decision to halt their migration, at least for a time, and establish themselves in northern Uganda on the banks of the River Nile.

Before the arrival of the Luo, this region in northern Uganda had been the land of the Madi tribe whose homesteads extended on both sides of the White Nile. Soon the Luo were sending out raiding expeditions from Pubungu, and their warriors brought back plunder and captives from the Madi and other local tribes. This dramatically swelled the Luo's numbers and increased their enthusiasm for conquest. Over time, these captives became part of the Luo tribe, and this process of integration was to become a common feature of their society over many centuries.

It was from Pubungu that the Luo also pushed into Bantu territory. The

Bantu are a tribal group which originated from the area of Nigeria and Cameroon in West Africa, and from around 1500 BC they expanded southwards and eastwards across central Africa. By 1000 BC the Bantu had established themselves around the great lakes of East Africa, where this rich region of grassland and savannah supported a prosperous kingdom called Kitara, with a population of several tens of thousands of people and hundreds of thousands of cattle.[15] In the oral tradition of the region, this was home to the Chwezi, pastoralists whose kingdom was at its peak between the fourteenth and sixteenth centuries. The Luo were still on their warlike rampage, and the Chwezi proved to be no match for bellicose Luo. According to Luo tradition, the attack on Kitara was led by Olum Labong'o, who is remembered in Bantu traditions as Rukidi – 'the naked man from the north'. Oral history tells us that the Luo armies moved south from Pubungu and attacked Kitara; the Chwezi king and his people fled the area, and by all accounts the Luo became the barbarian conquerors of a more cultured society. For a time, Olum Labong'o and the victorious Luo occupied the area, but the Luo reign was not to last, and in time they moved on.

It was during their most belligerent period in Pubungu that one of the most powerful and enduring Luo legends is claimed to have arisen: the fabled story of the lost spear and the bead.[16] It is a story which was told to me many times by several different people in Nyanza, and it takes on many forms among different African groups who originated in southern Sudan. Although the story cannot be true in all its variations, the legend nevertheless gives us a fascinating insight into the beliefs and customs of the Luo, which have endured for centuries.

One common version of the spear and the bead story is said to have occurred between two brothers, Aruwa and Podho II, who lived in Pubungu in the second half of the fifteenth century. (Podho II is said to be the (15) great grandfather of President Obama.) The story goes that when their father, Ramogi I, died (perhaps around 1480–90), his eldest son Aruwa took over the chiefdom and the two brothers lived in relative harmony.[17] However, one day an elephant came into their fields and began to trample through the crops. One of Aruwa's nephews was sitting on a raised platform watching over the millet field. When he raised the alarm, Podho rushed out to protect his son and chase away the elephant. As he did so, he grabbed the nearest weapon, which happened to be a spear belonging to Aruwa. Podho wounded the elephant, but not fatally, and it escaped into the forest with Aruwa's spear still hanging from its side. What Podho had not realised in the rush to protect his son was that the weapon he had grabbed was Aruwa's sacred spear. He confessed his mistake to his brother, but Aruwa was furious; he refused any substitute and insisted that Podho should go and retrieve the missing weapon. Podho had no choice but to honour his brother's demand.

The next morning at the first crow of the cock, Podho set off alone for the forest, taking with him his own spear and shield, and food prepared by his wife: some *kuon anang'a* (ground maize cooked in milk), grilled meat and sweet potatoes. It was a dangerous journey for anyone to undertake alone, and he decided the best course of action was to follow the setting sun. After travelling west for several days, Podho left behind 'the land of human beings' and entered 'the kingdom of the animals'. He then changed his course and walked to the south-west. He roamed the remote forest for many days and became exhausted, miserable at his failure. One afternoon he dozed off under a tree, worn weary, and woke to find an old woman watching him. (In some versions of the legend she is referred to as the Queen of the Elephants.) She led Podho to her *kiru* or shelter, where she fed him and allowed him to rest. Then she took him to a larger *kiru*, where she kept all the spears that had been hurled at her elephants at various times in the past. The old woman told Podho that he would find his brother's weapon among them. Podho spent several days looking for the sacred spear before he eventually found it. As he thanked the woman and prepared to leave, she presented him with a handful of magnificent beads, unique in pattern and colour.

Podho's return journey was difficult, and he was sick with exhaustion by the time he reached Pubungu. He called a village meeting and cere-moniously presented his brother with his sacred spear. There was general unease among the family at the dispute between the two brothers, but everyone hoped that, now the spear was found, the animosity between them would diminish. Time passed and the argument seemed to be forgotten until another confrontation opened the old wound. Aruwa's children were playing with Podho's prized beads, when one of Aruwa's daughters acci-dentally swallowed one. Podho was still feeling aggrieved about being forced to recover his brother's spear, and he demanded that Aruwa return his bead, refusing any substitute or replacement. Aruwa waited for three days to allow nature to take its course, but the bead did not emerge. Podho continued to insist that the bead should be returned, and in a blind fury and with no other option available to him, Aruwa took a knife and cut open his own daughter's stomach to recover it.

After this traumatic event, the brothers realised they could no longer live together, and their families would have to separate, otherwise they risked civil war. Together they walked down to the Nile at Pubungu and drove an axe into the river bed as a symbol of their separation. Aruwa went west with his family from Pubungu and Podho travelled east of the Nile towards western Kenya. A third brother, Olak, is said to have remained behind in Pubungu and his descendants became farmers and fishermen.

The legend of the spear and the bead is, of course, apocryphal and similar stories are told by many tribes as far afield as the Congo. Often the names of the participants change, sometimes a python takes the place of the elephant, and in other versions the stories of the spear and the bead are told as separate events. Because the story is widespread across many tribal cultures and has been preserved down the generations with such tenacity, it suggests that it performs a valuable function in a society with strong oral traditions. Like all myths, these stories have many dimensions: as with Shakespeare's *The Merchant of Venice*, there is the folly of insisting on having your pound of flesh at any price, and the child's death is a reminder that human life is infinitely more precious than property; Podho's journey into the forest is a classic tale of personal, heroic challenge; and the old woman, the Queen of the Elephants, is thought to be a metaphor for the creation of a society.

These stories of the Luo are all about the migration of families, lineages, and clanship. They often contain threads of historical detail, but they are really as much about the present as they are about the past. This was important in a society which had no written language, and where a society's morals and principles needed to be defined. These migration stories also explore a wide range of issues and emotions that ordinary people experience in their daily lives. Common themes include tolerance; another is jealousy. However, at its most simplistic level, the spear and the bead story is a reminder of the historic separation of the clans at Pubungu, and it was this new migration that eventually brought Podho's people to western Kenya.

According to the oral history of the Luo, when Podho II left Pubungu he did so with the whole of his extended family, and they travelled east from what is now Lake Albert. This was the beginning of the third stage of the

Luo diaspora, and it represented the first of several 'pulses' of Luo migration into western Kenya, which took place between about 1450 and 1720.[18]
This movement of the Luo has been described as being like the shunting
of a goods train in a marshalling yard; as one wagon is pushed, so it
knocks into another, which in turn pushes a third and fourth, and so on.
In this way the Luo clans 'nudged' their way into Kenya, and as more
people came later, so the early settlers were nudged further east. That is
not to suggest this was an entirely peaceful process, but compared with
what happened in Pubungu, and what was to happen with later waves of
Luo coming into the region, Podho's migration east towards Kenya was
relatively passive.

The Luo reverted to form when they left Pubungu, and Podho's clan
stayed close to the waterways to the east of the settlement. First, they followed
what is now known as the Victoria Nile from Lake Albert, through the
forest which today makes up the Murchison Falls National Park, before
arriving at the swamplands at the western end of Lake Kyoga. From here
they followed the northern shore of the lake, always making sure that their
three main priorities were always met: water, food and shelter. At no time
did they stray far from a river or lake.[19] Along the way they built temporary
kiru from branches and leaves, they lived off their cattle, caught what fish
they could in the rivers and lakes, and hunted in the forests. The younger
men, the clan's warriors, scouted ahead for game and suitable places for
their next stop, before returning to give advice to their clan leader. The
migration from Pubungu to western Kenya took at least three generations,
and the Luo speakers settled for a period at a place called Tororo, which
is close to the present-day border between Uganda and Kenya and lies to
the south-west of Mount Elgon. On the way from Pubungu to Tororo,
Podho II had at least six sons; we can reasonably assume that the eldest,
Ramogi II, must have died around Tororo, because his second son was
named Ajwang', which denotes a child who is born *after* the death of its
father.

It was not until the early part of the sixteenth century, perhaps around
1530, that Ramogi Ajwang' made his historic crossing into Nyanza with his
clan. These people were called the Joka-Jok; they were the pioneers and
they represented the first of three main waves of Luo-speaking people who
moved into western Kenya. There is some uncertainty exactly when they
pushed eastwards to establish the first Luo group in Kenya. The doyen of
Luo historians, Bethwell Ogot, gives a date of between 1490 and 1517, but
with an accuracy of only ±52 years.[20] The American historian David Cohen

suggests that the Luo reached Nyanza sometime around 1500 to 1550.[21] The Obama ancestry on page viii suggests that Ramogi Ajwang' was probably born around 1510, therefore his arrival in western Kenya is in keeping with a date of between 1530 and 1550.

Bethwell Ogot suggests that Ajwang's move to his settlement in Nyanza was not straightforward.[22] From their base in Tororo, Ogot claims the clan travelled first in a north-easterly direction towards Mount Elgon before curving south-eastwards towards the northern Ugenya region in western Kenya. Throughout this migration, Ogot suggests that the Luo were under constant population pressure from all directions, which is why they continued moving until they established a permanent settlement in western Kenya. It was here, on the ridge that is now called Got Ramogi (Ramogi Hill), that Ajwang' built his first defensive stronghold on a good strategic high point.

The region that Ramogi Ajwang' chose for his new settlement resembled the original environment which the Luo left in Sudan some half dozen generations before. The densely forested ridge of Got Ramogi towers above the snake-infested swampy grasslands of Gangu (pronounced 'Gang') like a vast, sprawling medieval fortress. It is the perfect position from which to view the surrounding countryside. The two hills on which Got Ramogi was established rise to over 1,310 metres above sea level, and they are protected on three sides by water; to the north is the Yala swamp, to the east the Yala River, and to the south the great lake, Lake Victoria, which the Luo call Nam Lolwe. Here, there was plenty of water for their cattle, space to establish their farms, abundant wildlife in the forest for hunting, and above all, a good strategic position from which to defend themselves against hostile attack. It was also a good position from which to mount an offensive into new territory. After nearly two centuries of travelling, it is not surprising that Ramogi Ajwang' has taken on a mythical status among the Kenyan Luo, and today every school child learns about their famous warrior ancestor; if Ramogi was their King Arthur, then Got Ramogi became his Camelot.

Life was not easy for the newcomers. According to the historian William Ochieng', the region was extensively populated by Bantu people.[23] Ramogi and his clan faced a hostile reception from the indigenous tribes, and this soon turned into open warfare; granted, this was caused mainly by the Luo getting up to their old tricks of raiding the Bantu homesteads for cattle, and, no doubt, for their women as well. Traditionally the Bantu are a farming people of medium stature, and they were no match for

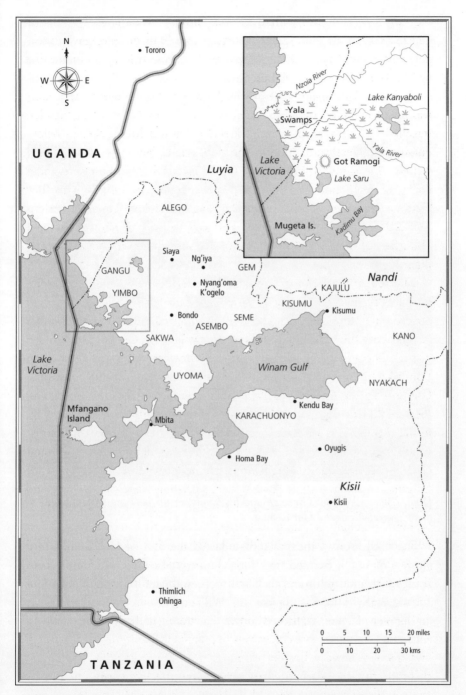

Nyanza Province (Luoland) and the region into which the Luo ancestors
migrated between 1530 and 1830; also showing the adjacent Luyia, Nandi
and Kisii tribal areas.

the tall, powerful Luo with their long history of warfare. The Bantu
fled the region; in some cases the tribes moved on to another location
only to find themselves being displaced a second time a generation or
two later by new waves of Luo invaders. In this way the Luo consolidated their hold on this part of western Kenya over a period of several
generations.

*Dudi, home of William Onyango and his family; in the background is the
densely-wooded ridge of Got Ramogi.*

Scattered around the flatlands today at the foot of Got Ramogi are
clusters of small, isolated traditional homesteads; these are simple Luo
houses with mud walls and thatched roofs, and with a sprinkling of cattle
grazing lazily in the hot tropical sun. William Onyango, a local farmer in
the hamlet of Dudi, explained to me that this is no longer good land to
cultivate:

'In the past, this place used not to be swampy. Here it used to be very
good. We were farming these lands, but there came some very big rains
about 50 years ago that made this place become swampy.'

Today, William Onyango struggles to make even a basic living from his land:

'In this place I grow my maize – you can see my maize here. You call it corn – corn on a cob! Then we have cabbages, onions, and all this. That is what I do here to survive. I have ten children to look after – I'm not like you who might have two children. I am a real African! I have one wife and ten children. Six boys and four daughters!'

Like most subsistence farmers in Kenya, William Onyango struggles to find the money for even the most basic necessities in life:

'Peter, getting money here is like getting gold. What little we earn is through our hard work. We make sure that we plant crops, we have vegetables. What we do then is take them to the market, but this can take a long time because we also use this for food. So getting money is not easy. That is why you can see the type of homes we have. We have lots of land here, but because we do not have machinery, we have to use our hands.'

Lack of money is only one of William's concerns. This is a very remote part of western Kenya, just a few kilometres from the Ugandan border and accessible only along rough dirt tracks, which become virtually impassable in the wet season:

'We have many animals here, and the most common here are the warthogs. We have antelope, gazelles, and we have lots of hare. We also have hyenas and leopards – these are the most common ones. And the snakes – we have lots of snakes here. We have the puff adder, the cobras and the spitting cobras, the rock pythons, the green and black mambas. We really fear the three main ones: the cobra because they can spit a long distance and blind you, the puff adders because they are so aggressive, and the mambas because they are so poisonous.'

It struck me that, in many ways, William's lifestyle has changed little from how his ancestors lived a dozen generations ago. I asked him why Ramogi Ajwang' had first settled in the area some four centuries previously:

'Ramogi is my very great-grandfather. He passed through the River Nile to this place, Got Ramogi, and he settled at the topmost part of the hill. I asked my grandfather what is the significance of the top of Got Ramogi. He told me that in those times, there used to be many enemies. So he liked this place because it was like a castle, and he could use this to view all parts of these lower lands. That is where he stayed. Now his people have migrated to other places to try to find land. Even the descendants of great-grandfathers in South Nyanza came from this place. So from here, people moved northwards, southwards and to the east to occupy other parts of Luo Nyanza.

'We have different Gots here, different hills, but it has only one major name which is Got Ramogi. But [Ramogi's] children and descendants used to occupy different hills. Like this is a different one at your back, it's a very green one. If you look behind me, you see another hill. So when Ramogi conquered here and settled, he allowed his sons to take other hills. Then they could help him to see what was happening if the enemies were coming. We are told that the people Ramogi drove out of this place were called the Lang'i people, a sub-clan of the Kalenjins.'

According to local tradition, Ramogi Ajwang' made his first settlement at the very top of the main hill at Got Ramogi, the hill they call Mienjera. But it was a hand-to-mouth existence, and William explained to me what life was like for Ramogi Ajwang' and his people four hundred years previously:

'One of my great-grandfather's grandfathers used to say that Ramogi and the olden people, and even he himself, they never had the [traditional Luo] round houses. They used to have what is called *kiru*. These are temporary houses; you cut trees and place the branches around other trees to make a temporary settlement. They were made without nails, you just put leaves and twigs together, then you tie them using plant rope.'

There are several features around the site of Ramogi's first settlement which the Luo consider to be sacred; these include Muanda, the sacred tree, the Asumbi or rock of rain, and the Rapongi, or whetstone used by Ramogi and his warriors to sharpen their knives. This hilltop is considered to be the ancestral home of both the Kenyan and the Tanzanian Luo, a sacred place of pilgrimage for believers in the traditional Luo religion, and a source of rare plants used in traditional medicine. It is even said that Raila Odinga, the Prime Minister of Kenya, makes regular visits to the site. Traditionally the area is guarded and maintained by William Onyango and other direct descendants of Ramogi Ajwang', who come from the Unyenjra and Idhi clans, but the Kenyan government has also now established a national museum here, which is charged with managing and protecting the Ramogi Hills.

According to Luo oral history, Ramogi Ajwang' decided to leave Got Ramogi and return to Tororo in his later life. When he was born, Ramogi's mother buried his placenta within the confines of his father's compound, and the desire to return 'home' to die is entirely consistent with Luo tradition. Even today, all Luos want to return to be buried in their homestead. However, Ramogi had been a strong and powerful leader, and he is said to have left behind in Got Ramogi the greatest gift of all – fifteen sons, who went on to consolidate their hold on the region and to establish a powerful clan. It was from Got Ramogi that small groups of young warriors spread out on scouting expeditions to 'test' the region. They would report back about the strength and displacement of other tribes in the area, the diversity and numbers of wild animals for hunting, and the availability of water for their cattle. If an area looked promising, then whole families and sub-clans would move out and establish new homesteads. In this way the Luo began to spread out throughout the region to the north of Winam Gulf.

Sometimes their movement into an area was peaceful but at other times there would be skirmishes and battles; cattle would be taken to swell the herds of the clan leaders and women, too, would be assimilated into the growing Luo sub-clans. Within a period of three generations, the Joka-Jok had spread in all directions, but they always stayed close to the lake, both to water their cattle and to fish.[24] Each settlement represented the potential for a future sub-tribe, but for the moment, the newcomers had no concept that they were the forerunners of the Luo tribe who would, by the end of the twentieth century, grow their number to nearly 5 million people.

One of the new expansion settlements in the area was situated just north of Lake Gangu. This was only a few kilometres from Got Ramogi and still in the Luo's golden triangle, that sacred spot wedged between swamp, river and lake. At Gangu, seven trench and wall settlements were excavated by archaeologists, and the site is thought to date from around 1600, which puts it firmly in the early decades of Luo settlement in the region.[25] These settlements were called *gundni bur*, ancient fortified communities which were built by Ramogi's ancestors, each with an earthen wall three to five metres high, and about one metre thick. In this respect it was similar to the fortification in Thimlich Ohinga, except that the defensive wall was earth, and not stone. This wall was surrounded by a ditch two to three metres deep, and inside the compound were scores if not hundreds of huts, home to large numbers of men, women and children. The land immediately around the homestead was reserved for cultivation by women and their daughters, whilst the elders and male warriors grazed their herds further away from the homestead. These *gundni bur* were compact settlements, providing an element of security for quite large numbers of people, together with their stores of foodstuffs and cattle.

From oral history passed down through the generations, it seems likely that each of the seven settlements at Gangu experienced a series of 'micro-conquests' or occupations. Some occupants reinforced the fortifications during their stay, whereas others probably did not stop long enough to do much rebuilding. Nearby and overlooking the settlement is a large rock outcrop which served as a look-out post for warriors and sentries. Even today, broken shards of earthenware pots may be seen scattered around on the ground, all dating from the early days of the Luo in Kenya. From the top of the rocks, Got Ramogi and the other Luo strategic settlements are plainly visible across the low-lying ground, making this the perfect springboard for more incursions into hostile territory.

For the next several generations the descendants of Ramogi Ajwang' expanded throughout the region; they were the Joka-Jok who had migrated from Uganda between about 1530 and 1680. This was only the beginning of the movement of Luo speakers into the region, and between the early sixteenth century and about 1720, scores of families and sub-clans left the Pubungu area and spread throughout the region, many of them moving eastwards through Uganda and into western Kenya.[26] Many of these migrants passed through Got Ramogi on their way to more permanent settlements. Over time, Ramogi Ajwang's great hill evolved from a defensive medieval fortress to something more resembling Ellis Island, the famous migrant screening station in New York through which generations of people passed on their way to a new life in the USA.

In the early years of the seventeenth century the Joka-Jok were followed by a new wave of migrants, the Jok'Owiny. A third major Luo group, the Jok'Omolo, arrived in Nyanza later in the seventeenth century. As these new people moved into the area, so the established groups moved on. This was one of the biggest movements of people in the history of this part of Africa. Hundreds of thousands of people moved out of southern Sudan over a period of several generations, but it was not a great, organised trans-continental migration, rather a gradual, disjointed drift of families and sub-clans, moving on when it suited them, and with very little coordination with like-minded people. It was only later, in the eighteenth century, that the Luo began to organise themselves into anything resembling an established tribe. Until that transition took place, the Luo were a disparate group of clans and sub-clans, fighting other tribes, and often each other, in an attempt to carve out a new life in an unfamiliar place.

The main expansion along the northern shore of Winam Gulf occurred between about 1590 and 1790, when the second major group of Luo migrants, the Jok'Owiny, arrived.[27] This group was led by Owiny the Great, a venerated leader and warrior who was the great-great-grandson of Podho II, and the great-grandson of Podho's youngest son, Muwiru. It is through Owiny's lineage that the Obama family trace their ancestry, and President Obama is believed to be the (11) great-grandson of Owiny.

The new arrivals tended to acknowledge those who had preceded them as the dominant group, and this helped them to establish larger and stronger clan groupings. Over time, the Luo sub-clans went through a transformation from a group of disparate families into larger groups who identified and looked towards an individual as their leader, and in which feelings of loyalty and cooperation began to emerge.[28] They organised themselves to wage war together, and to defend their territory. It was from this process of social assimilation that the concept of a defined Luo tribe began to emerge. Often the tribe took the name of the dominant leader and in this way, between 1550 and 1750, a number of strong sub-tribes established themselves in northern and central Nyanza.

However, despite their success in suppressing other tribes, the cantankerous Luo frequently squabbled among themselves. One major, and infamous, confrontation occurred with the Jok'Owiny in the middle of the seventeenth century. The dispute arose between the sons of Kisodhi, who was the eldest son of Owiny the Great. Kisodhi is (10) great-grandfather to President Obama, and at the time his family were still living in Gangu, in western Kenya, very close to Got Ramogi at a place called Rengho. Kisodhi had two wives, Nyaika and Jong'a, and between them they bore him eight sons and an unknown number of daughters. In many ways Kisodhi was a classic example of the powerful and successful warrior who was consolidating the Luos' hold on the region. Kisodhi probably died sometime around 1660, and by tradition he was buried in his compound in Rengho. His eldest son, Ogelo, naturally assumed that he would take his father's position as head of the family, but as the extended family gathered at the funeral, a serious confrontation broke out among the eight brothers which led to a split in the clan that lasted for generations. To get the full story, I went back to Gangu, to the site where Ogelo's younger brother, Ager, had established his fortification.

Got Ager is the ancestral home to Ager, second son of Kisodhi, and in many ways it is very similar to Got Ramogi. At the foot of the steep, wooded ridge I found a single hut, home to Zablon Odhiambo and his wife and three children. Zablon claimed to be directly descended from Ager himself, and he acts as keeper of the ancestral home. As we walked together up the slope to the summit of the ridge, I asked him how many *wazungu* (white people, the plural of *mzungu*) had been to Got Ager. 'You are the first,' he said with a chuckle, 'but I am expecting many more tourists to come in the future!' We began the long climb up towards the high ridge, walking first up the gentle lower slopes, which showed signs of having been grazing land in the past. We squeezed through overgrown thorn hedges which had obviously been there for many decades, and Zablon told me these had been planted by his great-grandfather. Further ahead I could see that the steeper upper slopes were covered in dense primary forest towards the summit. Zablon explained that leopard, hyena and snakes were still very common in the higher woodland.

It was a typically hot, tropical afternoon, and we sat down together on some exposed rocks on the upper slope of Got Ager and looked out across the flat grazing land, swamp and lake, a view which had not changed since Ager lived there, 350 years ago. I was interested to know from Zablon what he knew about the infamous family dispute:

'It is traditional with the Luo that a family goes into mourning for four days following the death of a male elder. On the fourth day, the family must have their heads shaven as a mark of respect, and to show to others that they are in mourning. I know that when Kisodhi died, he was the father and he had two wives who gave him eight sons. Ogelo was the eldest. Ogelo was somebody who was very quiet, and when he had been sat down to be shaved, the sisters of his two wives started talking to him. They were saying that because he was sitting down to be shaved, everybody else was going hungry.

'They had already started shaving him, but they hadn't finished when he stood up to distribute food to all these women. All his brothers became furious at this, because the women were praising Ogelo as the man with a good heart, as it was only him who got up to give people food. Ager, who was Kisodhi's second son, was leading this onslaught against him, so Ogelo then became angry with Ager.

'Now Ager was a very harsh man, and when Ogelo went off for food, Ager sat down and was shaved. When Ogelo came back, he found that his brother had taken his traditional birthright, and he was furious.'

Tempers became heated and insults were exchanged as different members of the extended family took sides in the dispute. It was a typical Luo family confrontation. Throughout all this turmoil, the drummer continued his performance at the funeral, seemingly oblivious to the family fracas going on around him. This infuriated Owiny Sigoma, who was the youngest son of Kisodhi's second wife, and he drew his spear and killed the ill-fated drummer on the spot:

'This started all the problems and this is why people had to leave to other places. So people started fighting and Ogelo ran away, taking all the family's cattle. Everyone chased after him. Ogelo ran away to a place called Mwer. Ager pursued him, but when Ogelo heard that Ager was after him, he kept going, past Siaya [a town 30km to the east]. So the people who went there with him became known as the Jok'Ogelo. That is why the place today is still called K'ogelo, the village where the step-grandmother to the President, Sarah Obama, still lives.'

Looking due west from where Zablon and I were sitting, I could just make out the hills which marked the modern border with Uganda, and the famous triangle through which the ancestral Luo had passed four centuries before. Zablon was keen to explain more about Got Ager:

'As we're sitting here, we are facing Uganda. Kisodhi, Ager's father, was near here close to the border, but not in Uganda itself. So it was here that the brothers separated. We're told in history that Ager had five wives, and that twenty-one men lived here at Got Ager, but we don't know how many women and children there were, because they are not recorded. Only the old man had a traditional round hut, but the rest who were helping Ager to protect this place, they had what we called *kiru*. These are very, very light houses made with just tree branches and leaves.'

In many ways, the altercation at Kisodhi's funeral is a typical Luo story, combining as it does pride, arrogance, family arguments and bloodshed. But the story doesn't end here, and the clash at the funeral of Kishodi led to a major succession dispute among the Luo.

Following the great family confrontation and the challenge to Ogelo's succession, it was actually Owiny Sigoma who became the undisputed leader of his clan. He was by far the most aggressive and belligerent of the local leaders – it could even be argued that he was a psychopath. As Owiny Sigoma continued to expand his territory east, so he transferred his power base from his father's settlement in Rengho to a site which he named after himself, Sigoma, near the modern town of Uranga Market in western Alego. The area into which Sigoma's people expanded was ruled by the Seje people, another Luo clan who claim descent from the people who first came to Nyanza with Ramogi Ajwang'. They had been settled in the area for a couple of generations, under their leader, *Ruoth* Seje.

However, Owiny Sigoma was not the type of man to meekly accept the leadership of Seje, and this led to a bitter and acrimonious dispute between the two groups. It was effectively a civil war between two Luo clans; at first, Owiny Sigoma was successful, and for a short period he became the undisputed ruler of the whole region. But he ruled by fear, and his dictatorial and repressive leadership style made the inter-clan rivalry worse than ever. Leo Odera, a local journalist in Kisumu, explained some of Owiny Sigoma's brutal tactics:

'Owiny Sigoma was a very cruel man. One of the things that he did was feed his enemies to the hyenas. This frightened people, because if they died, it was important for them to be buried in their homestead, otherwise their spirits would haunt the clan members. The hyenas used to cry out at night, and Owiny Sigoma used to boast, "These are my hyenas!"'

Eventually his people tired of Sigoma's repressive style and they rose up against him. Owiny Sigoma and his close entourage escaped from the region and regrouped. When Sigoma returned to Alego, he attempted to impose his ruthless authority again on the local population, but he was challenged by the Ugenya people and a full-scale war broke out again between opposing Luo clans. The inter-clan warfare was so widespread that it is inevitable that President Obama's ancestors became involved, and according to the Obama family history, Okoth ((7) great-grandfather to the President), fought in this historic and decisive battle. During the fight, Owiny Sigoma's warriors deserted him and he was killed on the battlefield, speared through the chest by an opponent. His death finally brought relative peace to the region.

Meanwhile, according to their family history, President Obama's (9) great-grandfather Ogelo, after fleeing the family dispute at his father's funeral, had settled in relative peace on a low hill called Nyang'oma overlooking the Yala river. It was a good spot to establish his roots; there was water for the cattle, the red soil was fertile, and the area was raised up above the swampy land, for nyang'oma means 'raised up' or 'on stilts' in Dholuo. In time, the village became known as Nyang'oma K'ogelo, and today the village of K'ogelo is recognised as the ancestral home of President Obama's family.

At the same time the Luo continued to migrate into Nyanza from eastern Uganda. Sometime between 1760 and 1820, a third major group called the Jok'Omolo, under the leadership of Rading Omolo, started to move into western Alego. This new wave of migration caused a rapid increase in population, and within five generations – less than two hundred years – the area north of the Winam Gulf became overpopulated. This inevitably led to more frequent clashes between the clans, and often to open warfare. The problem of overpopulation in the region was further compounded by a severe drought and famine in most parts of northern Nyanza during the early and middle eighteenth century.[29] Between 1750 and 1800 the feuding among the Luo became so acute that the clan structure began to disintegrate, and many of the sub-clans adopted the same solution their ancestors had several generations before them – they packed their bags and moved on. This time, the Luo moved across the Winam Gulf into south Nyanza, which was still a relatively underpopulated part of western Kenya.

In the Obama family, it was Obong'o, (3) great-grandfather to President Obama, who took the plunge and left his ancestral home in K'ogelo and established a homestead in south Nyanza. Obong'o was probably born around 1802, and he is thought to have left K'ogelo before he was even married. It must have been a big decision to make for any young man, but the pressure on land and resources was so great in central Nyanza that large numbers of people moved south over a period of two generations. According to Obama family history, Obong'o established his settlement in Kendu Bay, on the southern shores of Winam Gulf. This would have been the most logical thing for him to have done; the lake provided food for the family, and water for his cattle.

Charles Olouch lives in Kendu Bay and he is the great-great grandson of Obong'o, and cousin to President Obama. He explained to me how his great-great-grandfather took the drastic step to leave the ancestral home in K'ogelo, and take a chance in the new area in south Nyanza:

'At that time there was a lot of wrangling, and there were various people fighting within the family. The K'ogelo people were many now, and they came looking for land. Some people thought it would be easier to come this side [of the Gulf], because in this particular place, there were not many people, not settled areas, not so many around south Nyanza.

'Obong'o crossed to this side when he was around thirty years old. I heard he came before he was married. It was very hard to carry your family to go to a foreign land. And he came and found that the place was good, so he decided to find a family and settle.

'There was a lot of forest on this side. There was forest everywhere, wild animals, but most of the Kalenjins were up there in the mountains. They used to just come down, maybe to bring their cows to drink water sometimes when it was dry. But most of the time this land was not inhabited.'

Late in his life, after he had established a family and three sons in Kendu Bay, Obong'o returned to his family compound in K'ogelo. The Luo have a tradition of burying the placenta of a newborn within its father's compound, which gives rise to the saying *Oyik biecha kaluo kae* – 'My placenta is buried here in Luoland'. The expression is a confirmation of the importance they attach to the ancestral home, and regardless of how far people might journey from Luoland, they are always drawn back, even in death. So late in his life when he was over fifty, Obong'o returned to die in K'ogelo, the place of his birth.

We know that Obong'o had at least three sons; Obama, Opiyo and Aguk, and all three of them were born in Kendu Bay; they stayed to establish the Obama presence there. It was Obong'o's second son, Opiyo, who would become the great ancestor of the Obamas of Kendu Bay, for it was Opiyo Obong'o who became the grandfather of Onyango Obama, and the great-great grandfather of the President of the United States.

A portrait of a Luo father and son from 1902; they are wearing large metal arm and leg rings (minyonge) *as well as elaborate necklaces of cowrie shells.*

3

THE LIFE
AND DEATH OF
OPIYO OBAMA

Adong arom gi bao ma kanera
May I grow as tall as the Eucalyptus tree in my
uncle's homestead

**The diverse traditions which govern Luo life,
as seen through the life of Opiyo Obama**

Sometime around 1830, in a homestead to the south of Winam Gulf in
what is now Nyanza in western Kenya, a young woman gave birth to a boy
behind her simple mud hut. By tradition, she was probably alone for the
birth, but older women were at hand in case she got into difficulty. The
baby was the second son of Obong'o, a local Luo farmer. Nobody can recall
the name of the baby's mother, nor the names of his sisters, for the Luo
are a patrilineal society and women don't figure in their genealogy. Nor
does anybody know the exact year the baby was born, least of all the month
or the day. Yet we know from his name, Opiyo, that he was the first-born
of twins (*piyo* means quick).[1] The Luo have a tradition of giving their children a name which describes something about their birth. Yet Opiyo's
family have no record of the name of the second-born twin, who would,
by tradition, have been called Odongo if a boy, or Adongo if a girl (*dong*
means to be left behind). Therefore we can only assume that if the twin
was a boy, he died as an infant; if the baby was a girl, then her name would
not usually be recorded in the oral history of the family.

Opiyo grew to be a strong and respected leader within the Luo community
of south Nyanza and his family went on to prosper in their settlement in
Kendu Bay. In time, Opiyo fathered three sons, the second of whom he
called Obama; Obama would, in time, become the great-grandfather of the
man who is now the President of the United States of America.

However, Opiyo's birth was not greeted with the universal joy usually associated with a newborn son. In Luo society, the arrival of twins is seen as a
bad omen for a family, and as is customary among the Luo, his birth was
accompanied by a loud cry and wailing from the women; the noise is intended
to scare away the evil spirits which had brought about the double birth. This
unwelcome news was also taken immediately to the mother's parents, for it
was important that they too knew about the calamity which had befallen the
family. There were also many more rituals which the family had to perform,
which were intended to give protection to the children in their vulnerable
first few days of life, and which would also relieve the parents of the taboo
and social stigma attached to bringing twins into the world. Obong'o and his
wife had to give up their normal clothing and they wrapped tree-creepers
around themselves for several days after the birth. Obong'o's wife was confined
to her hut for several days, and she relieved herself in a large earthenware
pot hidden at the rear of her hut. If Opiyo's younger sibling had actually
died during these early days, then its body would have been callously tossed
into the pot. This period of taboo could not be broken until a special ceremony was performed by the family several days after the birth.

These complex and elaborate ceremonies surrounding the birth of the
twins were only the beginning of a lifetime of rituals which the young
Opiyo faced. They are an essential part of Luo life, and to ignore them
would result in not only vulnerability to the forces of evil which were everywhere, but ostracism by family and neighbours for not conforming to their
traditions. Despite the fact that the Christian Church now exerts a powerful
influence on the lives of most Luo, I was surprised to discover that many
of these rituals are still as important and relevant today as they were when
Opiyo was born, more than 180 years ago.

Opiyo's birth was governed by strict rules and tribal ceremonies. Traditionally, a Luo woman usually marries long before she reaches her twentieth birthday, and she usually gives birth to her first-born within a year of
marriage. Although Opiyo was his mother's second son, it is likely that she
was still very young when she gave birth. Opiyo's father, Obong'o, had three
wives, and he spent three or four nights with each woman before directing
his attentions to another. He was expected to have sex with one of his

women every night, and there was often rivalry between his wives, who competed for his attention.

Aloyce Achayo is a retired headmaster and a Luo cultural historian, and he explained to me the subtle ways in which the wives would vie for Obong'o's attention:

> 'Let's say that you have four or five wives, and you come back to your homestead at the end of the day. As you are coming in, an astute wife will send her children to help her husband. In this way, the children will bring their father back to their mother's hut, and so the man will now go to that home first.'

Children are prized in Luo society, and women were expected and encouraged to have many children. Obong'o's first wife, Aoko, would sometimes advise him to sleep with his younger wife, whom she knew was coming into the fertile stage of her monthly cycle. Like all Luo men, Obong'o slept in a small hut called a *duol*, and he would creep out after dark to discreetly visit the wife of his choice for the night – but he would always return to his *duol* before daybreak.

When Obong'o's wife gave birth to Opiyo behind her hut in the homestead, she cut the umbilical cord with a piece of sharpened corn husk called a *muruich*, and then smeared her newborn son with butter – a tradition which was both symbolic and practical, as the grease gave the newborn protection and reduced the loss of body heat. Opiyo's mother then dug a shallow pit and buried the placenta within the family compound. This was another important symbolic gesture, as the child was now a member of the family and he had become an inherent part of the homestead; it was even more significant because he was a male.

After giving birth, Opiyo's mother brought her baby into her hut, where she was confined for four days (it would be three days if she had given birth to a girl). It was believed that anybody with bad intentions towards the family could harm the baby in those early days, so during this period of purdah, Opiyo's mother was not seen outside her hut and nobody except her husband Obong'o could visit her. This confinement also had a practical advantage, as it allowed the baby and his mother to rest and bond before the celebrations began. However, people still brought copious quantities of food to the hut, because it was believed that mothers who had just given birth needed lots of food; in fact, new Luo mothers are called *ondiek*: hyena! For the next six months Opiyo was breast-fed, and during this time his mother gradually weaned him off her milk and began to feed him a gruel made from finely ground millet flour and water. By the time he was two years old, Opiyo was eating the same food as adults.

On the fourth day after his birth, Opiyo was brought out at dawn and placed just outside the door to the hut, carefully watched by his parents who sat a safe distance away. This ceremony is called *golo nyathi*, literally 'removing the baby', and it represented Opiyo's introduction to the world. *Golo nyathi* usually marks the start of a great celebration, particularly for a healthy newborn male. But as Opiyo was the first-born of twins, the family participated in a different type of drunken ritual, designed to relieve them of the disgrace of having given birth to twins. Several days after the birth, Obong'o and his wife joined the rest of their extended family in a ceremony where large quantities of beer were consumed. By tradition, the dancing which accompanied the revelry was intentionally licentious, and the family referred to the couple in the foulest and most obscene language imaginable. All these proceedings were intended to lift the taboo from the parents, but the ignominy of being a twin would haunt Opiyo for the rest of his life.

On the fourth day after the birth, Obong'o had sexual intercourse with his wife; this was another Luo tradition. The couple carefully placed Opiyo between them before making love, a ritual which is called *kalo nyathi*, literally, 'jumping over the child'. There are many events in the life of the Luo which need to be consummated by sexual intercourse; in this case it symbolised that the child belonged to the couple, and sex was a form of cleansing after the birth, in the hope that another baby would soon follow. It was generally believed that if Obong'o had sex with any of his other wives before *kalo nyathi*, then Opiyo's mother would never conceive again. So for a period of several weeks Obong'o was not allowed to sleep away from the mother's hut. Opiyo's final birthing ceremony occurred just a few weeks after he was born. It was called *lielo fwada*, 'the first shaving of the child', when all of the baby's hair was removed. This is a ceremony which is still practised today in many parts of Luoland.

Opiyo was given his birth name through a simple and logical system adopted by the Luo, and the names of children can tell you a lot about the individual and their family. Traditionally, Luo babies are given two names (or sometimes more), and nicknames are also commonly used as well. In each case their first, personal name says something about their birth: Otieno is a boy born at night, Ochola is born after the death of his father, Okoth is somebody born during the rainy season, and Odero is a boy whose mother gave birth by the grain store. The child also takes their father's personal name as their own surname, so Opiyo's full name was Opiyo Obong'o.

In the case of girls, their personal name begins with an 'A'; so Atieno is a girl born at night; Anyango was born between mid-morning and midday, Achieng' is a girl born shortly after midday, and so on. When a woman marries, she becomes known by her husband's surname. For example, Sarah, the third wife of Hussein Onyango Obama (the name Onyango indicates that grand-father Obama was born at midday or shortly before), was born Sarah Ogwel (Ogwel is a boy born with bowed legs), but after her marriage to President Obama's grandfather, she became known as Sarah Hussein Obama.

Although there are exceptions to this rule, the vast majority of Luos, probably more than three-quarters of them, have this unique form of naming. However, since the early twentieth century, when missionaries brought Christianity to Luoland, people often took a Christian name when they were baptised, and they used this before their tribal name. Therefore Charles, Winston, Roy and David are all common first names for boys, and Mary, Sarah, Pamela and Magdalene are typical girls' names. Barack (which means 'blessed one' in Arabic) is unusual. President Obama's grandfather, Onyango Obama, converted to Islam whilst in Zanzibar during the First World War and took the first name Hussein. He named his first son Barack Obama, who sub-sequently used the same name for his own son, the President. (On the day that Barack Obama defeated John McCain in the US election, practically every child that was born in Nyanza that night was called Barack or Michelle, and both names have remained very common since. It is something which will cause chaos in Nyanza's primary schools in about four years' time!)

The name Obama is thought to have been passed down through the generations from the early eighteenth century. Opiyo's great-great-grandfather was called Onyango Mobam – *mobam* means 'born with a crooked back', so he was probably born with curvature of the spine. The name Mobam is then thought to have become corrupted to Obama.

Any form of physical or mental disability challenges people's under-standing of the world, and the Luo use traditional morality tales to help explain how to manage difficult events in life, such as death, suffering, or the birth of a deformed child. There is one pertinent story which is told about a woman who constantly gave birth to monitor lizards instead of human babies.[2] After each birth, the couple abandoned the lizard-babies because they were hideous to look at. However, the parents decided to keep one child, and in time he grew to be a young adolescent. Their child loved to bathe secretly in the river, and before swimming he would remove his monitor skin; underneath he was a normal human being, but only for the time he was in the water. One day a neighbour was passing and saw the boy in the water, and returned to the village to tell his parents that their son was a perfectly formed human being. Secretly his parents followed him on his next outing and discovered that it was indeed true; his skin was only a superficial covering and underneath their boy was normal. So they destroyed his skin, their son became accepted and loved by the whole community, and the couple lived to mourn all the monitor-lizard children they had discarded. The moral of this traditional tale, of course, is that people should show compassion towards children with physical defects.

Opiyo's younger brother was probably born around 1835, and he was called Aguk. Normally this is a female name (the male version being Oguk, meaning a boy born with a humped back, which suggests that there might be a genetic abnormality in the family). However, occasionally a boy is given a female name (or a girl a boy's name) to indicate something significant or prestigious about their birth. For example, the only boy born into a large family of girls might be given his mother's name to mark the honour of giving birth to a male heir; conversely, a girl could be given the name of her grandfather if he was particularly respected within the community, or was a renowned warrior and hunter. This reversal of names confers a special status on the individual. A woman with a man's name, for example, will often be offered a chair to sit down on when she is waiting in line, or she will be given special treatment when shopping, such as a small discount on her purchases. The cultural historian Aloyce Achayo was given a woman's name, and I asked him about its significance. He told me that his grandmother Achayo had died just before he was born, and for that reason he was given her name. (The name Achayo, or Ochayo, is given following an unexpected birth; this might be because the mother was thought to be infertile, or close to the menopause, or to a child not expected to survive – perhaps following a premature birth.)

There is yet another layer of naming which is very common in Luoland, but which is quite independent of family names. The Luo frequently give people nicknames, which are related to where they live. A man from Kendu Bay might be referred to as 'Jakendu' – in this case the preface 'Ja' is used in combination with the village or township of a man. A woman from the same location might be nicknamed 'Nyakendu'.

As a young boy, Opiyo grew up in a large, extended family, with lots of brothers and sisters, who were all offspring of his father's three wives. The family homestead was also home to all the widowed grandmothers in the family, and the girls would gather in her home, called the *siwindhe*, to listen to stories and learn from their grandmother and the older girls in the family about what was considered to be appropriate behaviour for a Luo girl, the mores of the clan and the sexual and social duties expected of them.[3] In a society which predates formal education, the *siwindhe* became a classroom for the young girls of the homestead, and they would usually move out of their mother's hut at a relatively young age, so as not to disturb their mother and father when he visited at night. The girls would live in the *siwindhe* with their grandmother until they married. Here, Opiyo's grandmother presided over the storytelling and verbal games. Friendly arguments often broke out over the precise interpretations of riddles or *ngeche* (singular *ngero*), and the youngsters competed to find clever answers to common questions. One riddle, for example, asks: 'Which is the pot whose inside is never washed?' and the standard answer is 'Your stomach'. Sometimes the children were asked to solve a riddle which had several potential answers: 'What is the four-legged sitting on the three-legged waiting for the four-legged?' The standard answer would be a cat sitting on a stool waiting for a rat, but children would compete to find alternative answers.

In the evenings after everyone was through with their day's work, Opiyo and his brothers would join their father in his hut for their evening meal. The men always ate separately from the women and girls, and Obong'o's three wives would cook in the evening and bring the food to his hut. This was one of the few occasions they would ever come to his *duol*, which was always the preserve of the male members of the clan. The staple food was *kuon* (called *ugali* in Swahili), a dough made from hot water and maize flour; it is usually rolled into a lump and dipped into a sauce or stew. Everyone ate with their fingers (and still do), and the *ugali* is used in a variety of creative ways when eating; sometimes a thumb-depression is made in the dough which is then used as a scoop, or the *ugali* is flattened into a thin pancake and wrapped around pieces of hot meat, making it easier to pick up. Fish too was popular, and it was eaten either fresh or sun-dried, and then stewed or roasted. The meal was supplemented with vegetables and pulses from the home garden, or anything that could be collected in the forest, including mushrooms, fruit, honey and even termites.

The most important area in the compound for Obong'o's first wife was the *agola* or veranda, outside her hut. It was created by extending the thatched roof beyond the mud wall, and supporting it with pillars. It was here that most of the domestic activities took place, including grinding flour, cooking and tending to the chickens. It was on the *agola* that Obong'o's wives cooked,

using traditional earthenware pots of varying sizes, with each pot kept exclu-
sively for one particular food. Even today, the Luo will tell you that cooking
in an earthenware pot is far superior to using aluminium saucepans.

The food was cooked on a traditional hearth, comprising three large stones
which raised the pots above the fire. The meal was taken communally, but
with the wives, daughters and the other women eating separately from the
menfolk. This is still common in the rural areas, and I have taken many meals
where the men eat together and the women sit to one side, watching, but
never partaking. Traditionally, certain foods were not eaten by certain members
of the family; women, for example, would not eat eggs, chicken, elephant
meat or porcupine and men would never eat kidneys. Obong'o, as head of
the household, was always served the best meat, such as the cuts from around
the chest of the animal, the tongue, liver and heart. The women ate the intes-
tines and other offal. The skin of the carcass would then be tanned and used
for clothing or bedding. After the meal, Opiyo's father would talk to his sons
about Luo legends and stories of their ancestors. The discussions in his *duol*
would dwell mainly on heroes, battles, bravery and hunting; this was all part
of the rich Luo culture, and in this way the oral traditions of the tribe were
passed down through the generations. Like the girls, the boys too would play
verbal games, asking riddles and telling stories. After their anecdote, each of
the storytellers would close with the phrase, *Adong arom gi bao ma kanera* –
'May I grow as tall as the Eucalyptus tree in my uncle's homestead'.

The Luo have a long tradition of entertainment and partying, and even
today, Luos are some of the best musicians and dancers in Kenya. During
important ceremonies such as marriages and funerals, Obong'o would invite
a musician to play the *nyatiti*, an eight-stringed wooden lyre. This was played
either as a solo instrument, or with an assistant who would accompany the
musician on the drums or some other percussion. The *nyatiti* sessions were
great social occasions, and people would make requests or ask the player to
repeat a piece. However, the golden rule was that any request had to be
paid for, often with a chicken or a useful household object. Other musical
instruments included the *ohangla* (a drum made from the skin of a monitor
lizard), horns, flutes and various other types of drum.

Beer drinking was also an important part of these social events. The best
Luo beer is called *otia*, and it is brewed from sorghum flour. This is first
fermented, then dried in the sun, cooked and fermented again before
being strained and drunk warm. The men drink the beer from a large
communal pot from which they sip with a long wooden straw called an
oseke, sometimes up to three metres long. The men always use their right

hand to hold the straw, because this is the hand which represents strength and integrity. (Left-handedness is viewed with suspicion by the Luo, and left-handed children are forced to use their right hand for eating and to greet people.) Another type of beer is *mbare*, which is made from brown finger-millet flour called *kal*. This is not cooked but, like *otia*, it is dried and refermented. (The grain left over from beer-making is a useful by-product which I've seen used even today; the fermented residue is still potent, and it is left outside for wild guinea fowl to eat – the birds become intoxicated and are therefore much easier to catch.)

Often the adults also smoked tobacco or took snuff during these social events, and they also smoked *bhang* (marihuana) from calabashes. These parties were also a chance for Opiyo to play with his brothers and sisters, and to spend time getting to know their neighbours. *Ajua* is still a popular game in Luoland, played with small pebbles on a board with two rows of eight holes; *adhula*, a form of hockey, was also popular. Sometimes the young men would play a type of soccer using a ball made from rolled banana leaves, and they would also challenge each other to wrestling matches, called *olengo*; this was a golden opportunity for young men to show off their strength and physique to the girls from neighbouring villages.

When he was around fifteen, Opiyo faced one of the most important ordeals of his life. Most African tribes practise some form of initiation into adult-hood around this age, and the Luo are no exception. In Africa, the most common initiation is male circumcision, and often a clitorectemy for girls. The Luo were unusual in this respect and have never practised genital mutilation; instead they traditionally removed the six lower teeth of both boys and girls in a ceremony called *nak*, the teeth being extracted by specialists in the community called *janak*. By tradition, Opiyo's parents were not given advance notice that their son was being prepared for his initiation into adulthood. The practice was widespread in Luoland until the middle of the twentieth century, when both the government and missionaries tried to discourage it. However, *nak* is still performed today in some rural villages in Luoland, and even in certain churches in the main city, Kisumu.

It is still very common to see older men with their lower teeth removed. Joseph Otieno is a retired farmer in his late sixties and he lives in a remote community in Gangu in western Kenya. He still remembers with total clarity the day of his *nak*:

'The ceremony was usually done during the summer in August. The night before the ceremony, I crept into my mother's granary and stole a basket full of millet. This was my "prize".

'My sister came to my hut, and she escorted me the next morning to the ceremony. That morning when I went, I felt brave because it was my initiation into manhood. So you go willingly, otherwise you would not be considered to be a man in our society. So I had to be very brave to face it, because all the Luos go through the same thing. I had to kneel down, my sister held my shoulders, and I opened my mouth. The way they did it was to use a thin, flattened nail to remove my teeth. They forced the flattened nail into my gums to loosen each tooth. You can't be afraid – you must be strong.

'Many young people came to the same function, and there were many boys there to have their teeth removed. You could not reach the age of twenty without your teeth being removed. There were some people there who were afraid, so they put a stick in their mouth to keep it open. If you are too fearful, which some people were, then a group of boys would come and hold you down.'

Joseph Otieno displays the gap created when his six front lower teeth were removed when a teenager during nak, *his Luo initiation ceremony.*

I was interested to know from Joseph what the significance was to a Luo of having their front six teeth removed:

> 'Number one, the reason why they were removing this is that sometimes people can get sick, and this would be a gap where they could feed you food or drink.
>
> 'Number two, if you die anywhere [away from home], then people would know you were a Luo. So the symbolism was important; they would know that this here is a Luo.
>
> 'The third one, it was an initiation into adulthood, and it shows that you are now no longer a child. Luos are not circumcised, so this was our initiation. It was a very painful experience, but we had to do it. If you didn't do it, then your age-mates would not walk with you. It was symbolic, and if it was not done, you could not mix with other people. If it wasn't done, I would have to stay in the house all day. It was painful, but we had to go through it. You just have to persevere.
>
> 'Afterwards, my mouth bled for eight days.'

Joseph made the whole experience sound straightforward and perfectly normal, but I knew that the *nak* ceremonies didn't always go quite so smoothly. Leo Odera Omolo is a Luo journalist who lives in Kisumu. He too had his lower teeth removed, but against his will:

> 'When I was young, I lived away from home a lot of the time, and I did not want my teeth removed. When I was about eighteen, I returned to my parents' house one day for a short visit. That night I was grabbed by several young men from the village and they dragged me from my bed. My parents insisted that I should have my teeth removed, otherwise it would bring shame to my family. It was done forcibly. The boys held me down and the *janak* pulled out my six lower teeth with pliers.'

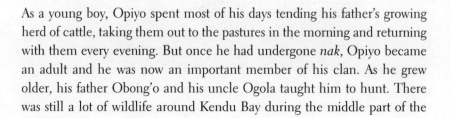

As a young boy, Opiyo spent most of his days tending his father's growing herd of cattle, taking them out to the pastures in the morning and returning with them every evening. But once he had undergone *nak*, Opiyo became an adult and he was now an important member of his clan. As he grew older, his father Obong'o and his uncle Ogola taught him to hunt. There was still a lot of wildlife around Kendu Bay during the middle part of the nineteenth century, and the animals were an essential source of food and protein for the family. Opiyo was taught how to throw a spear accurately, and how to use a bow and arrow, and he went off on regular hunting trips with his brothers. Antelope were common in the area, as well as buffalo, warthog and birds. But these hunting expeditions were not without risk; buffalo, for example, are one of the most dangerous animals in Africa because of their unpredictable nature, and an animal will often turn and attack with little provocation. (Today, only the hippo and the crocodile kill more humans in Africa.) Lions, leopards, hyenas and poisonous snakes also made Opiyo's hunting forays risky affairs.

It was, however, as a fighter that Opiyo could really make a name for himself. One of the reasons the young men did not marry until they were nearly thirty was because of their responsibilities as warriors; the defence of the clan was a priority and being a warrior was a form of 'national service' expected of all young men (except only sons whose family lineage depended on them producing an heir; such boys might be married as young as fifteen and would not be expected to fight). The young Luos were always prepared for war, and there were constant skirmishes between clans, and with other tribes. In practice, inter-clan conflict was a fact of life among the Luo, and as a young man Opiyo was expected to prove himself as a fearless warrior. Disputes frequently arose from competition over land, cows, resources (such as grazing rights for cattle), and sometimes women, and the young men of a tribe were always prepared for battle. Quite often disagreements arose during social gatherings such as funerals and marriage celebrations, such as the succession fight between Owiny Sigoma and his older brother Ogelo, who was (9) great-grandfather to Opiyo.

When war was declared, platoons of warriors were organised along family lines, based on the principle that kinship strengthens the bond between combatants. The fighters were called by blowing a small sheep's horn called a *tung'*; this made a high-pitched wailing sound which could be heard a long distance away. Once the warriors were assembled and ready to fight, the *oporo* was blown; this was a low-pitched booming horn from a bull or buffalo. This sounded the attack, and the young men of the clan, often high from smoking *bhang*, would advance on the enemy. The fighters were armed with spears (*tong'*), war clubs (*arungu*) and arrows (*asere*). For protection, the men carried a shield or *okumba*. The *kuot* was an even larger, body-sized shield which was made from three layers of buffalo skin, and this would deflect even the most powerful spear or arrow. As a strategy to disable their enemy, a village elder would select a spear and fold its blade in on itself; this was the first missile to be thrown at the enemy, and it was believed that this act would render the spears of their enemies ineffectual.

The battles could be bloody affairs, and in the aftermath the job of recovering the dead and wounded fell to the women, who remained safe from attack by the enemy under their widely accepted rules of warfare. The women carried the dead and injured back to the homestead where they were greeted with loud wailing; if the clan was victorious in battle, there was general elation and the returning warriors would stomp their way back to the compound, thrusting their spears skyward and chanting the *agoro* – the victory song. It was taboo for those fighters who had killed in battle to enter the homestead through the main gate; instead, they waited outside the compound until a new opening was made in the thick euphorbia hedge for them to enter. Inside, their wives and mothers waited for them, smeared with dust to celebrate their safe return. The fighters then had to go through a cleansing ceremony which involved swallowing strips of raw lung from a billy goat; the goat skin was also cut into strips, which were tied to the wrist of the successful warrior and around his spear, one strip for every man he had killed in battle. The goat's heart was then removed and the warriors also ate this raw, before their heads were symbolically shaved as a mark of a victorious warrior.

The next major episode in Opiyo's life was his marriage. Usually, Luo men take their first wife in their late twenties, and very few men are unmarried by the time they reach thirty-five. As with all Luo ceremonies, Opiyo's marriage followed a strict protocol which was designed to strengthen family ties. A suitable girl was selected by an aunt or a marriage-maker, called a *jagam* or 'pathfinder'. The Luo are strict about this selection and they do not allow marriage with even a distant relative. Opiyo's first wife, who was called Auko Nyakadiang'a, came from the Kadiang'a clan, who lived several kilometres away. Opiyo visited the family and met the chosen girl; either one of them could refuse the union at this stage. Traditionally the girl is coy about the approach, and is expected to play hard to get. After several refusals, she then agrees to the marriage.

The lineage of a prospective partner is keenly scrutinised by both the family and the village elders. If, for example, the prospective bride's father was known to practise witchcraft or be a habitual liar, then a marriage into that family would be considered unwise. Likewise any genetic conditions

such as epilepsy would have negative connotations for the union. Despite
this, every member of the Luo community is expected to marry and anybody
who remains unwed is viewed with suspicion. As with all Luo betrothals,
final approval for Opiyo and Auko's union rested with the village elders,
who decide if the marriage is appropriate.

The next stage is the negotiation of the bride price, which would have
been paid by Opiyo's father to Auko's family. Once a girl marries, she leaves
her homestead and becomes part of another clan, and her value to her
family is the potential bride price which she might command. Sometimes
the dowry takes up to three years to organise, and is often paid in instal-
ments. It typically involves the payment of twelve cows or more, and at
least one goat (for ceremonial purposes). Once the bride price is paid, the
groom can claim his bride. Once again, Opiyo had to fulfil an elaborate
ritual. One day he stole off to Auko's village with his two brothers, Obama
and Aguk; their intention was to kidnap his intended in a ritual known as
'pulling the bride'. Auko would have moved out of her mother's hut when
she reached puberty, so she was now living in her grandmother's *siwindhe*
in preparation for her marriage. It is likely that Opiyo bribed Auko's grandmother to be conveniently away from her hut at the crucial time for him
to claim his bride. As part of the ritual, the girl must always resist the
attempt to be taken, and there is every chance that her screams will be
heard by her brothers, in which case a fist-fight will ensue. This is no token
skirmish – the young men in the girl's village are determined to prove their
mettle by putting up a serious resistance to the kidnapping; in return, the
kidnappers are expected to show their determination to take the girl.

Opiyo was successful in 'pulling' his bride, and he took Auko back to
his *simba*, inside his father's compound. That night they consummated
their marriage, but even this is part of an elaborate ritual. As he brought
his bride home, the couple was pursued by a group of girls from Auko's
village. Aloyce Achayo explained the elaborate procedure which occurred
on that first night:

'The very day the lady is brought back, they are married. What will happen
now is that a group of girls will come at night, maybe forty or fifty girls.
They'll come, following this girl who was pulled. And that is called *omo
wer*. So it is on that night that the man and the woman will meet sexually.
This is now the beginning of the marriage. If those girls don't come, there
is no sex.

'The bride and the bridegroom come into the house for their first experience, and the consummation has to be witnessed by two or three girls who are almost the same age as the one who is being married. Outside, the other girls are singing all night. They don't sleep. If this particular girl is found to be a virgin, there is very big joy from the girl's side. A big, big joy.

'Very early in the morning, these girls will go back [to their village] with the news that she was or wasn't a virgin. During our olden times the majority used to be virgins. On their first meeting, the blood will show. She will sit on a stool, which will then be carried back to the girl's home to be shown to the mother. And this was a very big joy.'

The third stage of the wedding ceremony occurs on the morning after the consummation. As the *omo wer* girls return to the village, they meet the older women coming in the opposite direction to celebrate the marriage. This is called the *diero* of the women. The next day there is a *diero* of the young men – the very people who forcibly resisted the pulling of the bride – and they now come to the husband's home to celebrate.

The final ceremony occurs a few weeks after the wedding day. After the marriage has been consummated, the bride asks a handful of her friends to remain behind in the village to keep her company in her new home; they stay for anything up to a month. Then the bride's girlfriends return to their village for a final celebration, the *jodong*. Opiyo would have taken Auko back to her home to visit her family, and as many as sixty people would have joined in the celebrations. Auko was given a goat, which led her back to her parents' home. The animal was then slaughtered to mark the beginning of the *jodong*, followed by much eating, drinking, dancing and singing. (By Luo tradition, a goat slaughtered for ceremonial reasons always has its neck cut from the back.)

The homestead where Opiyo grew up in Kendu Bay was laid out in exactly the same way as that of all his neighbours. All the huts were ringed with a thick euphorbia thorn hedge which gave the occupants some degree of protection against both their enemies and wild animals. There were usually two entrances through the hedge: a formal, main gate which was always used by visitors, and a smaller gap in the hedge at the rear of the compound which allowed people to take a short cut through to their fields. The largest hut in the compound, perhaps five metres in diameter, belonged to Opiyo's father's first wife, and the door to this hut faced the main entrance to the compound. In this way, any visitors to the homestead were directed to the hut of Obong'o's senior wife; here they would introduce themselves, for it was the first wife who always ran the compound. To the left of the big hut was the house of Obong'o's second wife, identical in every way to that of his first wife, but slightly smaller. To the right of the big hut was the home of Obong'o's third wife, again slightly smaller still. In this way, the huts of all the wives were built on alternate sides of the first wife's hut, but each slightly smaller in size. Each wife also had her own granary or *dero* next to her hut, but generally they would work together to cook meals for the whole family.

Obong'o's hut was smaller even than that of his youngest wife, but as he spent most nights elsewhere, there was little point in having anything too grand. However, as head of the homestead, he used his hut for holding council with his fellow elders, and for discussing family business with his three sons. Women never came to Obong'o's hut unless they were summoned, or to bring food to the men.

Once Obong'o's sons reached puberty, they moved out of their mother's hut and built their own place inside the compound. Obama was Obong'o's eldest son, and he built his *simba* first, close to the main gate to the compound and just to the left of the entrance. A *simba* is essentially a bachelor pad, so when Opiyo came of age, he too built his own *simba*, but this time to the right of the main gate, thus following the same pattern as the women's huts. When his younger brother Aguk came of age, he too built a *simba*, but this time to the left of the entrance to the homestead, but further away from the gate than that of his oldest brother, Obama. In this way, the young men of the family guarded the entrance to the family compound. The space between the huts in the 'upper' part of the compound where the parents lived, and the sons' houses near the entrance to the compound, was deliberately arranged to be a respectable distance apart.

The sons also had to get married in order of seniority and once Obama took a wife, she moved into his *simba*. In time, each of the sons would marry, and their respective wives would move in and start a family of their own. Only when Opiyo had a son could he leave his father's compound and establish a homestead of his own.

Opiyo's hut was built in exactly the same way as all the others in the compound. His *simba* was circular, with thick mud walls and a pointed, thatched roof. Visitors had to stoop low to enter the doorway, and the inside was cool and very dark, as the huts had no windows. There was no furniture to speak of, but a raised mud platform served as a bed, and scattered animal skins and blankets gave a little comfort for sleeping. A small fire could be lit to give some warmth, and the smoke rose up into the rafters and helped to fumigate the thatch. Before he was married, Opiyo enticed local girls into his *simba*. This was expected of him, and periodically Obong'o would pass quietly by his son's *simba* at night to check that his son's social (and sexual) development was on course. Although both boy and girl gained sexual experience in this way, the girl would almost always draw the line at full penetrative sex, for virginity was, and still is today, expected of all brides.

Such is the power of the tradition of the *simba* that in early 2008 one of Kenya's leading national papers, the *Standard*, ran a story about Barack Obama. At the time, he was running against Hillary Clinton to win the Democratic Party nomination. The newspaper ran a front-page special, with the headline: 'EXCLUSIVE: Obama's one-day visit to Kenya':

> Senator Barack Obama, the man who has caused a sensation in the presidential nomination race in the US, is in Kenya for a one-day visit . . . Obama will make a public appearance at KICC [Kenya International Conference Centre] where he will sign autographs and speak on peace.
>
> He is later scheduled to leave for his father's home in Kogelo, Siaya District shortly after midday.

Within minutes of the paper hitting the news stands, crowds were flocking to the conference centre in Nairobi to hear the great man speak, and the switchboards at radio stations running talk shows were jammed with hundreds of callers wanting to speak. The rumour soon spread that Obama had been advised that he would greatly increase his chances of success with the American electorate if he returned to Kenya and built himself a *simba*. This, people claimed, would show that he was a true Luo.

What nobody noticed was the date on the top of the paper: 1 April.

There comes a time in the life of any young male Luo when he moves out of his father's homestead and establishes himself in his own compound. There is always a strict order of seniority, and Opiyo's brother Obama had to move out first, before Opiyo could do the same. The youngest son in the family, in this case Aguk, never leaves. Instead, he stays behind to look after his ageing parents and, in time, he inherits his father's compound.

With the exception of the youngest, practically all the other sons move out of their father's compound once they have a family, although certain young men do not qualify. A man without a family of his own could never move out; nor if he had only daughters, as both a son and a wife are necessary to perform some of the complex rituals involved in establishing a new homestead. Nor can a left-handed person set up his own home, for this is seen as a bad omen and it was believed that if a left-hander were to establish his own compound, it would lead to the death of his siblings. Traditionally, it was also believed that left-handed people were easy prey to their enemies, and they were vulnerable to magic and witchcraft. (It is worth noting that according to strict Luo tradition, President Obama would never be allowed to establish his own homestead in Luoland on two accounts: he has only daughters, and he is also left-handed.)

For several weeks before setting out to build his own compound in Kendu Bay, Opiyo surreptitiously looked round for a suitable location, but he had to be careful not to be seen to be too interested, in case others moved there first, or put a curse on the site. The area to the south of Winam Gulf was relatively sparsely populated in the mid-nineteenth century – that was why his father had moved to the region nearly forty years previously. In those days, most of the land had not been cleared and the area was covered in thick, tropical forest. There were wild animals too, and encounters with leopards, cheetahs and hyenas were common.

The establishment of a new homestead is one of the highlights in the social development of any male Luo. On the eve before he set out to build his new home, Opiyo had sex with Auko, his first wife; this was a long-established Luo tradition. The next morning he rose before dawn and walked out of the family compound, accompanied by his father Obong'o, his uncle, his wife Auko, and Obilo, his eldest son. Everyone had their own specific roles to play that day. Opiyo carried a large cockerel, Obilo a new axe, and Auko had a small fire smouldering in an earthenware pot. On arrival at his chosen place, his uncle selected the precise location for the new home, then drove a forked pole into the ground where the very centre of Opiyo's hut would be. His uncle then hung a bird cage on one branch of the forked pole, and at the base of the post he carefully placed a piece of soil taken from an ant hill which they had passed on the way. Inside the bird cage was a selection of items to bring good fortune to the homestead:

a rotten egg to dispel sorcery, star-grass for prosperity, and stalks of millet and maize to attract wealth. Opiyo's uncle then took blades of *modhno* grass, tied them into a knot, and cast them down on to the ground; the grass symbolises a blessing for a new home, and protects it from evil forces.

Only now could the real work begin on the new hut. First Obilo, Opiyo's eldest son, cut a pole using his father's new axe. Opiyo then cleared the site of undergrowth and dug the first hole, into which he placed the pole which his young son had cut; this first hole in the ground always coincides with the sleeping side of the house. Opiyo then marked out the outline of his circular *duol*, and the rest of the party joined in to dig holes at regular intervals to take the remaining poles which would form the main reinforcement for the mud walls. Opiyo then fitted the door posts, being careful to put cow dung, *modhno* grass and *bware* (a medicinal plant) into the holes for the door poles. For the door post, he cut down a *powo* tree and removed the bark, leaving a very smooth surface. The Luo believe that a smooth door post keeps away the evil effects of witchcraft, as these negative forces simply roll off the post to the ground and never enter the house.

With the door pillars in place, the rest of the family and the neighbours joined in to help Opiyo complete his house before nightfall. All day there was a steady supply of help; women carried water and cooked food for the men, and they also helped carry some of the lighter building materials, such as reeds. The men did all the heavy construction work, such as softening mud to build the walls; they also climbed up and thatched the roof. The house had to be finished by the end of the first day, and when it was completed, Opiyo lit a fire and placed the cockerel inside the *duol* to crow the next morning. Meanwhile, the family returned to the old home, leaving Opiyo and his son to spend the first night together in their new hut. It was traditional that only one simple house was erected on the first day. Opiyo spent four nights in his new *duol* with his young son, Obilo. This gave him time to build a grander hut for Auko. On the fifth day, his wife moved in, and by Luo tradition, the couple consummated the new hut by having sex on that first night together.

In time, Opiyo took a second wife; her name was Saoke from the Wasake clan and she came from a village 90km away, on the border between Kenya and Tanzania. We know that Opiyo must have become a wealthy man with many cows for him to be able to afford the bride price for a second wife; but because she came from such a distant village, his reputation must have been very widespread throughout south Nyanza. When he married Saoke,

Opiyo built a hut for her in the family compound. In time, Opiyo fathered three sons in total; Obilo, Obama and Aginga, and two daughters. His middle son Obama was born around 1860, and he became the great-grand-father of President Obama.

Living as we do in the twenty-first century, it is difficult for us to fully appreciate just how independent and self-sufficient Opiyo and his family had to be to survive. They lived in a remote part of western Kenya during the middle and latter part of the nineteenth century, a full fifty years before the Luo were introduced to any form of modern technology by the white colonists. Opiyo and his family grew all their own food, built their own houses and made their own clothes (such as they were), as well as making many of their farming implements and weapons. Opiyo was a traditional subsistence farmer, but living nearby were a wide variety of specialists who traded their goods and produce; there were weavers, blacksmiths, potters, medicine men and exorcists. Opiyo could call upon these people to protect his family against snake bites and evil curses, and he would trade for ropes and fishing baskets, cooking pots and knives. There was no money in circulation, for that was not introduced until the early twentieth century (by the British); instead, the Luo economy functioned on a system of elaborate bartering.

Opiyo's family grew or hunted for practically everything they needed. They had two areas of cultivated land; the kitchen garden, or *orundu*, was usually located behind the family compound and accessible through a narrow back gate. The *orundu* was fenced off to keep animals away from the produce, and it was here that Opiyo's two wives, Auko and Saoke, grew vegetables, pulses (peas and beans), groundnuts (peanuts), simsim (the Arabic word for sesame), maize, millet, cassava and sweet potatoes. The food grown here was usually for immediate consumption. Further away from the compound was their main farm. This was the preserve of Opiyo himself, and here he grew cereals and pulses for long-term storage, thus creating a strategic reserve for his family for use during times of drought and famine.

In addition to the crops, the family reared cattle, goats, sheep and chickens. Cattle were, and still are, considered to be the most important livestock for an African and the main indication of a man's wealth. The head of the family has to accumulate cattle to pay the bride price for his sons, but he also receives animals when his daughters are married off. The importance of cattle to an African can never be underestimated; apart from their prestige value, they also represent an invaluable resource for the family, for they provide milk, meat, skins and fuel. Sheep are also prized by the Luo, and are used mostly as food, or as gifts for friends. The responsibility for looking after the livestock falls on the young males in the family, and Opiyo's sons took turns to look after the animals, usually for three days at a time, before being relieved by one of their siblings. (President Obama's father Barack Snr is often referred to as being a 'goat herd' during his youth. In practice, he looked after all of his father's livestock.) The women always looked after the chickens and other fowl, and they would take cone-shaped fishing baskets down to the nearest river to catch what they could.

A successful farmer can produce a surplus of food, which is traded for items he cannot produce himself, such as knives and salt. Bartering among the Luo was a sophisticated form of exchange, and there were specific exchange rates, for example between grain and meat. Sometimes an owner would slaughter a bull to exchange for cereals, and each part of the animal was valued differently. The Luo also had a special form of barter called *singo*, which was a form of promissory note. If a man needed to slaughter a bull for a specific ceremony such as a funeral, but did not have one of his own available, he would strike a deal with a neighbour to exchange one of his cows for a bull. Under the *singo* system the neighbour would keep the cow until such time as it produced a calf, which the neighbour then kept for himself.

One important area of expertise in the Luo community was traditional herbal medicine, which was used to treat both physical and psychological illnesses. Common medical problems included fractures and other physical injuries from accidents or battles, parasites, snake bites, eye infections and tropical diseases, such as malaria, sleeping sickness (trypanosomiasis) and bilharzia, which is a parasitic fluke caught from a water snail which can damage internal organs and impair a child's growth. Some traditional remedies were inevitably more successful than others, but the importance of tropical herbs and plants in the search for the development of new medicines is legendary, and there is no doubt that there is more that modern pharmaceutical companies can learn from traditional remedies. For example, among the Luo there is a wide variety of treatments for snake bites, both herbal and non-herbal. They include mystical therapies as well as concoctions made from twenty-four different herbaceous plants; the treatment usually involves cutting, sucking and binding the injury, followed by the application of a poultice made from leaves or roots, which is held in place over the wound with strips of cloth or tree bark. I have been assured that the different remedies can be very effective, and each one is tailor-made specifically for the particular snake venom involved.

Like all Africans, Opiyo also believed in the spiritual world. Before the coming of the Christian missionaries at the start of the twentieth century, the Luo believed in a supreme God or life-force called Nyasaye, the creator. Nyasaye is all powerful, and he intervenes directly in the daily activities of humans. He can both create and destroy, and when angry, he can generate sickness and bring disaster as a punishment. The mystery of Nyasaye is all encompassing, and he can be found not only in the sun and moon, but in rivers, lakes, mountains, large rock structures, trees and even snakes (especially the python) – these are all natural conduits for his divinity. In this sense, the Luo are traditional animists.

It was believed that the sun could appear to people in a dream, and the individual would become very agitated and might have to be physically restrained as he or she reached out to ask for the sun's blessing. The individual might also throw cow dung, human excrement or plant seeds towards the sun, and in return they would be blessed with wealth in the form of a good harvest or many cattle. The power of the moon was also invoked: old men prayed for more wives, young men for a bride, young women for a husband, and married women for satisfaction. Sometimes, a large goat was kept in the house as a living embodiment of Nyasaye. Celestial bodies were also consulted to help forecast the weather and to predict the future. For example, a ring appearing around the sun was seen as signifying that an important person had just died. Solar and lunar eclipses were viewed with awe and forecast a major event. In response to these portentous signs, the village elders would gather and deliberate over the most appropriate action to take to avoid disaster.

Belief in the power of Nyasaye is still common among the Luo. In 2003, a six-metre-long python appeared in a village on the banks of Lake Victoria and its presence exposed rifts in the community, pitting traditionalists against modernists. The snake was found by a thirty-five-year-old mother of five called Benta Atieno, who considered it was her divine duty to ensure that

The Luo believe that their God, Nyasaye, resides in all natural things including rock formations such as this one outside of Kisumu, called Kit Mikayi *or 'Stones of the first wife'. Legend has it that Mikayi went up to the hill when her husband took a second wife, and she has been weeping there ever since.*

the female python safely hatched its dozens of eggs. When she first discovered the snake, she ran to tell other people in the village about her find, and the elders told her that the serpent's presence could signify good news. The locals considered this to be a special snake, an *omieri*, and welcomed it as a harbinger of good fortune. They believed it was a sign that the rains would come, that their harvests would be bountiful, and that their livestock would produce healthy offspring. If the *omieri* was cared for, they claimed, good things would ensue, but if it was harmed, then bad luck would befall the village. This, they believed, is what had happened seven years previously when another large python was killed in the village, and a severe drought subsequently struck the area. However, there was opposition to *omieri* and some people, including senior church leaders, called for the snake to be destroyed, fearing that it would take livestock or could even be a danger to small children. The appearance of large pythons in Kenyan villages is a common event, especially during the rainy season, and what usually happens in these cases is that the Kenya Wildlife Service removes the snake, and releases it well away from human habitation.

The Luo also worship their ancestral spirits, both male and female. They believe that man is made up of visible and invisible parts; the invisible part, known as *tipo* or shadow, and the visible part (the human body) combine to create life. When an individual dies, their body becomes dust, and the *tipo* becomes a spirit, which retains the individual's mortal identity but becomes even more powerful and intelligent in the afterlife. Thus the most potent spirits were important people when they were alive, and this is why powerful male ancestors are usually the most respected and the most feared. However, only the spirits of a particular clan can haunt the living relatives of that family, and the Luo believe that this ancestral spirit continues to exist for as long as those who recognise it are still alive. People perceive these spirits to be agents of both good and evil, and they might claim to see, hear, or smell them when awake, or encounter them in their dreams. A spirit can become a demon, *jachien*, when the circumstances of his death and burial are not honoured correctly. For this reason, the strict rituals and customs of the tribe must always be followed to avoid a *jachien* being created.

In many African societies, ritual sacrifice is frequently made to ancestors or gods, and the Luo are no exception. Their sacrificial ritual involves the consecration of an animal before killing it and sharing the meat among the members of the clan. If the spirits are offended, the head of the family must seek expert help from someone who can best advise what course of action to take, and for this purpose there are witch-doctors, shamans, magicians and medicine men in Luo society who claim to have unique powers. Throughout his whole life, Opiyo lived under the constant fear that a curse could be cast on his family, and he took elaborate precautions to guard against these evil powers.

Opiyo felt overwhelmed by the many powers that could bring evil upon him or his family, and if he needed advice about the future, or had worries about his ancestral spirits, then he would turn to traditional diviners for help. The diviner, or *ajuoga*, is an expert in dispensing medicine and magic; he can diagnose illnesses, prescribe cures, and appease the spirits using sacrifice or the powers of cleansing. Whenever Opiyo visited a diviner, he took with him a present, or *chiwo*. A diviner might contact the ancestral spirits using a number of different techniques, including *gagi* – literally 'casting pebbles' – or *mbofwa*, meaning 'the board'. This last method involves rubbing two flat, wooden blocks together, one of which is much bigger than the other, and summoning the spirits by name. The diviner knows that he has contacted the spirit when the smaller piece of wood begins to stick to the bigger piece. Another technique, called *gagi*, involves using wild beans or cowrie shells; the diviner tosses them onto the ground and interprets the message according to the pattern they make. He will use both methods to identify the rebellious spirit that is causing the problem. Most diviners rely on the ancestral spirits for their knowledge, and any consultation with the dead is done in darkness, and only the diviner can see and talk to the spirits.

However, it was not only the ancestral spirits which Opiyo feared; his neighbours too could bring harm and death to his family through the use of sorcery and witchcraft. (In witchcraft practitioners use mystical powers to harm or kill others, whereas sorcery achieves the same objective through the use of material objects.) Witches, sorcerers and magicians among the Luo are called *jojuogi*, and to Opiyo and his family they represented a powerful threat although they could also use the *jojuogi* to their own advantage. People would engage a witch or a sorcerer for a number of reasons; there might be rivalry over land or a woman, or someone might simply resent the success of a neighbour, or covet the cows he owned. It was generally believed that by cursing and killing a successful neighbour, you would benefit from their death. Whatever the reason for the dispute, magicians were simply hired hands who, for a fee (usually three cows), could summon death or pestilence on demand.

The powers of magicians and sorcerers were inherited from their fathers and grandfathers, and their techniques would vary; some could simply stare at an individual to bestow a fatal curse, or would point the dried forearm of a gorilla to have the same effect. Others would summon lightning to strike, or they would slaughter a black sheep or a cockerel and their curse would strike morbid fear into the individual concerned. Some sorcerers would mix the blood of a sheep with secret ingredients and leave it in front of the hut of the targeted individual, or alongside a path where they would be sure to pass. In many respects, these techniques are similar to those used in many African societies, and also in voodoo, and they work because people believe in the power of the magic.

However, there was a protection against witchcraft and sorcery which could be summoned, and that was to find a practitioner at least as powerful as the protagonist, who (for another fee) would conjure up an antidote to the spell, to give you and your family protection. Not unnaturally, these people were the most feared individuals in Luo society, for they literally had the power of life and death over ordinary people, and are also among the wealthiest from the fees people paid for their services. However, because of their unique position in Luo society, they were also considered to be outside the normal social structure of the Luo tribe, and they did not live a normal family life.

Belief in witchcraft persists today. Roy Samo is a local councillor in Kajulu, a sprawling village north of Kisumu. He told me how people in his community feared witchcraft, and how only recently somebody had directed a bolt of lightning onto a neighbour's house. I knew Roy well, and I asked him almost jokingly what he thought about these traditional beliefs. I was astonished at his response. 'Oh I fully believe in them – they have the power of good as well as evil.' 'But Roy,' I said, 'you're an educated man, a devout Christian and a pastor at your local church!' 'Yes,' he laughed, 'but I am also an African.'

This was not an isolated case, and I discovered that the belief in magic is still very widespread among the Luo. As recently as May 2008 in Kisii district, south Nyanza, eleven elderly people – eight women and three men aged between eighty and ninety-six – were accused of being witches and burned to death by a mob. Villagers told reporters that they had evidence which proved the victims were witches; they claimed to have found an exercise book that contained the minutes of a 'witches' meeting', including details of who was going to be targeted next. In 2009 Kenya's *Daily Nation* claimed that 'an average of six people are lynched in different parts of Kisii on a monthly basis for allegedly practising witchcraft'.

Sometime around the end of the nineteenth century, Opiyo Obong'o died. Like many Luo men, he reached a good age from a combination of a high-protein fish diet and a lifetime of physical labour that kept him lean and fit. Indeed, it is not unusual for men in this part of Africa to live to be a hundred years or more. For the Luos, there is no such thing as a natural death, there must always be a cause. An old man dies, not of 'old age', but because he has been called by his ancestors to join them for further duties in the afterlife.

Opiyo's death marked the beginning of his last ritual on earth, an elaborate rite of passage for both the deceased and the family who survived him. Even in death, Opiyo was expected to conform to certain traditions; if his death occurred at any time other than between two o'clock and seven o'clock in the morning, then it was considered to be a very bad omen. Today it is possible to preserve a body with formalin, or failing that, the body is placed on a bed of sand covered in banana leaves to keep it cool. In the past, a body had to be buried very quickly, and certainly on the day of death before the midday heat. If Opiyo died in the evening and his body lay in his hut overnight, then three goats would have been sacrificed to dispel the bad omen and the evil spirits which would otherwise haunt the family. The goats would be provided by close members of his family, either his brothers or his cousins, and they would not have been killed in the usual way by cutting their throats, but instead brutally bludgeoned to death. Only by killing the goats in this gruesome way would the evil influences which had caused the man to die at an inappropriate time, be beaten away.

The first that the villagers knew about Opiyo's death was when his first wife, Auko, began wailing – a high-pitched howling cry called *nduru*. By tradition, she stripped naked and ran from her hut to the entrance of her compound and back again. Auko then dressed in her husband's clothes, which she continued to wear throughout the protracted mourning period. This was the first ritual, which only the first wife could perform; it not only alerted everyone to Opiyo's death, but it also started what would become a long period of mourning. Opiyo's other wife, Saoke, also showed respect towards her dead husband by wearing his old clothes, and this also served as a sign to others that they were in mourning. Saoke joined Auko in *nduru*, and their noise alerted other members of the family to Opiyo's death, as well as their neighbours; soon people began to congregate outside Opiyo's hut. Meanwhile, Opiyo's two married daughters had been told about their father's death, and they came to the family compound as quickly as possible. By tradition, the eldest daughter had to arrive first; her younger sister could not enter the compound until after the older daughter had arrived.

Ever since he was a young man, Opiyo had kept the skin of his biggest bull ready for this occasion. He had not only killed the bull himself, but he also lavished great care in curing the skin ready for the day when it would be wrapped around his naked body as a burial shroud. A man never used the skin of a cow – that would only ever be used for a woman. (This practice has now largely died out over the years from the influence of European missionaries, and most Christian Luos are today buried in a wooden coffin.) Opiyo's body lay inside his *duol* to the right of the door until later that morning, when he was buried within the confines of his homestead.

On the day of Opiyo's burial, his relatives built a bonfire next to his grave to honour the deceased. The fire was called *magenga*, and the big logs burned for several days as friends and relatives came to pay their respects. The *magenga* always has to be lit by a cousin and the eldest son of the dead man. During the lighting ceremony, a big cockerel is killed and then roasted on the flames. Like the skin of the bull, Opiyo kept an old cockerel in his hut ready for the day of his burial. The sacrifice of the cockerel is symbolic that the man has now gone, and that he can no longer offer the household his protection. Along with the bird, Auko also prepared a traditional dish of *ugali* for the visitors.

By the evening, all Opiyo's relatives, his three sons and his two married daughters had congregated by his grave, and for the next four days neighbours brought food to the house to help feed the visitors. The next morning his family brought out Opiyo's three-legged stool, his fly whisk, and his clothes and placed them on his grave to accompany him to the next life. During the four-day mourning period, the women wailed and danced to chase away the 'death spirits'. For these four days after his death, the houses in the compound were left uncleaned, but on the fourth day, his two wives performed *yweyo liel* – the 'cleansing of the grave'. This marked the start of a spring clean throughout the whole compound. On that fourth day, Opiyo's three sons, their wives, and his daughters had their heads shaved. This symbolic act is called *kwer*, and indicates to others that a person is bereaved. Opiyo's wives too had their heads shaved, and they continued to wear his clothes for several more months.

On the fourth day the mourners prepared to leave. By tradition, Opiyo's son, Obama, had to leave first. Opiyo's eldest daughter too had to leave the compound before his other married daughter. As with other ceremonial functions with the Luo, sexual consummation was part of the ritual; Opiyo's eldest son Obilo returned to his homestead and had sex with his wife before his two younger brothers could leave their father's compound. This act set the brothers and sisters free from any curses which they might have acquired at the funeral. The two married sisters could then return home, again leaving the family compound in strict order of their birth. The brothers too returned home, and they also had to consummate the mourning period by having sex with their respective wives. If this is not done correctly, the Luo believe that you might have a child with physical or mental problems, or you can become sick yourself. (Most Christian Luos, even those living in the cities, still practise this custom today.) Meanwhile, Opiyo's two wives continued to mourn their dead husband, rising early at dawn to sing and praise him, extolling his virtues to anyone who was still listening.

Opiyo's widows, Auko and Saoke, were now restricted in what they could do and where they could go. They still wore his old clothes, but ever since his death they were considered to be unclean – tainted by his death and capable of putting a curse on people. They could not enter another's hut for fear of bringing bad luck to the owner, they could not stroll by a river for fear of it drying up, or walk through a field of maize for risk of it shrivelling, nor could they shake hands with their friends, eat with them, or pick up their children, otherwise they could bring bad luck to their neighbours. These women were in *chola*, and they could only be released from this restriction once they were 'inherited'.

During the first four days of mourning after Opiyo's death, his two brothers and his male cousins gathered in the family compound to decide which of them would inherit his wives. This is a process by which a dead man's wives are literally shared among his immediate relatives. It might be several weeks or even months before the women are finally inherited, but on the day of the inheritance, it is essential for the man to consummate the event with his new wife. Sometimes a man might inherit more than one wife, or even all of them, and would be obliged to have sex with all of the women on that first night, in strict order of seniority. Any woman towards whom the man failed in his obligation on that first night was required to remain confined to her hut until another husband could be found to rise to the occasion.

If her married sons had not already established their own homestead before their father's death, then they could not do so until after their mothers had been inherited. In this way, strong social pressure is brought on women to agree to inheritance, no matter how much they might prefer otherwise. A widow has the right to reject her inheritor, but this happens rarely. There are also restrictions over who can inherit a woman; if a prospective couple had previously had an extra-marital affair, then the woman could not be inherited. The woman might also object if she considered the man 'was of bad character', so there has always been some element of choice. However, in the past, the women would always be inherited by somebody and pressure is brought on anyone who might be reluctant to conform. This tradition of wife inheritance might seem bizarre, but in an environment where survival is tough and tenuous, it does guarantee that any widowed woman and her children will be looked after within an established family unit, and not abandoned.

Sometimes, a woman will resist inheritance. Hawa Auma, aunt to President Obama, told me that when her husband died, she refused to be inherited. Auma is a practising Muslim and many people in her mosque supported her firm stand. In the end, she agreed to a token inheritance, but refused to allow the union to be consummated. Auma is a very determined and strong-willed woman, but others are not quite so blessed. In the sprawling village of Kajulu in the outskirts of Kisumu, there was recently a case of a woman who was widowed, but as a devout Christian she spurned all attempts to be inherited. Tragically, her own son died quite suddenly, leaving the woman's daughter-in-law widowed as well. There is a Luo tradition that you cannot have two widows living in the same compound. So in order to bring pressure on the woman to be inherited and take new husband, the village elders refused to bury her son. Within a matter of weeks, the woman relented.

On the day that Auko and Saoke were inherited, the family slaughtered a bull in celebration, and the women discarded their dead husband's apparel and put on new clothes for the occasion. They were now free from the taboo of Opiyo's death. Restrictions placed on other members of the family were now also lifted. Within a few months of Opiyo's death, all of the huts of his wives were destroyed and new ones built adjacent to the old position in a ceremony called *loko ot*, or literally 'changing hut'. At some point after the funeral, there was also a big ceremony, called *romo* or *nindo liel* – literally 'stepping over the grave' – in remembrance of the deceased.

Today, most Luos are Christians, and they have been so for more than a century. Nevertheless, traditional rituals still play an important part in a funeral. Most people are now buried in a shroud or a suit, and their body is placed in a coffin. But it is still very important for any Luo to be buried in their own homestead. In 1987 an important legal battle was fought in the Nairobi courts to determine the final resting place of the Luo lawyer, S. M. Otieno. The trial held the attention of the nation for months. Otieno's widow, Virginia Wambui Otieno, was a member of the Kikuyu tribe and their marriage in 1963 – one of the first between a Kikuyu and a Luo – was considered to be shameful at the time. Mrs Otieno argued that because her husband had led a modern life and had no regard for tribal customs, she had the right to bury him in a place of her own choosing; in this case, she wanted a non-tribal burial on their farm near the Ngong Hills on the outskirts of Nairobi. The lawyer for Otieno's Luo clan argued that without a proper tribal burial in his homestead in Luoland, the ghost of Otieno would haunt and torment his survivors.

Otieno's body lay in a Nairobi mortuary for over four months whilst the dispute worked its way through the law courts, and eventually went to appeal. Finally, the Nairobi court ruled against the family and in favour of the Luo tribe, arguing that it was impossible for a Kenyan citizen to disassociate himself from his tribe and its customs, especially those of a tribe like the Luo, who still retain strong tribal traditions. The court claimed that a tribal burial was of paramount importance, and ordered that Otieno's body should be given to his fellow tribesmen for a traditional committal in his homeland near Lake Victoria. Although the judges said that tribal elders owed it to 'themselves and their communities to ensure that customary laws keep abreast of positive modern trends,' this important legal ruling highlighted the powerful force that tribalism still exerts in Kenya. To this day, neither Otieno's widow nor his children have visited his grave in Nyanza.

In my experience and without exception, every Luo wants and expects to be buried in his homestead. Even if the individual dies overseas after living abroad for many years, they would still want their body returned to their family compound. Many Luos now live and work in other parts of Kenya and especially in Nairobi, so when there is a death in the family, it can sometimes take several days for relatives and friends to return to the family home. It has therefore become customary to preserve the body, either in a hospital mortuary or at home, to allow people time to pay their last respects.

Leo Odera Omolo once told me that as a boy, he always looked forward to somebody in the village dying: 'We would look at the old people, waiting for them to die. That way there was lots of singing and dancing, and plenty for people to eat and drink. It was a good excuse for a party and we enjoyed ourselves!'

I have been to a few Luo funerals myself, and it is clear that people are there for many different reasons. The immediate family are grief stricken, but some others are in tears because the deceased owed them money and they were coming to terms with the fact that they would never be paid back. Local politicians use the events as opportunities to press the flesh and make promises to the electorate which they are never likely to keep, and most of the rest of the company are there to eat, drink and dance, or maybe just to pick an argument with somebody. Despite over a hundred years of Christianity, the indigenous Luo traditions have been absorbed and integrated into these rituals, and the tribal influence is still very much a part of these major life events.

In the rural areas, wife inheritance is still the norm and its practice is partly responsible for the high incidence of HIV/AIDS among the Luo population. There is still a great social stigma attached to being HIV positive. Often a man will keep his illness hidden from his family, and only take his medication at his place of work. When he dies, his wife might be quite oblivious to the fact that she is carrying the virus, and when she is inherited, she can pass it on to her new husband, and thence to his other wives.

There are many other strong Luo traditions which even today are never broken, even by modern city-dwellers. Sons-in-law and daughters-in-law have to respect rigid taboos when visiting the compound of their spouse's parents. For example, when one of a Luo's in-laws dies, he or she cannot visit their homestead until after the burial. To view the corpse would effectively be 'to see them naked'. Even when alive, there are rigid protocols which are still adhered to. If a son-in-law visits the house of his wife's parents, he must never look at the ceiling. If his wife's parents come to visit him, they must never sit opposite the door leading to the marital bedroom. Nor would they ever accept, or be offered, food in the other's homestead. To do so would break an indissoluble taboo. Nor must parents-in-law ever sleep in the home of their son-in-law when they come to visit; again it is something which is strictly forbidden, and there are serious consequences to be faced if the taboo is broken.

There was a very recent case, again in Kajulu, when a bad tropical storm prevented a wife's parents from returning home after visiting their daughter and son-in-law. They had no option but to stay the night; this was quite acceptable providing the parents-in-law sat upright all night and did not fall asleep. Unfortunately it was a long night, nature took its course, and both parents fell asleep. This was a serious breach of protocol, and there was only one possible outcome: the house had to be destroyed completely.

This protocol does raise serious problems, of course, for the President of the United States. When he moved to Washington DC with his family in January 2008, he invited his wife's mother, Marian Robinson, to live with them and help raise their two daughters. By Luo tradition, there is only one way to break the taboo created by such a rash decision – and that is to knock down the White House.

Henry Morton Stanley with his trusted African gun bearer and servant, Kalulu, a Swahili word for an antelope. Kalulu was originally a young slave who was given to Stanley during his first visit to Africa by an Arab merchant.

4

THE WAZUNGU ARRIVE

Rieko lo teko
Brain is mightier than brawn

**The arrival of the Europeans in the 1490s
through to 1884 and the start of colonisation**

Swahili is an East African Bantu language that has been greatly influenced by Arabic, including the loanword 'Swahili' itself, which comes from the Arabic *sawāhilī* (meaning 'of the coast'). Swahili has always been a living language, and this has enabled people speaking in different tongues and with different origins to come together, to communicate, and especially to trade. (In Swahili itself, the language is called *Kiswahili*.) In the nineteenth century, the Swahili speakers of East Africa had to find a new word to describe the increasing number of European traders who were appearing on their shores. They did not choose an obvious word linking the Europeans to their colour, because in their eyes, the odd-looking Caucasians could be anything from white, to pink, to red or brown, depending on how much time they spent in the sun. Instead, the Swahili speakers coined the word *wazungu* (singular *mzungu*) to describe the newcomers as 'people who move around'. (The actual word could have been derived from *zunguluka* or *zungusha*, which means to go round and round.)

The East African coast had been a place of contact with foreigners long before the Europeans first arrived at the end of the fifteenth century.

Historians believe that the Arabs were trading along the coast perhaps as early as two centuries before the Christian era, attracted by the lucrative trade in gold and ivory from the African continent. East African trade with India came later, around the seventh century, and then in 1414 a huge fleet of sixty-two Chinese trading galleons and 190 support ships under the command of Zheng He crossed the Indian Ocean and landed on the African coast.[1] The Chinese had fourteenth-century maps which showed the East African coast in great detail, which suggests that they had been sending trading missions to the region for some time before Zheng He's armada arrived. This trade with both Arab and Oriental traders should dispel the myth that Africa – the 'Dark Continent' – had little or no contact with the outside world until 'opened up' by Europeans.

Towards the end of the fifteenth century, just as the Luo were leaving their cradleland in Sudan and migrating south up the Nile valley towards Uganda, the Portuguese landed on East African shores. On 8 July 1497, just five years after Columbus set sail for the New World, the Portuguese mariner Vasco da Gama set sail from Lisbon in a small fleet of four ships and a crew of 170 men. His objective, as it was with Columbus, was to find a sea route to the spices and other riches of the Orient. Da Gama, however, chose to sail east around the southern cape of Africa. It was a longer and much more challenging task than sailing across the Atlantic. By the time da Gama's fleet rounded the Cape of Good Hope in November 1497, his crew were dying of scurvy; one ship was abandoned after it was damaged in a storm, reducing the fleet to just three vessels. As they voyaged north into the Indian Ocean, they were sailing into unknown territory, for no white-skinned European had travelled so far. In the late fifteenth century, the Arabs dominated trade in the Indian Ocean and da Gama feared that the local population would be hostile to Christians. So when he arrived in Mozambique, he impersonated a Muslim to gain an audience with the Sultan. The subterfuge failed spectacularly and his Portuguese fleet was forced to flee; da Gama vowed to return to teach the Arabs a lesson, and his parting gift was to fire his cannons into the city in retaliation for his inhospitable reception.

As the Portuguese fleet sailed, a small dhow set off ahead of them to warn fellow Arabs further north of what might be in store for them. When da Gama's fleet arrived at Mombasa, the Arabs were waiting, and they launched a seaborne attack to cut their anchor ropes. Da Gama retreated and sailed further north to Malindi where, finally, he found a friendly Sultan and a much warmer reception. The association between the

Portuguese and the town of Malindi lasted almost 200 years, and the Church of St Francis Xavier was built during da Gama's visit. The building survives to this day as one of the oldest churches on the continent.

Da Gama discovered that there was intense rivalry between the two Swahili cities of Malindi and Mombasa, and not for the last time in the history of colonisation in Africa, the Europeans decided to exploit this division to their own advantage.[2] Da Gama signed a trade agreement with the local rulers in Malindi, and this became the beginning of European involvement in East Africa. Two years later, in 1500, the Portuguese sacked Mombasa in retaliation for being snubbed; they returned in 1528 and attacked the town a second time. Between 1500 and 1700, the Portuguese established a series of trading posts and forts along the coast, including the construction of Fort Jesus in Mombasa in 1593. The Portuguese were adept at exploiting the rivalries between independently governed towns on the coast and they successfully dominated much of the coastal trade in the region. Then in 1696, the Arabs took their revenge and stormed Fort Jesus, finally taking posession after a siege lasting thirty-three months. From that point onwards, Portugal's power in East Africa began to wane.

However, trade between East Africa and the rest of the world continued to flourish; Indian cotton, Chinese porcelain, and metalwork from the Middle East were traded for slaves, ivory and gold. However, Africa south of the Sahara is not blessed with environmental conditions conducive to easy travel, and tsetse-fly was common in large areas of highland savannah, which severely limited the use of pack animals for transporting goods. Unlike many coastal countries such as Congo, Nigeria and Mozambique, East Africa has no large rivers running inland and the highland tributaries are too shallow and fast-flowing for the extended use of boats and canoes, so any exploration or trade inland relied on human porterage. Before the British eventually completed a railway at the beginning of the twentieth century, the only route inland from the coast to Lake Victoria was nothing more than a meandering track through dense tropical jungle, and the return journey could take as much as six or seven months. Food had to be purchased or hunted en route, tolls paid to ensure safe passage, and the loads were limited to what could be carried by human porters – effectively no more than 30kg. Therefore the trade to and from the interior was limited to items of high value and low weight; rare skins and ivory, copper and gold, glass beads and cotton textiles, and in later years, tobacco, guns and liquor. Slaves too were traded, and they had the additional advantage of not having to be carried.

Ever since the Spanish opened up the New World at the beginning of the sixteenth century, the European nations had been on an imperialist binge around the globe. But given the difficulties of access to the interior, they paid scant attention to East Africa – at least at the beginning. Colonisation of the Americas by Spain and Portugal in the 1500s was soon followed by the growing power of Great Britain, France and the Netherlands. India, China and other countries in the Far East became absorbed by the burgeoning European empires, who were all in search of new spheres of influence around the world, and a source of raw materials to fuel the rapid industrialisation back home. It was only after most of the rest of the world had been carved up by Western nations, that Europe turned its undivided attention to the division and colonisation of Africa.

After the Portuguese left the East African coast for good in 1720, bloody and bowed, the Sultan of Oman became the undisputed ruler of the coastal region, but he proved to be ineffectual. He appointed governors from the Nahaban family in Pate, the Mazruis in Mombasa and the El-Hathis in Zanzibar. Inevitably, these governors quarrelled among themselves and it was not until 1822 that the new ruler of Oman, Seyyid Sa'id, sent a fleet of heavily armed warships to subdue the querulous city-states. The Mazruis in Mombasa had no defence except for their puny muskets and the massive stone walls of Fort Jesus. At the time, two British survey ships, HMS *Leven* and HMS *Barracouta*, were on a Royal Navy mission to survey the east coast of Africa, under the command of Captain William Fitzwilliam Owen. Sulaiman bin Ali al-Mazrui, the Mazrui chief, pleaded that Mombasa become a protectorate of Britain as a defence against the threat from the Sultan of Oman. Owen, with imagination and foresight, realised what Britain could achieve in this part of Africa. In return for Mombasa becoming 'subject to the king of England', Suleiman bin Ali agreed to assist the British in ridding East Africa of the scourge of slavery.[3] On 7 February 1824, seventeen years after the Slave Trade Act received its Royal Assent, thereby abolishing the trade in slaves within the British Empire, the Royal Navy hoisted the Union flag over Fort Jesus; it was the start of Britain's domination of East Africa, which would last for the next 140 years.

The middle decades of the nineteenth century marked the beginning of the European exploration of the interior of East Africa. In early 1844,

Dr Johann Ludwig Krapf, a German Protestant missionary and accomplished linguist, arrived in Zanzibar. His ambition was to link the east and west coasts of Africa with a chain of Christian missions. He soon moved on to Mombasa where, tragically, his wife Rosine died of malaria, together with their newborn daughter. It was a shocking introduction to the realities of life for a European trying to survive in nineteenth-century Africa, but Krapf persevered and moved inland from the coast and established his first mission on higher ground at Rabai. However, Krapf fell into a deep depression following the loss of his family and his enthusiasm for establishing his pan-African missions was not rekindled until the arrival of a Swiss Lutheran missionary, Johannes Rebmann. Yet, it was not for their missionary work, nor for their translation of the Bible into Kiswahili that these missionaries became best known, but for their expeditions into the interior.

Together, Krapf and Rebmann set off inland and became the first Europeans to see the snow-capped Mount Kilimanjaro in 1848, and then Mount Kenya the following year. Krapf recorded the name originally as Kenia, which he learned from the indigenous tribes who live around the mountain. The Kikuyu call it *Kirinyaga*, or 'white mountain', the Embu call it *Kirenia*, the 'mountain of whiteness', and to the Kamba, it is known as *Kiinyaa*, literally 'mountain of the ostrich', as the speckled ice and rock resembled the tail feathers of the male ostrich. Krapf was told by the Embu people that they did not climb high on the mountain because of the intense cold, and that 'white matter' rolled down the mountains with a loud noise. This led Krapf and Rebmann to correctly deduce that glaciers existed on these equatorial mountains,[4] even though their initial report was greeted with derision by the scientific community.

Back at the recently founded Royal Geographical Society in Kensington Gore, London, armchair travellers who had never set foot in Africa argued fiercely about the findings of Krapf and Rebmann, and the missionaries' reports only further whetted the appetites of other European explorers. Krapf also noted that the rivers on the slopes of Mount Kenya flowed continuously, unlike other rivers in the area which dried up after the rainy season had ended. This reinforced his conviction that the source of water on the mountain was melting glaciers, but he mistakenly believed Mount Kenya to be the source of the White Nile. From information gleaned on their travels, Johannes Rebmann also co-created the 'slug map' – an ambitious but ultimately misleading representation of East Africa, which shows a single huge lake in the centre of Kenya. The map was presented to the

Royal Geographical Society in London in 1855, and did much to stimulate further interest in the region.

The significance of the legacy left by these two men is still debated by historians. Professor Roland Oliver wrote in 1952: 'These . . . sad and other-worldly men achieved no great evangelistic success among the scattered and socially incoherent Wanyika tribesmen.' But he did add that, 'Krapf and Rebmann, if they were somewhat impractical, had vision, tenacity and boundless courage.'[5]

The Scottish medical missionary and explorer David Livingstone first arrived in South Africa in 1841, but it was not until 1866 that he visited East Africa. Livingstone was intent on seeking the source of the Nile, but on landing in Zanzibar, he was subjected to the full scale and barbarity of the slave trade, which had continued in East Africa despite Captain Owen's attempts at containing it more than forty years previously. He was soon writing reports back to England about what he called the 'great open sore of the world':

> To overdraw its evils is a simple impossibility . . . We passed a slave woman shot or stabbed through the body and lying on the path. [Onlookers] said an Arab who passed early that morning had done it in anger at losing the price he had given for her, because she was unable to walk any longer. We passed a woman tied by the neck to a tree and dead . . . We came upon a man dead from starvation . . . The strangest disease I have seen in this country seems really to be broken heartedness, and it attacks free men who have been captured and made slaves.[6]

Slavery was not new in Africa and the use of forced labour goes back more than 5,000 years. The first hieroglyphic account of contact between the Egyptians and their black Nubian neighbours was inscribed on a rock during Egypt's first dynasty (i.e. before 3000 BC), and five centuries later the fourth-dynasty king Sneferu recorded that he had attacked Nubia and brought back 7,000 black slaves and 200,000 head of cattle.[7] The Arabs too traded extensively in human labour, and although the Prophet Muhammad laid down precise rules about the ownership of unbelievers, the Qur'ān does not explicitly forbid human bondage. So the practice of forced labour in Africa was established long before the trade to the Americas was started by the Portuguese and Spanish in the early sixteenth century. Elikia M'bokolo, a renowned Congolese historian, wrote about the trade in humans:

The African continent was bled of its human resources via all possible routes. Across the Sahara, through the Red Sea, from the Indian Ocean ports and across the Atlantic. At least ten centuries of slavery for the benefit of the Muslim countries (from the ninth to the nineteenth). Then more than four centuries (from the end of the fifteenth to the nineteenth) of a regular slave trade to build the Americas and the prosperity of the Christian states of Europe. The figures, even where hotly disputed, make your head spin. Four million slaves exported via the Red Sea, another four million through the Swahili ports of the Indian Ocean, perhaps as many as nine million along the trans-Saharan caravan route, and eleven to twenty million (depending on the author) across the Atlantic Ocean.[8]

Even by the end of the nineteenth century, it is estimated that 50,000 slaves still passed through the slave-trading centre of Zanzibar every year; from here, they were sent to the markets of Turkey, Arabia, India, and Persia. The Arab traders in East Africa also had a reputation for being more brutal than the Europeans, and they made less effort to keep the slaves from dying. It has been estimated that for every five Africans taken prisoner in the continental interior, perhaps only one reached the slave markets in the Middle East. Nor could the Arab slave traders have been quite so successful without the assistance of the Africans themselves. Since it was easier to buy slaves brought to the coast than to hunt them down and capture them inland, the Arabs relied heavily on the Kamba people, who lived between the coast and the central highlands in Kenya, to act as middlemen and organise huge caravans to bring slaves and ivory from the interior.[9]

The Swahili traders also made good trade with the Luhya people of western Kenya, and their leader Nabong'o Shiundu in particular was keen to find allies in his attempt to build his power in the region.[10] Nabong'o became notorious for capturing other Africans, including Luos, and selling them on to the Arab slave traders. The island of Zanzibar and the nearby port of Kilwa on the mainland became the largest African shipping points for the trade, and as demand continued, Arab slavers penetrated further and further inland, even as far as Uganda and Congo, in search of new supplies. In 1873 the British eventually forced the ruler of Zanzibar to close his slave market and to forbid the export of slaves from the regions under his control. (Enforcing this rule was not easy and even as late as the 1970s the United Nations received complaints of a thriving trade in black slaves from East Africa.)

I was interested to hear from Leo Odera about some of the personal encounters that his Luo ancestors had with the slave traders:

'It used to be very common in this part of the world. It caused chaos and whole families would move on to evade the traders. Many years back when my family were still in Busoga in Uganda, the slave traders took many people including Chwanya, one of my ancestors. The family did not expect him to return and they even held a mock funeral to mourn his passing. However, his son Onyango Rabala – he was a son of Chwanya's fourth wife – he followed the Arabs. Onyango found them feasting by the lake and with the slaves in chains in a dhow. The slavers were cooking a long way from the water because of the danger from crocodiles, so Onyango swam up to the boat and pushed it into the lake – and it had all their weapons on board too! In Dholuo, we have a saying: *rieko lo teko* – brain is mightier than brawn. The Arabs ran away, too frightened to retaliate, and Onyango rescued his father and two other slaves chained to him. When he returned, there was a great taboo because he had been mourned as dead and there were many rituals to be performed. He had to sleep in the granary for three days and eventually his second wife took him back.'

The slave trade continued in East Africa long after it was abolished by the British. These young Africans were sold into slavery by Arab merchants during the 1890s.

Krapf and Livingstone pioneered the early exploration of East Africa, but their travels only highlighted how little was known of the African interior, and they were soon followed by others. Next into East Africa were the British explorers Richard Burton and John Speke, fired up with enthusiasm to find the great lakes which were said to exist in the centre of the continent, and to locate the source of the White Nile. Burton and Speke mounted their expedition in 1856, a year after the 'slug map' came to London. Like Krapf and Rebmann before them, they found the travel arduous and both men fell ill from a variety of tropical diseases. On one occasion, Speke became temporarily deaf after a beetle crawled into his ear – he deftly removed the insect with his pocket knife. Burton and Speke persevered inland and became the first Europeans to visit Lake Tanganyika, although Speke was temporarily blind at the time and he never caught a proper sight of the lake. They were told of a second lake in the area, but by now Burton was too ill to travel and Speke – having recovered from his blindness – went alone and in 1858 he found a vast lake. He named it after the British Queen and claimed it to be the source of the Nile. This infuriated Burton, who considered the matter still unresolved, and a very public disagreement arose between the two men. This only generated even more interest in the issue by fuelling the debate among geographers back in Britain, as well as great interest by other explorers who were keen to either confirm or disprove Speke's claims.

By the middle of the nineteenth century, finding the exact location of the headwaters of the White Nile had taken on an importance which is difficult to comprehend today. It resulted not only from the excitement of exploring a continent hitherto unknown, but also from the British Government's obsession with the strategic control over large parts of the world. The significance of the region was further increased in 1858, when the Compagnie Universelle du Canal Maritime de Suez started work on a canal to connect the Mediterranean to the Red Sea. Although the canal was built by a French company (using the forced labour of Egyptians), the intention was that the canal would be open to all nations. The British considered this French-inspired project to be a threat to their geopolitical and financial interests in the region and they instigated a revolt among the workers, which soon brought the construction to a halt.[11] Despite these setbacks, the canal opened to shipping in November 1869, and it played an important role in speeding up the European colonisation of East Africa by offering a quicker route to the Indian Ocean.

Meanwhile, Livingstone returned to Africa in January 1866 with the express intent of identifying the source of the White Nile once and for all. Livingstone believed the Nile started further south than the great lakes, and he assembled a team of freed slaves to travel with him. One by one his porters deserted him, and by the time he reached Lake Malawi in early August 1866, most of his supplies had been stolen, together with all of his medicines. Livingstone then travelled north through difficult swampy terrain towards Lake Tanganyika, but with his health declining, ironically he had to join a group of slave traders to stay alive. Livingstone was ill for most of the last four years of his life, suffering pneumonia, cholera and tropical ulcers on his feet.

The journalist Henry Morton Stanley had arrived in Zanzibar in March 1871, sent by the *New York Herald* newspaper with instructions to find Livingstone, who had not been heard of for some years. Stanley was a Welshman, born in Denbigh; his father was either John Rowlands, the town drunk who later died from *delirium tremens*, or James Vaughan, a married lawyer from London and a regular customer of Stanley's mother, Betsy Parry, a nineteen-year-old prostitute. The baby's name was entered into the birth register of St Hilary's Church as 'John Rowlands, Bastard', and Stanley spent his life trying to live down the shame of being born illegitimate. As a five-year-old, he was given up to a workhouse; when he was released as a young man he fled Wales for America at the age of seventeen and changed his name in an attempt to erase his past. Stanley landed in New Orleans in 1858, and during the American Civil War he fought first for the Confederacy before being taken prisoner, whereupon he changed sides and fought for the Union. He covered the Indian Wars as a journalist and gained a reputation for taking on risky assignments, but the thought of going to Africa terrified him. He called it an 'eternal, feverish region', and had nightmares about what he might experience – he even contemplated suicide. Nevertheless, he persevered with the task and assembled one of the largest expeditions ever to set out from Zanzibar; his party was so large that he divided it into five separate caravans and staggered their departure to avoid attack and robbery. Before he left Zanzibar, he heard rumours that a white man had been seen in the region of Ujiji, about 1,200km inland, so he set off for the interior at the end of March in search of Livingstone with some 190 men, armed guards, and a guide carrying the American flag. On 4 July 1871 Stanley sent his first dispatch back to New York from Unnyanyembe district, in the form of a 5,000-word letter; it filled the front page of the *Herald*. The piece quoted Stanley's letter extensively, and ended with a promise from the journalist:

> Our explorer says (July 4):— 'If the Doctor is at Ujiji, in one month more and I will see him, then the race for home will begin'; but that 'until I hear more of him, or see the long-absent old man face to face, I bid farewell. But wherever he is be sure I shall not give up on the chase'. Good words these from a trusty man.[12]

In one of the great encounters in history, Stanley found Livingstone in the settlement of Ujiji on the shores of Lake Tanganyika, on 10 November 1871. Stanley greeted the explorer with the now famous words, 'Dr Livingstone, I presume?', to which Livingstone apparently responded, 'Yes, and I feel thankful that I am here to welcome you.' There is no direct record of this exchange – Stanley had torn the pages of this encounter out of his diary, and Livingstone does not mention these words in his own account. However, they do appear in the first description of the meeting, published in the *New York Times*, dated 2 July 1872:

> I noticed in the centre of a group of Arabs, strongly contrasting their sun-burnt faces, a hale-looking, gray-bearded white man, wearing a naval cap, with a faded gold band, and a red woolen shirt, preserving a calmness of exterior before the Arabs. I enquired, 'DR. LIVINGSTONE, I presume?'
> He, smiling, answered yes.[13]

Stanley urged the missionary to return to the coast with him, but Livingstone was determined not to leave until his task to find the source of the Nile was complete. However, it was not to be; Livingstone died in Zambia, in the village of Ilala on 1 May 1873, from a combination of malaria and internal bleeding caused by dysentery. Two of Livingstone's loyal servants, Chuma and Susi, buried his heart at the foot of a nearby tree. They then dried and wrapped his body, which, along with his papers and instruments, they carried back to the island of Zanzibar – a trip which took them nine months to complete. In April 1874 Livingstone's remains reached England by ship and he was buried in Westminster Abbey in London.

Henry Stanley was inspired by the expeditions of Livingstone and others, and in 1874, the *New York Herald*, in partnership with the *Daily Telegraph* in London, provided the finance for Stanley to return to Africa. He had several objectives: firstly, to circumnavigate Lake Victoria and confirm that it was a single body of water and the source of the White Nile; secondly, to finish Livingstone's work of mapping the Lualaba river, which Livingstone thought might be the Nile itself; and finally and most ambitiously of all, to traverse the continent from east to west and thereby trace the course of the River Congo to the Atlantic. By circumnavigating Lake Victoria, he almost certainly became the first European to make direct contact with the Luo of western Kenya.

The difficulty of the challenge that Stanley set himself to circumnavigate Lake Victoria and then cross the continent to the Atlantic is hard to overstate, even by the extraordinary standards set by his predecessors. The preparation back in England for his expedition was hopelessly rushed and he later wrote: 'Two weeks were allowed me for purchasing boats – a yawl, a gig, and a barge – for giving orders for pontoons, medical stores, and provisions; for making investments in gifts for native chiefs; for obtaining scientific instruments, stationery, &c., &c.'[14] Stanley eventually left England for Zanzibar on 21 September 1874, accompanied by three other Englishmen: Frederick Barker and the brothers Francis and Edward Pocock.

By the time that Stanley started his expedition, the Luo had long finished their migration from Uganda and, due to a rapidly increasing population throughout the century, the Luo clans had spread both north and south of the Winam Gulf. Although there were other tribes in the area, the Luo were by far the most dominant group, having very effectively assimilated many of the indigenous people into their tribe. In Alego to the north of the Gulf, the descendants of the great leaders Owiny and Kishodi were still living in K'ogelo. However, around 1830, Obong'o, (3) great-grandfather to President Obama, left Alego and established a new sub-clan in the Kendu Bay area of south Nyanza. By 1874 his three sons, Obama, Opiyo and Aguk, were in their prime and their families were well established on the southern shore of Winam Gulf. I asked Charles Oluoch what life was like for his ancestors, who had moved into virgin territory in south Nyanza in the first half of the nineteenth century:

'Obong'o crossed to this side when he was around thirty years old. People told him there was big land here, so these young men came and checked and saw this place. You know, they were front runners. He came and found that this place was good, so he decided to start a family and settled.

'There was a lot of forest on this side. There was forest everywhere, wild animals. Most of the Kalenjin were up there in the mountains. They used to just come down, maybe to bring their cows to drink water sometimes when it was dry. But most of the time this land was not inhabited. There was no fighting involved.

'Obong'o had three sons; Obama, Opiyo and Aguk. Obama Opiyo is special because now his great great-grandson is the President of the United States. It's because of the line. All these three brothers are buried here – the sons of Obong'o.'

Back on the coast, Stanley left Zanzibar on 12 November 1874 for the mainland and began his remarkable trek across Africa, with his porters carrying his boats in sections overland as far as Lake Victoria. This first stage of his expedition took 103 days and his pedometers recorded a distance of 1,150km through dense equatorial jungle. The expedition eventually reached Kagehyi on the south-eastern shore of Lake Victoria, where their first task was to assemble their boats. The biggest vessel was a steam powered sailing sloop, the *Lady Allice*, which had been carried from Zanzibar in four parts. On 8 March 1875, Stanley wrote in his diary:

At 1 p.m. after vainly endeavouring to persuade Kaduma Chief of Kagehyi to accompany me as a guide as far as Ururi, I sailed from Kagehyi with 10 stout sailors of the Expedition in the *Lady Allice*, a cedar boat 24 feet long and 6 feet wide which we have carried in sections from the Coast for the purpose of exploring the Lakes of Central Africa. The men were rather downhearted and rowed reluctantly, as we have had many a grievous prophecy that we shall all drown in the Lake, or die at the hands of some of the ferocious people living.[15]

In little more than two weeks, the expedition had sailed up the east coast of the lake and Stanley was approaching Luoland. At first, his main concern were hippos in the water – as always, they were unpredictable, sometimes benign and at other times potentially very dangerous. Then, on 22 March, he stopped at what he called Bridge Island and wrote:

The island is covered with mangrove trees, whose branches extend far into the water, under which our boat might be screened by their deep shade . . . From the summit of the island which is easy of access we obtained a fine view of lofty Ugingo Island and the tall steep mountains of Ugeyeya with the level plain of Wagansu and Wigassi.

Ugingo Island (now called Migingo Island), is about 20km off the lakeshore in the extreme south-west corner of what is now Kenya. From this point onwards, Stanley was in Nyanza – Luoland. He wanted to go ashore to learn the names of some of the villages, but a large gathering of men carrying spears caused him to think better of it. The security of a small, unpopulated island a safe distance away seemed a wiser choice to spend the night. Then, on 24 March, the group landed at a place Stanley called Muiwanda, and he negotiated with the people to bring food to them:

> . . . we anchored within an arrow's flight from the shore and began to persuade the natives to bring food to us, by holding out a bunch of beads . . . Finally trade was opened, and while trading for food I found the people very friendly and disposed to answer all my questions. They spoke the language of Usoga with a slight dialectic difference. Neither men nor women wore anything, save a kirtle of grass, or plantain leaves which the latter wore. Men had extracted two front teeth of lower jaw, had bracelets of iron rings, rings above elbows and in ears. Shaved their heads in eccentric fashion . . .

The Usoga people are now called the Wasoga, and they result from inter-marriage between the Luo and the Luhya. (The Luhya remove two lower teeth as an initiation, unlike the Luo's six.) However, a close examination of Stanley's map of Lake Victoria shows that he completely missed the extent of Winam Gulf, and he might have assumed that the narrow entrance to this large bay was only the mouth of a small river.

Three days later, on 27 March, Stanley finally made contact with another group, but this time on the northern side of Winam Gulf:

> They came to repeat the request of Kamoydah, the King, but we begged to be excused from moving from our present safe anchorage, the waves were rough, the wind was strong. They begged, they implored and all but threatened. Three more canoes now came up loaded with men, and these added their united voices to invite us on the part of the King to his shore. Finding us still obstinate, they laid hands on the boat, and their insolence increased almost to fighting pitch . . . We continued on our way for five

miles in the direction of Usuguru and then lowered sail and prepared to rough it in the open Lake. At dusk the gale abated and an hour afterwards was a perfect calm, but from the south-east at 8 p.m. blew the most horrible tempest — hailstones as large as filberts, and rain in such torrents that all hands were required to bail the boat out, lest we sank at our anchorage.

Usuguru is an island on the border between Kenya and Uganda and is now called Sigulu. The following day, they had a dangerous encounter with the locals:

In the morning while sailing close to the shore we were stoned by the people. Two great rocks came near to crushing the boat's sides, but a few revolver shots stopped that game. Arriving between the islands of Bugeyeya and Uvuma, we had the misfortune to come across a nest of Lake pirates who make navigation impossible for the Waganda. Ignorant of their character we allowed 13 canoes to range alongside and commenced a friendly conversation with them, but I was soon informed of their character when they made an indiscriminate rush upon the boat. Again I beat them off with my revolver, and having got them a little distance off opened fire with my elephant rifle — with which I smashed three canoes, and killed four men. We continued on our way hence immediately to the Napoleon Channel, and after a look at the great river outflowing northwards [the Victoria Nile at the Ripon Falls], sailed to Marida where we rested secure and comfortable.

It was an inauspicious start to British involvement in western Kenya and there was outspoken criticism of Stanley back in Britain. In his later years, he was obliged to defend himself against the charge that his African expeditions had been marked by cruelty and gratuitous violence. In his defence, he argued that 'the savage only respects force, power, boldness, and decision'.[16] In many ways, Henry Stanley was an enigma; from his writings, it is clear that he had an endearing attitude towards many of the Africans he travelled with, to whom he owed both his success and his survival in Africa. This included Kalulu, his boy servant who loyally stayed with Stanley from 1882 to 1887 – Stanley even wrote a children's book about Kalulu's life, and dedicated it to the end of slavery.[17] On the other hand, he was capable of using excessive violence, racial abuse and condescending language towards Africans. He was, essentially, a man of his time.

Stanley's expedition succeeded in circumnavigating Lake Victoria before heading west to trace the course of the River Congo to the Atlantic.

He eventually reached a Portuguese outpost at the mouth of the river in August 1877, 999 days after leaving Zanzibar. It had been a remarkable feat to cross central Africa; however, of the 359 people who started on the expedition, only 108 survived. Stanley's three British companions, Frederick Barker and Francis and Edward Pocock, all died during the expedition, along with his trusted servant, Kalulu.

Stanley resolved the long-standing question of whether Lake Victoria really was the source of the Nile (something the Arabs had long known, for the lake is clearly shown on a map dating from the 1160s drawn by the cartographer Al Idrisi). Although the lake is not quite as impressive as depicted on the 'slug map', it is still a vast body of water, more than twice the size of Belgium and the second largest freshwater lake in the world, after Lake Superior. (Strictly speaking, Lake Victoria is only a feeder lake to the Nile; it is now claimed that the true source of the Nile is the longest river to flow into Lake Victoria, the Luvironza (or Ruvyironza), which is said to bubble up from high ground in the mountains of Burundi before flowing into the lake.)

Towards the end of the nineteenth century, a new imperialism was beginning to emerge among the industrialised nations, each seeking a slice of the colonial pie. Germany, the United States, Belgium, Italy, and, for the first time, an Asian power, Japan, were all beginning to compete for what little 'unclaimed space' there was left around the world. As the rivalry among the colonising nations reached new heights, so the nations with established empires – mainly Great Britain and France – consolidated their territorial gains. Technology too began to have an effect; the Suez Canal was now open and modern steamships could sail from Europe to East Africa in a fraction of the time that it had previously taken to sail around the Cape of Good Hope. The railway and the telegraph were revolutionising transport and communication on land, and new advances in medicines to treat tropical diseases – especially quinine as an effective treatment for malaria – now allowed vast regions of the tropics to be accessed more safely by whites. The time was ripe for the biggest land grab in history.

The division of Africa – the last continent to be carved up by the European nations – was essentially a product of this 'new imperialism'. Prior to 1880, the colonial possessions of European nations in Africa were relatively modest and were mainly limited to the coastal areas, leaving almost all the interior still independent; by 1900, Africa was almost entirely divided into separate territories under the administration of various European nations.

In East Africa the colonial powers were particularly slow to establish a real presence, which is no surprise considering the privations experienced by the early missionaries and explorers. Malaria and other tropical diseases had taken their toll of the pioneers, and there was no easy river route into the interior. Furthermore, it was clear from the reports of Krapf and Burton that the East African region of modern Kenya and northern Tanzania was the least suited to peaceful infiltration, since this was the province of the Maasai and other warring tribes, through whose land even the armed caravans of the Arab traders feared to travel.

The first traders from overseas who were not interested in slaves or ivory were American merchants from ports in New England and New York. By 1805, forty-eight trading ships from Salem, Massachusetts were reported to have sailed around the Cape of Good Hope into the Indian Ocean, and the first American vessel is believed to have reached Zanzibar in 1817. The New Hampshire merchant Edmund D. Roberts arrived in Zanzibar in the *Mary Ann* in 1828, and complained to the Sultan about the taxes his officials were demanding on traded goods. President Andrew Jackson himself took an interest in the Zanzibar trade, and he commissioned Roberts to negotiate a trade treaty with Sultan Seyyid Sa'id. By 1833 the two nations had exchanged 'most favoured nation' status, and in 1835 Richard P. Waters became the first US trade-consul to Zanzibar.[18] Several US trading companies soon opened offices on the island, including John Bertram & Co. of Salem, Massachusetts, and Arnold Hines & Co. of New York.

The American trading initiative was soon followed by Great Britain in 1841, and France in 1844. By 1856, there were three American merchants with agents based in Zanzibar, all trading in cheap calico; four German companies developed a triangular trade with West Africa to ship cowrie shells there to use as currency and a couple of French firms imported brandy in exchange for sesame seeds.[19] The US dominance of the East African trade lasted until the Civil War period, when the country lost its pre-eminent position to British, German and Indian traders. However, trade was generally slow, and Britain showed little interest in the region; by the middle of the nineteenth century, East Africa was still a backwater.

The great stimulus in Victorian Britain to opening up East Africa was Livingstone's emotional reports about the Arab slave trade, which touched the public mood back home. In particular, his last journey to Africa and his subsequent death in 1873 fired the imagination of missionaries to come and work in Africa; but without the Bible translated into the language of potential converts, any mission work was limited. It was the linguistic labours of people like Krapf and Livingstone himself which laid the groundwork for all those who came afterwards – whether they were missionaries, traders or colonialists. Roman Catholic missionaries first came to Zanzibar in 1860, but it was the Anglicans in the mid-1870s, inspired by Livingstone, who established new mission stations in the interior, and particularly in Buganda – the lakes region of Central Uganda. These early efforts were ad hoc attempts to spread the Gospel to the 'African heathens'. Even a missionary who arrived with a few dozen porters to establish a mission in a native village had to set up what amounted to a small independent state, where he was recognised as a kind of chief by the other local headmen.[20] By 1885 there were nearly three hundred Europeans living in East Africa,[21] most of them Catholic or Anglican missionaries. Initially, however, they won few converts. Islam had long been established on the coast, and this too began to spread into the interior through the influence of Arab traders. After 1880, however, Christian missionaries made significant inroads in the Buganda region, and by the end of the nineteenth century, Christianity was beginning to spread quickly throughout the region.

Around the middle part of the nineteenth century, the perceived wisdom in London was that African possessions were too expensive to run, and the potential yields were too low to make a profit. As Europe's foremost imperial political power, Britain pursued a policy of 'paramount importance' in Africa – it was keen to maintain an influence in the region, but not really interested in exercising any real power.[22] Instead, Britain considered its priorities were to close the slave trade with the Middle East, encourage the expansion of Christianity, and allow legitimate trade to flourish. Missionaries tried to encourage British merchants and ship owners to establish a commercial presence in East Africa. Although the financial prospects were not encouraging, there was some limited response, mainly from Scottish entrepreneurs inspired by David Livingstone. For example, William Mackinnon, a Glaswegian ship owner and member of the Free Church of Scotland (who started out in life as a grocer's assistant and rose to become one of the wealthiest men in Britain), began to run vessels from his British India Steam Navigation Company to and from Zanzibar from 1872.

But it was in 1885 that a turning point was reached. Up until that year, 80 per cent of the continent remained under traditional and local control, with foreign interests confined almost entirely to the coastal areas. By the

middle of 1885, in one of the most cynical and avaricious moves ever under-
taken by colonial powers, a new map of the continent was superimposed
over more than a thousand indigenous cultures and regions. The new
national boundaries that were created in Africa lacked any logic or rationale,
save for political expediency by the European nations.

It was an unseemly scramble by the countries of Europe to seize vast
areas of the continent, much of which was largely unknown to them, and
the change it brought would have far-reaching consequences for every single
individual living in Africa.

The World's Plunderers: 'It's English, you know.' A cartoon from Harper's Weekly, *published 20 June 1885.*

5

THE NEW
IMPERIALISM

Kik ilaw winy ariyo
Don't chase two birds at once

**The Berlin Conference of 1885 and the division of East Africa;
colonial rule in Kenya and the arrival of white settlers
through to the First World War in Africa**

In 1885 the face of East Africa and much of the rest of the continent was
changed, almost single-handedly, by the actions of just one individual – a
reckless, hot-headed young German student called Karl Peters. He was born
in the small village of Neuhaus on the banks of the River Elbe, about
80km south-east of Hamburg in northern Germany. Peters was the son of
a Lutheran minister and in 1879 he left Berlin University with a degree in
history and moved to London, where he stayed with a wealthy uncle. During
his four years in London, Peters studied British history and its colonial policies, and the experience left him with a deep contempt and loathing of
the British; but he also became passionate about German nationalism and
the new opportunities that existed for imperialist expansion. In 1884 his
uncle committed suicide and Peters returned to Germany. Fired up with
the nationalistic zeal of a twenty-eight-year-old, and with the support of
like-minded contemporaries, he established the Gesellschaft für Deutsche
Kolonisation – the Society for German Colonisation. At its first executive
committee meeting, the group clearly defined its objectives as 'the founding

of German plantation and commercial colonies by securing adequate
capital for colonisation, by finding and securing possession of regions
suitable for colonisation, and by attracting German immigrants to those
regions."[1]

The express aim of their society was to propel Germany headlong into
rivalry with the two leading imperial nations in Europe – Britain and France
– and it did not take long for them to realise their ambitions. In 1884
Germany made its first real bid for membership of the colonial club when
it announced territorial claims in South West Africa, in Togoland and
Cameroon, and (courtesy of Peters and his friends) part of the East African
coast opposite Zanzibar. Belgium and Italy – two small European nations
with no previous colonial ambitions – joined the club and declared an
interest in Congo and the Red Sea region respectively; even Portugal and
Spain once again became interested in claiming bits of African territory.
As more European nations piled in, rivalry intensified, and so began the
unseemly European land-grab in Africa.

It soon became clear that the territorial ambitions of the European
nations in Africa could easily get out of hand and lead to military confrontation and war. So when the Portuguese requested that Germany convene a
meeting of European powers to resolve their interests in Africa, Chancellor
Bismarck readily agreed to organise a conference of the major Western
powers to discuss the partition of the continent. The German leader previously had frequently declared that he had no wish to acquire overseas
colonies,[2] but as more European countries boarded the bandwagon, public
opinion in Germany shifted; by 1884, Bismarck had changed his position
and was ready to act.

The conference opened in Berlin on 15 November 1884, and fourteen
countries were represented by a plethora of ambassadors and politicians,
few, if any, of whom had ever set foot in Africa. The conference lasted
until 26 February 1885 – a full three months – during which time the European nations haggled over the geographical divisions of the continent and
completely ignored any of the cultural or linguistic boundaries already
established by the indigenous population. At the start of the conference,
80 per cent of the continent was under traditional African governance; by
the end of February 1885, Africa had been carved up into fifty irregular
countries. This new 'imperial' map of Africa was imposed on a thousand
indigenous cultures and regions; borders were often drawn arbitrarily, with
little or no regard for ethnic unity, regional economic ties, migratory patterns
of people, or even natural boundaries. The new 'African' map had no logic

or reason except that of political expediency around the conference table in Berlin. It was an extraordinarily arrogant act for the participating nations to make, and the boundaries established in 1885 have created tribal tension and conflict in Africa ever since.

The Berlin Conference as depicted in L'Illustration, *1884.*

On 4 November 1884 – just two weeks before the negotiations began in Berlin – Karl Peters and his two companions, Karl Ludwig Jühlke and Count Joachim von Pfeil (all three still under the age of thirty) arrived in Zanzibar intent on realising their imperial ambitions. Their trip had not been sanctioned by the German government, and the German consul in Zanzibar showed Peters a communication that he had received from the German Foreign Office which stated that Peters could expect from the government 'neither Imperial protection nor any guarantees for his safety'.[3] Undeterred, they disguised themselves as mechanics and crossed over to the mainland at Bagamoyo, where they began to establish a German colonial presence in East Africa. Within days, they succeeded in negotiating their first treaty with an African chief on behalf of the Gesellschaft für Deutsche Kolonisation. It was an extraordinarily audacious act, and the three young Germans pushed on and made several more treaties with neighbouring tribes. It is said that Sultan Mangunguy of Msovero, a local chief in Usagara, agreed to offer 'all his territories with all its civil and public appurtenances to Dr Karl Peters . . . for all time', whilst in return, Peters

agreed to 'give special attention to Msovero when colonising Usagara'.[4]
Peters later wrote about this initiative:

> As the Gesellschaft wanted to found independent German colonies under
> the German flag, its activity naturally was limited to those areas which at
> that time had not yet been taken. In fact, only Africa was suitable . . .
> Already in November 1884 this task basically had been fulfilled by the
> expedition sent via Zanzibar. On December 14th 1884 I found myself, as
> representative of the Society for German Colonisation, as the rightful
> owner of 2,500 square miles of very lush tropical land, located to the west
> of Zanzibar.[5]

By the middle of December – after just six weeks in East Africa – Peters
had signed a total of twelve agreements with the 'sultans' of four inland
regions, which gave him theoretical control over 155,400 square kilometres
of the East African mainland – an area half the size of Italy. In practice,
of course, these treaties were hardly worth the paper they were written on,
as it is unlikely that the Africans had any idea of what they were actually
ceding; but their real value was to demonstrate to other colonial powers
that Germany had prior claim to the region. The young German had
achieved exactly what he needed.

Peters returned to Germany as quickly as possible and on 12 February
1885, two weeks before the conclusion of the Berlin Conference, he
founded the Deutsche Ost-Afrika Gesellschaft – the German East Africa
Company – to which he assigned all his African territories. The Berlin
Conference was coming to a close, and at first Bismarck refused to accept
responsibility for the new acquisitions in Africa. But Peters played his
trump card and threatened to cede the land to King Leopold II of
Belgium. On 17 February – still ten days before the end of the talks –
Bismarck agreed to issue an imperial charter – a *Schutzbrief* — which
gave all the territories acquired by the German East Africa Company
the protection of Emperor Kaiser Wilhelm I. It was an impudent but
brilliant move by the young German adventurer, which inevitably
provoked vociferous complaints from the established British companies
and overseas interests in Zanzibar. The British had previously acquired
treaties inland around the foothills of Mount Kilimanjaro, and a group
of entrepreneurs had already talked of ambitious plans to acquire land
to build a railway between the coast and Lake Victoria. Now they had
some real competition.

In response to Karl Peters' inspired initiative with the Deutsche Ost-Afrika Gesellschaft and the creation of a German protectorate, the British responded by forming the British East Africa Association (BEAA). After several months of sabre-rattling in London and Berlin, the Anglo-German Agreement was signed in 1886, followed by a second treaty in 1890 which consolidated the arrangements. With these two treaties, Britain and Germany agreed on their spheres of influence in East Africa. The region was divided by a line running from the coast south of Mombasa, then north of Kilimanjaro to a point on the eastern shore of Lake Victoria. The border cut straight across East Africa in a north-westerly direction, except in one place where it kinked around Mount Kilimanjaro – this is because Queen Victoria wanted her grandson, the German Kaiser, to have his own 'big mountain' in Africa. Everywhere north of the border became the Protectorate of British East Africa, and Germany took the area south of the line.

In 1891 Peters was made *Reichskommissar* (Imperial High Commissioner) to German East Africa, but by 1895 rumours began to reach Berlin of his cruel and inhumane treatment of Africans. He is said to have used local girls as concubines, and when he discovered that one of his lovers had had an affair with his manservant, he had them both hanged and their home villages destroyed. This earned him the name *mukono wa damu* – 'the man with blood on his hands'. He was recalled to Berlin, where a judicial hearing officially condemned him for his violent attacks on Africans; he was dismissed from government service and deprived of his government pension. Ironically, Peters sought refuge in London, where he continued to develop further interests elsewhere in Africa, but back home in Germany many people considered him to be a national hero. Kaiser Wilhelm II later reinstated his position as an Imperial Commissioner and awarded him a pension from his own private budget. Twenty years after his death in 1918, Peters was officially rehabilitated by the personal decree of Adolf Hitler, who feted him as an ideological hero, and in 1941 he commissioned a Nazi propaganda film about Peters' life. He remains a controversial figure to this day.

The creation of British East Africa took place on two levels; the first, on paper, had already been hammered out in diplomatic meetings in London and Berlin; now the second stage was about to begin, as Britain came to terms with taking control of an area of East Africa that was bigger than metropolitan France and nearly twice the size of German East Africa.[6] In

1888, with an investment of £240,000, the British East Africa Association was granted a royal charter and was renamed the Imperial British East Africa Company (IBEAC). Initially, the ambitions of IBEAC were impressive; the company would act as a trading and development agency, with a special emphasis on the improvement of the well-being of ordinary Africans. However, neither the British nor the German government had any intention of spending state funds on colonial administration and the formation of IBEAC was an attempt by the British to devolve responsibility for governance to a chartered company.

Both the Deutsche Ost-Afrika Gesellschaft and the Imperial British East Africa Company started badly. In German East Africa, Karl Peters' personal misconduct focussed attention on what was generally an arrogant and overbearing contempt by the Germans for Africans. In British East Africa, the problem was one of incompetent management and a lack of any real business acumen. William Mackinnon – the Scottish ship owner who had been inspired by Livingstone to open trade in Zanzibar in 1872 – was made chairman of the IBEAC, and he bore the brunt of complaints about the mismanagement of the company. Every visitor to Mombasa seemed to comment on the disorganisation of his administration. The Foreign Secretary, Lord Salisbury, who never had much faith in Mackinnon, once commented that he 'had no quality for pushing an enterprise which depends on decision and smartness'.[7] By 1890, even his fellow directors had become maddened by Mackinnon's unrealistic ideas and poor planning.

In 1890 a young man called Charles William Hobley arrived in Mombasa to begin work as an IBEAC transport superintendent on the coast. First-Class Assistant Hobley would later join the colonial government and become the provincial commissioner of the Kavirondo region near Lake Victoria, the homeland of the Luo, but he came to Africa as an inexperienced twenty-three-year-old. His memoirs give a fascinating insight into what Mombasa was like towards the end of the nineteenth century:

> It could not have been healthy, for it was surrounded on three sides by the native town, and the mosquitoes were very trying to a newcomer. A mosque stood about fifty yards away, and the frequent calls to prayer, by the muezzin, were at first a novelty, but soon became tiresome monotony. Shortly before my arrival it was said that the wailing tones of the call to the faithful so frayed the nerves of a young assistant who was confined to bed with fever that he hurled a bottle at the muezzin, an injudicious act which took much explaining.[8]

Mombasa had always been a multi-cultural melting pot and it had long been a strategically important harbour on the East African coast. Now, it became the heart of imperial power in British East Africa. Its local name, Kisiwa M'vita, means Island of War – a reference to centuries of bloody battles between the Portuguese, Arabs and Africans. The old town, which had grown up on the northern side of the island, is shown on a map by Ptolemy dated AD 150. It was here that the Portuguese built Fort Jesus in 1593, and the huge castle still dominates the old town. Even today, old Mombasa is a maze of narrow coral-pink streets with whitewashed houses on either side, each with a traditional heavily carved wooden front door and a balcony overhead; it is little changed from Hobley's time, except for the unsightly electricity cables that festoon the alleyways.

The old town's narrow streets and tall houses were designed to give some relief from the sun, and it was here that the traders set up their stalls, selling anything from fruit to carpets to brassware, forerunners of the tourist curio shops that continue to turn a profit for their Arab owners. The modern port still serves Kenya and Uganda today, with shipping containers stacked high, waiting to be dispatched inland. In 1895 it was not freighters but countless numbers of dhows from Oman, Arabia, Somaliland and India which jostled for position in the old harbour, ready to take on their cargoes of ivory, gold, frankincense, mangrove poles – and even slaves. The British government decided that it had to take control of the whole region from Uganda to the coast in order to safeguard the lines of communication to Mombasa and to maintain strategic control over the Upper Nile valley. Mombasa became the gateway to East Africa for the British, and the city was placed under colonial rule on 1 July 1895.

As the nineteenth century came to a close, the IBEAC had two major objectives: first, to organise trading caravans into the interior; second, to collect customs revenues from a string of seven company agents stationed along the coast from Vanga in the south to Lamu in the north. It also faced two major obstacles: first, unlike other parts of Africa, British East Africa had no profitable mineral resources to exploit; second, there were no large navigable rivers which reached inland. Not much had changed since Krapf had penetrated the interior fifty years previously, and a return journey from Mombasa to Lake Victoria remained a perilous undertaking which still took six months to complete. The main interest of the IBEAC was in Buganda (now part of Central Uganda), not Kenya. At the time, the cost of human porterage from Lake Victoria to the coast was £250 a ton,[9] and now that slavery had been abolished in the region, the only financially viable export from the interior at this price was ivory. It was a recipe for economic disaster.

During the 1890s, the IBEAC made several attempts to find alternatives to the Zanzibari porters who brought goods out from the interior, and to find a more cost effective solution to transportation within the protectorate. Donkeys and camels were imported and used as pack animals, and Cape oxen were brought up from South Africa to pull carts. A few roads were constructed, and a steamer was chartered to use on the small rivers that were navigable for a short distance inland. Even a few kilometres of narrow-gauge tramway were laid from the port of Mombasa, the wagons being pushed by Africans. It was a pathetic attempt to open up the interior and the tramway was never used for any effective purpose other than what one visitor referred to as 'occasional picnic parties'.

Throughout the mid-nineteenth century, the Maasai were at the peak of their power and they were considered to be one of the most dangerous and belligerent of the central East African tribes. Like the Luo, the Maasai are a Nilotic tribe who migrated from southern Sudan several centuries previously, albeit by a different route and at a different time. The young Maasai warriors would roam freely throughout the region in large war parties, raiding for cattle whenever they could. These warriors used spears and shields, but their most feared weapon was a throwing club, or *orinka*, which could be hurled accurately up to 100 metres. Johann Krapf first encountered the Maasai when he and Johannes Rebmann first travelled into the interior in 1848, and he wrote that the Maasai 'are dreaded as warriors, laying all to waste with fire and sword, so that the weaker tribes do not venture to resist them in the open field, but leave them in possession of their herds, and seek only to save themselves by the quickest possible flight'.[10]

However, as the nineteenth century came to a close, the indigenous tribes of East Africa were subjected to a series of epidemics of almost biblical proportions, including smallpox, rinderpest, and contagious bovine pleuro-pneumonia. These infections affected all the East African tribes, but particularly those whose livelihoods depended on cattle – and the Maasai were particularly badly hit.

A generation after Krapf explored central Kenya, the Austrian explorer Oscar Baumann travelled extensively through Maasai lands, and in 1891 he witnessed at first hand the devastation that had been wreaked on the region:

'There were women wasted to skeletons from whose eyes the madness of starvation glared . . . warriors scarcely able to crawl on all fours, and apathetic, languishing elders. Swarms of vultures followed them from high, awaiting their certain victims.'[11] Weakened by disease and famine, as well as the loss of their cattle, the Maasai never recovered their numbers, and one estimate suggests that two-thirds of the Maasai died during this period.

In western Kenya, the Luo too were suffering from similar epidemics, but there were no Europeans there to witness the catastrophic effects of these highly infectious diseases. However, among the Luo such traumatic events are passed down by word of mouth, and John Ndalo, a close Obama relative from Kendu Bay, recalls what his father and grandfathers told him of what happened when cattle plague and famine arrived in Luoland:

> 'Many homes lost their family. People were fighting, and if you had even a little food, people would come in a great number and invade your family and take everything away, and this led to conflicts. For those whose cattle survived, we organised raids and went in big numbers with spears and arrows, and we would go and invade them and beat them and bring back all their cattle.
>
> 'This brought rivalry both between communities and also between tribes. When we had exhausted the food within the other clans of the Luo we went to attack other tribes, including the Luhyas, who are our immediate neighbours, and even some of the cattle we got from the Maasai.'

The pressure on food supplies and the threat of starvation and famine resulted in the escalation of warfare within the Luo community itself:

> 'The famine also led to more wars and the invention of the buffalo shield. We were taking the buffalo skin and making a very good and strong shield. The buffalo skin was very strong, and we knew it would resist any spear, so it led to a lot of rearmament in the African society. So we were looking everywhere for the buffalo, everywhere, because there used to be many more here in this area. So the young men had to kill them.
>
> 'Apart from helping us get out of famine, the war also trained our young men to believe that we were good warriors. Because before then, we were not fighting on that scale. So we made a lot of spears, a lot of arrows and shields, and we attacked all the communities who had food. This fighting was between our communities, and it was also tribal. So these are the stories that I was told.'

In Mombasa, the British had altogether different worries. They were becoming increasingly desperate about the financial viability of British East Africa, and the directors of the IBEAC began to lobby the British Tory government for a subsidy to build a proper railway. Political resistance to this 'gigantic folly' was voiced immediately, with people claiming that the railway 'started from nowhere' and 'went nowhere'. Furthermore, the Liberal Opposition claimed that the British government had no right to build a railway through land owned by African tribes. Despite claims that the venture would also be a monumental waste of taxpayers' money, the Tories found support from an old ally; in an article published in September 1891 *The Times* of London thought: 'It is not, after all, a very serious matter to build four or five hundred miles of railway over land that costs nothing.'[12] The editorial could not have been more misguided, but the minority Tory government won the day and agreed to fund the enterprise. It would, they argued, bring an end to the East African slave trade, secure British control over the headwaters of the White Nile, and advance 'the cause of civilisation throughout the interior of the continent'.

The cost of the construction was estimated to be £2.24 million, equivalent to over £200 million ($340 million) today.[13] When the railway was eventually completed, the final cost was more than double at £5.5 million, equivalent to over half a billion pounds ($850 million) today.[14]

The inaugural plate-laying ceremony was performed on 30 May 1896 and the British tabloid newspapers of the day soon began to call it the 'Lunatic Line', and not without good reason. In order to build the railway, the British shipped in some 32,000 workers from India;[15] the paradox of using indentured labourers to build a railway to rid Africa of slavery seemed to be lost on the IBEAC. In addition, the company needed an additional 5,000 more educated workers, including clerks, draughtsmen, drivers, firemen, mechanics, stationmasters and policemen to service the project.[16] It has been estimated that 20 per cent of these Asians remained in East Africa, and their descendants still account for a substantial part of the Asian community now living permanently in Kenya.

The railway was intended to provide a modern transport link to transport raw materials out of the Uganda colony, and to carry manufactured British goods back in. The senior British diplomat in Uganda, Sir Harry Johnston, described the enterprise as 'the driving of a wedge of India two miles broad right across East Africa from Mombasa to the Victoria Nyanza'.[17] The workers were paid a pittance and they laboured under intense heat and poor working conditions; in all, 2,500 died during the construction – averaging nearly five deaths for every mile of laid track.

The British started their railway line at the new station on Mombasa Island, before crossing to the mainland over Salisbury Bridge – diplomatically named after the British prime minister of the day. Once on the mainland, the first challenge was to cross the waterless Taru plain. The Scottish explorer Joseph Thomson was the first traveller to write about the desert:

> Weird and ghastly is the aspect of the greyish-coloured trees and bushes; for they are almost destitute of tender, waving branch or quivering leaf. No pliant twig or graceful foliage responds to the pleasing influence of the passing breeze. Stern and unbending, they present rigid arms or formidable thorns, as if bidding defiance to drought or storm. To heighten the sombre effect of the scene, dead trees are observable in every direction raising their shattered forms among the living, unable to hold their own in the struggle for existence.[18]

The first technical challenge of the construction was how to sustain the workers whilst they built the railway across the Taru plain, where every drop of fresh water had to be transported from the coast to the camps. But there was worse in store; by 1898, the line had reached the Tsavo river, 200km from Mombasa. Here the construction was delayed for nine months by two maneless lions who hunted together, mainly at night, and which had developed a taste for human flesh. The lions terrorised the Indian workers and hundreds fled the construction camps. It is claimed that these two animals killed at least 28 Indian and African labourers – although some accounts put the number as high as 135.[19] Eventually the lions were hunted down and shot by Chief Engineer John Henry Patterson, who sold the skins to the Field Museum of Natural History in Chicago for $5,000. The curators laboriously repaired the skins and stuffed the two animals, and they are still on display in the museum today.

This was not, however, the last time that lions disrupted construction. A year later, a road engineer called O'Hara was dragged from his tent near Voi and killed by a lion, and in June 1900 Police Superintendent C. H. Ryall was sleeping in his observation saloon at Kima station when a lion entered his carriage and killed him, dragging his body through a window and into the bush. Fortunately man-eating lions are a rare occurrence in Africa, and one theory suggests that the many railway workers who died of injury or disease were often poorly buried – or not buried at all – and so scavenging lions stumbled across an easy meal, and so developed a taste for human flesh.

By 1899 nearly 500km of track had been laid and the line reached the foothills of the Kenya highlands – an area of swampy ground called En Kare Nyrobi by the Maasai. This was over halfway from the coast to Lake Victoria, and the company decided to build a railway depot here which would facilitate further construction up into the highlands. The railway headquarters were also moved from Mombasa; what started out as a tented encampment built on a fetid swamp soon became a permanent township, when proper houses were constructed for the staff. This attracted the Asian merchants who supplied goods and services to the workforce, and a year later, the spelling of the town was changed to Nairobi. Kenya's capital city was born.

The next challenge for the engineers was to tackle the Rift Valley, which dropped 450 metres from the highlands in just a few kilometres. Gradients of up to fifty degrees had to be negotiated and an innovative counter-balanced system was used to lower wagons and equipment down to the valley floor to allow the railway to push ahead, whilst the permanent track was built down into the rift. The railhead finally reached Lake Victoria on 19 December 1901 – a distance of 930km from Mombasa. The terminal

The SS Nyanza was one of two steamships built in Kisumu in 1905; the cargo boats were used to link the railhead at Kisumu with other parts of Lake Victoria.

was called Port Florence after Florence Preston, the wife of the chief foreman platelayer, Ronald Preston; she had tenaciously stayed with her husband during the whole of the five-year construction period. However, even here the railway had not reached the final destination, Kampala, on the opposite side of the lake, and a fleet of steamers and dhows were needed to complete the journey. Port Florence was later renamed Kisumu. Later still, several branch lines were built, but it was not until 1931 that the line was extended to both Mount Kenya in the highlands and Kampala in Uganda.

Even though the railway was complete, there continued to be opposition from some of the local tribes across whose land the line had been constructed. Those tribes who were less dependent on cattle were not so badly affected by the bovine infections, and at the end of the nineteenth century it was the Nandi of central Kenya (a sub-group of the Kalenjin) who led the fight against the Uganda Railway. The Nandi had long had a reputation for maintaining their independence and were particularly fearsome during this period. Long before the railway line to Lake Victoria was even started, a Nandi *Orkoiyot* or spiritual leader caller Kimnyole arap Turukat had predicted that a big snake would come from the eastern lake (interpreted as the Indian Ocean), belching smoke and fire, and would go on to quench its thirst in the western lake (Lake Victoria). Kimnyole also prophesied that foreigners would one day rule the Nandi lands. These forecasts only reinforced the fear among the Nandi about foreign intervention, and for years they had harassed anyone who tried to cross their lands – the Arab caravans generally took a longer, safer detour either north or south of Nandi territory to avoid trouble. The Nandi would not even allow individual Europeans to pass through their country without the correct papers, and in 1896 they killed a British traveller called Peter West and his twenty-three porters when he attempted an unauthorised crossing – an event which sparked off an eleven-year war between the Nandi and the British.

By 1900 the Nandi were led by a new *orkoiyot*, supreme chief Koitalel arap Samoei.[20] The Nandi believed the railway was a fulfilment of Kimnyole's prophecy, and they united behind Koitalel to oppose the line. They proved to be excellent guerrilla fighters in the dense forests and steep ravines of the rift valley, where the superior firepower of the Europeans was less effective. When the railway arrived, the Nandi stepped up their harassment and regularly stole the shiny copper telegraph wire to wind around their necks and arms as body ornaments.

Despite several 'punitive expeditions' by the British, the Nandi were determined to maintain their independence by keeping foreigners away. Charles Hobley, who had now been promoted and moved to Nyanza, later commented: 'The Wanandi [Nandi], with the exception of a few in the vicinity of the station, have all along viewed our presence in the country with veiled repugnance ... We were unwittingly living on the edge of a volcano.'[21]

This constant harassment was too much for the British; in October 1905 they sent a military intelligence officer, Colonel Richard Meinertzhagen, to negotiate with the Nandi leader. Unfortunately, one of Koitalel's other prophesies – that British bullets would turn to water – proved not to be correct.[22] According to tribal legend, as Meinertzhagen moved forward to shake hands with the Nandi leader, he withdrew his pistol and shot Koitalel dead. This was a signal to British troops hiding nearby to open fire on the assembled tribesmen, and at least twenty-three more Nandi warriors were killed. Some reports claim that Meinertzhagen beheaded Koitalel as he lay on the ground. There was, apparently, one survivor from the massacre who managed to escape and report what had happened. After complaints from other British officers who accused Meinertzhagen of treachery, the Colonel was called before a military inquiry. Meinertzhagen claimed the shooting was in self-defence and the tribunal found him not guilty – but he was later transferred out of the area. Koitalel's death had exactly the effect the British had hoped for; the Nandi's resistance was broken, and they were no longer a threat to the construction of the railway.

However, the railway was not the only focus for opposition by the Africans, and the British found that the imposition of colonial rule was opposed practically everywhere. Between 1895 and 1914 the British organised a number of military raids – 'punitive expeditions' – against what they called 'recalcitrant tribes'. Everywhere, the British used well-armed soldiers and crackshot mercenaries against the spears and arrows of the Kenyan tribes. For the next couple of decades, British rule in East Africa could be established with the use of force.

In the Luo heartland of Nyanza, the arrival of the British could not have come at a worse time. In the early 1880s the region had been hit by the same series of natural disasters which had drastically reduced other tribal populations. First was contagious bovine pleuropneumonia (CBPP) or lung plague, which had particularly devastating consequences in Maasailand. CBPP is a bacterial disease that attacks the lungs of cattle; then, between 1885 and 1890 a succession of locust invasions devastated the crops in Luoland and brought the onset of the Ong'ong'a famine of 1889; in 1890–91 another cattle infection, this time great rinderpest (an infectious viral disease), virtually wiped out the Luo's cattle; two years later, anthrax killed off most of the few remaining animals.[23] It was a devastating period for the Luo and the pressure on the population brought about by the disease created a virtual civil war throughout Luoland, as clan fought neighbouring clan over cattle, land and grazing.

Weakened by famine, the Luo were then hit by a smallpox endemic – the same epidemic which devastated the Maasai. The death rate in the area was so high that it led to widespread depopulation throughout the lake region and thousands of people were forced to move to new areas. This movement and displacement of people led to the tsetse fly returning to areas previously free of the insects; between 1902 and 1908 it is estimated that at least 250,000 people died from an epidemic of human trypanosomiasis, or sleeping sickness. John Ndalo remembers the days when trypanosomiasis was common around Kendu Bay:

> 'The sickness name in Dholuo is called *nyalolwe* – sleeping sickness. Even around here, the sickness killed people and cattle at that time. We were taught to clear all the bushes where the animals were, because the tsetse fly was in the bushes and if they bit the cattle, the cows would die.
>
> 'When a tsetse fly bites a human being and you are out there tending your cattle, you fall asleep suddenly, and when you are sleeping all the cattle will just wander off! When it bites, it happens so quickly and the same day you fall asleep. So for you to keep a little awake, they would give you stories all the time.'

It was the imposition of colonial rule that brought an end to the migration of the Luo, who were forced to settle under the new British administration. In 1895, the year that President Obama's grandfather, Onyango Obama was born, the British appointed Charles William Hobley to be the new regional colonial administrator in Nyanza. Hobley was becoming an old hand in Kenya, as he had been stationed in Mombasa, working for the IBEAC since 1890. Hobley soon established his administrative headquarters in Mumias, about 65km north of Winam Gulf, where he found the reaction of the Luo to colonisation was mixed. Hobley believed that the only way for the British to exert control over the region was through the use of force, as he later claimed: 'The reaction of a native race to control

by a civilised Government varies according to their nature, and to their
form of government, but in every case a conflict of some kind is inevitable,
before the lower race fully accepts the dictum of the ruling power.'[24]

Starting in 1896, Hobley mounted a series of vicious punitive expeditions
against the Luo clans who opposed British rule. He referred to the Luo as
'the Kavirondo', and on several occasions between 1896 and 1900 the British
confronted what they called 'recalcitrant Kavirondo sections' in open battle.
The Luo's arrows and spears were no match for the Maxim machine gun
and the Hotchkiss cannon, and on each occasion several hundred Luo
warriors were killed. Usually the British followed up their attacks by confis-
cating the livestock and destroying the houses of the Luo. In this way the
British established a form of colonial dictatorship, imposed and maintained
by violence, and totally indifferent to the needs or wishes of the Africans.

However, not all the Luo clans were hostile to the British and the colonists
became adept at 'divide and rule' as they pitted clan against clan – the Luo
have a saying for it, *Kik ilaw winy ariyo* – 'Don't chase two birds at once.'
Those groups who accepted British authority were treated as 'friendlies'
and were given special privileges. They recruited local labour to work for
the whites, and collected the taxes which were beginning to be imposed
on the Africans. It was British policy that their administration in the region
should be based on the Luo political system, and the new administrative
borders were designed to overlap the boundaries of the *pinje*, or Luo clan
system. However, unlike the traditional Luo *ruoth* who acted as guardian
of traditional laws and customs, the new chiefs were effectively African civil
servants, paid for and given their wide-ranging powers by the British.

One such chief was Paul Mboya, who governed the Kendu Bay area
when Onyango Obama was living there in the 1930s. Paul Mboya was an
important man in the community. He became the first Luo to be ordained
as a pastor in the Seventh Day Adventist church, before the British made
him chief in Karachuonyo in south Nyanza, and then secretary of the
African District Council in that region.[25] Sarah Obama's youngest brother,
Abdo Omar Okech, once told me that Onyango had made an enemy of
Mboya, by standing up to him over forced labour:

'Onyango wanted Africans to walk freely. So he had this argument with
Paul, because during those times, there was forced labour, which was introduced by the white men. The chief's representatives would come around
and take you to work on the farms. And Onyango was against this. Paul
organised this because he was the chief, but Onyango opposed this.

'Onyango was anti-government and anti-chief. When Paul sent the
askaris around, Onyango told them, "The workers must be allowed to go
willingly, no forced labour," so that is why he was against this system. Paul
was very obedient, very loyal to the whites, and Onyango was against that.
Paul was misusing his power. If somebody said they were sick and could
not go out and work for the white men, Paul would just take you force-
fully because he was a powerful man.'

Another of the Luo chiefs who was highly favoured by the British was
Ng'ong'a Odima. Hobley put him in charge of the whole of the Alego
region, north of Winam Gulf, and Odima proved to be a reliable and enthusiastic supporter of colonial rule. Ng'ong'a grew wealthy and powerful from
the benevolence of the colonial administration, and like many of the new
breed of African officials, he abused his position. Often these chiefs were
employed as hut counters and tax collectors. However, they often over-
charged villagers, refused to issue them receipts for payments, and forced
people to feed them during the course of their administrative duties.[26] The
Luo historian Bethwell Ogot believes this early form of patronage ultimately
led to the entrenchment of dishonest profiteering in Kenyan society:

> Thus new allies were co-opted by the British and new pivots of patronage
> were created at different levels of the social and political system. In this
> way, corruption began to manifest itself [in Kenya] in various forms such
> as nepotism, bribery, looting and gradually it became entrenched and toler-
> ated as an essential ingredient of governance.[27]

The system worked very effectively for the British, and within a very few
years the Luo were pacified and became loyal supporters of British rule in
Kenya. According to Hobley, the great advantage of the 'Kavirondo' was:

> Once they were beaten they readily made peace and, once they had made
> peace, it was peace, for within a few hours the women were in camp selling
> food, and one had no anxiety about a subsequent treacherous attack
> either at night or on the road. Under these circumstances mutual respect
> gradually supervened and we became great friends.[28]

With the opposition of the Luo and other tribes quelled by the early twentieth century, the IBEAC turned its attention to the finances of the railway.
The final cost of over £5.5 million was more than double the original

estimate and the British realised that the line had no chance of being financially viable. Elspeth Huxley, the British-Kenyan writer and journalist, wrote, 'Never before or since has such an impracticable, extravagant and uneconomical railway been planned. There was not the slightest chance of its paying, so far as anyone could see, within any measurable distance of time.'[29]

Shortly before the line was completed in late 1901, a new governor was installed by the British Foreign Office. Sir Charles Norton Edgecumbe Eliot was an experienced career diplomat and a brilliant linguist who had previously served in Russia, Morocco, Turkey and the USA, before being posted to Kenya in February 1901. Eliot realised immediately that the Uganda Railway was a white elephant, but he also insisted that the protectorate had to be self-financing and that the railway would have to pay its full running costs. Eliot was an arrogant, conceited man, who held the indigenous Africans in contempt. According to the new governor:

> The African is greedy and covetous enough ... he is too indolent in his ways, and too disconnected in his ideas, to make any attempt to better himself, or to undertake any labour which does not produce a speedy visible result ... [The African's mind] is far nearer the animal world than is that of the European or Asiatic, and exhibits something of the animal's placidity and want of desire to rise beyond the stage he has reached.'[30]

As Eliot sought to find solutions to develop British East Africa and make it financially viable, he effectively ignored the role of the Africans in his plans, except as a source of tax revenue. Instead, he proposed to resolve the fiscal problems of the railway by the colonisation of the rich land in the Kenyan highlands by Europeans. It was a bold and imaginative proposal, but other diplomats and politicians had different ideas, none of which involved the participation of the indigenous Africans. Lord Lugard, then High Commissioner of the Protectorate of Northern Nigeria, suggested that British East Africa be given over to the Indians and Harry Johnston, the new special commissioner in Uganda, even referred to Kenya as the 'America of the Hindu'; the Colonial Secretary in London at the time, Joseph Chamberlain, had other ideas, and even went so far as to offer the protectorate to the Jews as a permanent home.[31] However, none of these ideas actually addressed the problem of paying for the railway, and the only viable option open to the British was Eliot's proposal to populate the highlands with white farmers in the hope that they would produce cash crops for export, thereby making the railway financially viable.

Eliot also expected the Africans to contribute to the cost of running the protectorate, and he introduced what was called a 'hut tax' – a tax on every dwelling payable in hard currency. If a man had several wives, then a tax was paid on each of their houses. This was an iniquitous levy on a society which did not have a cash economy. It not only succeeded in raising money for the Uganda Railway but also effectively forced the Africans to work for the British, whether they wanted to or not, in order to earn the money to pay their dues to the colonial administration. It was a tax which was bitterly resented by the Africans and the historian Bethwell Ogot claims that it marked 'the beginning [of] rural–urban migration and the breakdown of the closely-knit family structure and values'.[32]

Eliot's proposals to solve the financial crisis in British East Africa did not get universal support back in London, but he was unrepentant and he responded to the accusation that Europeans had no moral or legal right to settle or colonise the Africans' land in his characteristically blunt manner:

> There seems to be something exaggerated in all this talk about 'their own country' and 'their immemorable rights'. No doubt on platforms and in reports we declare we have no intention of depriving the natives of their lands, but this has never prevented us from taking whatever land we want for Government purposes, or from settling Europeans on land not actually occupied by natives . . . The sooner [the native] disappears and is unknown, except in books of anthology, the better.[33]

By May 1901 – less than four months after taking up his tenure in Nairobi – Eliot submitted his first annual report to the Foreign Office back in London, in which he greatly exaggerated the agricultural potential of British East Africa. Nevertheless, it had the desired effect and the colonisation of the richest agricultural land in East Africa began. In 1903 large grants were made around Lake Naivasha in the central Rift Valley, regardless of the rights of the indigenous tribes in the area. In January of that year the Farmers and Planters Association was formed to export the first crop of potatoes from the area, but the association soon became political and it secured a guarantee to reserve the best land in the highlands for white settlers. Hugh Cholmondeley, better known as Lord Delamare, became a leading light in the Association, and together with Charles Eliot championed the interests of the white settlers.

The colonial administration declared the land to the north of Nairobi and in the central highlands that surrounded Mount Kenya, to be Crown land, and by 1904 white farmers from Europe and South Africa began to arrive, lured by the promise of good farming land being sold off for a pittance. Eliot wanted to stimulate the production of cash crops at almost any price; the original occupants of the land, predominantly the Kikuyu, Maasai and Kalenjin, were moved off their tribal territories and white settlers were given a ninety-nine-year lease on their land. Eliot wanted even greater independence from London over the allocation of land, so that he could speed up the process, and he claimed that 'the enormous land appetites of the colonists, particularly South Africa, should be considered, and this, without wasting time on African interests'.[34] This uncompromising attitude brought Eliot into direct conflict with the Foreign Office back in London, and he was forced to offer his resignation in 1904, but not without one final shot at his nemesis, the Foreign Secretary, Lord Lansdowne:

> Your lordship has opened this Protectorate to white immigration and colonisation, and I think it well that in confidential correspondence at least, we should face the undoubted issue, viz. that white mates black in a very few moves. There can be no doubt that the Masai and many other tribes must go under. It is a prospect which I view with equanimity and clear conscience. [Maasaidom] is a beastly, bloody system founded on raiding and immorality.[35]

Despite Eliot's departure, the settlement of what became known as the 'White Highlands' continued. By 1905, 700 Afrikaner farmers arrived from South Africa, together with more than 250 British and other settlers. Between 1904 and 1912 the South Africans outnumbered the British, and other Europeans arrived including Finns and European Jews. However, the pattern of colonisation in Kenya was different from that in other parts of the British Empire because of the availability of cheap labour, and it was never the intention of the newcomers to perform manual labour themselves, but instead to become planters – managers who would oversee the Africans doing the hard labour.

John Ainsworth was one of the early colonists and in 1906 he wrote, 'White people can live here and *will* live here, not . . . as colonists performing manual labour, as in Canada and New Zealand, but as planters, etc., overseeing natives doing the work of development.'[36]

These early settlers were, in their own way, just as pioneering as the

early Americans who took their families west in search of a new life. Jos
and Nellie Grant were typical of the enthusiastic but inexperienced British
hopefuls who moved to the protectorate in the early twentieth century.
They landed in Mombasa in December 1912, intent on starting a new life
in British East Africa. Jos bought 500 acres from an Englishman in a bar
at the Norfolk hotel in Nairobi, paying £4 an acre for the land. Many years
later, their daughter Elspeth Huxley wrote about their early years in *The
Flame Trees of Thika*. She recalls the family leaving Nairobi in 1913 to
establish their family home:

> I sat beside my mother, only a little less fortified in a pith helmet and a
> starched cotton dress. The oxen looked very thin and small for such a task
> but moved off with resignation, if not with speed, from the Norfolk hotel.
> Everything was dusty; one's feet descended with little plops into a soft,
> warm, red carpet, a red plume followed every wagon down the street, the
> dust had filmed over each brittle eucalyptus leaf and stained the seats and
> backs of rickshaws waiting under the trees.
>
> We were going to Thika, a name on a map where two rivers joined.
> Thika in those days – the year was 1913 – was a favourite camp for big-
> game hunters and beyond it there was only bush and plain. If you went
> on long enough you would come to mountains and forests no one had
> mapped and tribes whose languages no one could understand. We were
> not going as far as that, only two days' journey in the ox-cart to a bit of El
> Dorado my father had been fortunate enough to buy in the bar of the
> Norfolk hotel from a man wearing an Old Etonian tie.[37]

Thika was a small township about 30km north-east of Nairobi, on the
route 'up country' towards the popular farming land around the foothills
of Mount Kenya. Perhaps the British had not mapped the 'mountains
and forests' to the north, but the Kikuyus who were being displaced by
the white settlers certainly knew the area well enough, as they had lived
there for hundreds of years before the *wazungu* came.[38]

Wealthy British families such as the Delamares used their strong
political connections to buy up huge areas of land, and by 1912 just
five families owned 20 per cent of all the land held by whites. In 1901
there were thirteen white settler-farmers in British East Africa; by
1921 there were 9,651, and by then 20 million acres (about one-eighth of
the country) was designated as 'native reserves' and over 7.5 million acres
– by far the best quality farming land – was taken by the white farmers.

The Maasai reserve, for example, was only one-tenth of the area the tribe had occupied prior to 1883.

It had been an extraordinarily fast transition into the twentieth century for the Africans. In the ten years between 1895 and 1905, British East Africa grew from an isolated backwater to a colonial protectorate bigger in area than France; it was controlled by an administration that was prepared to use ruthless force where necessary, where the Africans now paid taxes to live in their own homes, where steamboats sailed on Lake Victoria, telegraphs crossed the land, and a steam railway connected the ocean to the interior. It was into this world of dramatic change that Onyango Obama, second son of Obama and Nyaoke, grandson to Opiyo was born in 1895; 114 years later, his grandson would become the President of the United States.

Onyango represented the very last generation of Luos to be born into an independent Luoland. Over the course of his life he would witness even greater changes; he started life in an Iron Age society whose people were catapulted into the twentieth century in less than a generation. During the course of his life, Onyango would fight in two world wars, witness a bloody national revolt against the colonial rulers, and eventually see his country gain independence from white rule. But for his first few years, life was the usual tough existence for any Luo in Nyanza. Already his family's cattle had been devastated by a decade of bovine infections, his parents had struggled through the 1889 famine, and now there was an epidemic of smallpox rampaging through the region. Many Luo families were forced to move on, but Onyango's father elected to stay in the family homestead in Kendu Bay.

When Onyango was nine there came a new influx of white people who would have just as much influence on the lifestyle of the Luo as the British administrators: the Christian missionaries. Although there had been Anglican and Catholic missions in East Africa for several decades, most of them were concentrated in central Uganda. This new influx of missionaries into Luoland came from a very different branch of the Christian church – they were the Seventh Day Adventists (SDAs), an evangelical Christian church which observes Saturday as the Sabbath and which puts strong emphasis on the imminent second coming of Jesus Christ. The church grew out of the Millerite movement in the USA in the middle part of the nineteenth

century and it was formally established in 1865. Today, the SDAs have a
missionary presence in 200 countries. In Kenya, the Seventh Day Adventists were late on the scene and only established their first mission in
1906. Under the leadership of the Canadian missionary Arthur Asa
Grandville Carscallen, the church focussed its attention on the region
around the eastern shores of Lake Victoria, where it established seven
mission stations.[39]

Carscallen arrived in Kisumu in November 1906, but he did not receive
the reception he was expecting – a colonial official told him that they had
missionaries of all shapes and sizes, and with all sorts of labels, and the last
thing they needed were any more. Undeterred, he began to scout for a
suitable place to establish his first mission, and his first trip took him to
Kendu Bay:

> Brother Enns, Brother Nyambo and myself took a small launch here and
> crossed over to the southern shores of the Kavirondo Bay where we pitched
> our tent close to the water's edge until we could have a look around the
> country. After a few days' search we decided to locate on a hill about two
> miles back from the bay. From this hill we have a fine view in every
> direction. To the north we can see across the Kavirondo Bay and get a
> good sweep of the country beyond. To the north-east we see Kisumu, and
> to the east we have a view of the country for fifteen miles; to the south we
> can see the hills for about thirty miles and to the west there is a valley
> spreading out below us for some ten miles, while beyond that the hills
> loom up one after another for many miles in the distance. We are well
> favoured by having a good river flowing along the foot of the hill, which
> winds its way through the valley to the bay.
>
> The country here is very thickly settled with a most friendly class of
> natives. We can stand on our hill and count about two hundred villages,
> each of the nearest ones sending us a present of at least a fowl. The natives
> have made friends with us quite quickly, and we now have a good deal of
> company every day. The chiefs have shown themselves most friendly and
> have come to see us several times. Whenever they come they bring us
> some little present. One brought a fine sheep the other day. Another, who
> wants two boys educated, brought us a fine young bullock, nearly full
> grown, to pay for the education of the boys. Other missionaries say it is
> best to take something that way from the chiefs as it makes people feel
> that the education is worth something.[40]

John Ndalo was born eighteen years after Arthur Carscallen established his mission in Kendu Bay, and like many of the residents of the area, he was baptised as a Seventh Day Adventist. He recalls his father telling him about the arrival of the first missionaries:

> 'When they first came, there was an old man called Mr Ougo. He was the first person to see them. So they asked Ougo to give them a place where they could settle. So in that place called Gendia, that's where they put their tent. Mr Ougo was the owner of all that land, and he gave them a place to stay. They gave us sweets and sugar, even clothes and blankets. They knew how to get the African people to be close to them.
>
> 'So these missionaries started getting into people's homes, to tell them about this foreign god. Initially, they were very suspicious of these white men. But you know, the white man knows how to go about making friends, giving them sweets and so on. But some of the Africans were very proud, so they said, "Forget about the white man" – some of them were taking bhang', so they were very strong-headed.
>
> 'Then they began by building a small settlement with a school, where they started teaching people the word of God. But there was a language barrier because people couldn't understand them. So they started teaching the older people of about thirty years of age, teaching them English so they could communicate.'

Arthur Carscallen was an accomplished linguist and he soon mastered the Dholuo language (which in itself was no mean feat), and he went on to become the first person to create a written language and dictionary for the Luo people. He even imported a small printing press, which he used to produce a Luo grammar textbook, and he also spent several years translating parts of the New Testament into Dholuo. (This original press is still working today in the SDA mission in Gendia.) With textbooks, the Luo could be given a formal education. The Seventh Day Adventists also stress the importance of good diet and health, and part of the mission's objectives was to administer medical care. John Ndalo himself has benefited from the medical centre introduced by Carscallen: 'During this time there were sicknesses like malaria and even cholera, and so they built a hospital where they could treat the people, and it was free. There was a man called Majwek – if he heard that you were sick in your home, he would come to visit you there.'

A year after arriving in Luoland, Carscallen was joined by his fiancée,

Helen. As an accomplished seamstress, she was less concerned about the lack of a written language and more troubled by the lack of any clothing worn by the locals. Determined to change the situation, she began to grow cotton, and made her own material to clothe the Africans. However John Ndalo recalls that his older relatives found the new clothing provided by the missionaries had several disadvantages over their traditional attire:

> 'They used to wear skins, so when the white man came, they started to give them clothes. They had a very hard time with these clothes, because every time they wanted to go for a "long shot", they had a big problem taking off their clothes. It was difficult to handle the European clothes, so we were struggling for a long time. We could not get them on, and they tried very hard to get people to wear them by giving us sweets and sugar. But people refused because they didn't want to wear them, they were cumbersome to us.'

This stalwart independence and a focus on corporeal as well as spiritual matters brought the missionaries into conflict with some of the local traders who were trying to establish a presence in the region. Carscallen in particular came under some criticism. The first permanent British settler and trader to arrive in Kisii, in south Nyanza, was Richard Gethin, and he complained that Carscallen and his other missionaries were 'more interested in trading in buffalo hides' than in saving souls, and that their mission houses were used mainly to store hides and other trade goods for export, rather than being havens of spiritual devotion and learning:

> Preaching of the Gospel was conspicuous by its absence. Carscallen would see an old Jaluo [Luo] native asleep in the shade of a tree. He would approach him, put his hands on his head and if he still slept, give him a kick on the backside saying, 'Son you are saved and you can thank the Lord it is me who has saved you; if it were one of the others you would be condemned to terrible torture when you died.' With this, the convert would be roped into carrying a load on the next safari.[41]

For the young Onyango Obama, the arrival of the white missionaries was an exciting diversion from the monotony of village life. His last wife Sarah tells the story of when the white man first arrived in Kisumu.[42] Onyango was only eleven when Carscallen established his first mission in Gendia, but he was fascinated by these white strangers from the beginning. Sarah always says that Onyango was different from the others, even as a young boy. As a child he would wander off by himself for days on end and nobody would know where he had been – nor would he tell them anything when he got back. Sarah maintains that he was always very serious as a child, he never laughed or joked around, or even played games with the other children. He was, and, as I later found out, would always remain, an outsider.

But Onyango had one powerful redeeming feature, and that was his curiosity; he wanted to learn and understand about everything around him. It was his innate inquisitiveness which drew him to the white missionaries like iron to a magnet. At a time when most of the Africans were doing their best to ignore these new visitors, thinking that, like the Arab traders, their presence would be only temporary, Onyango went off alone to find out more about these strange new people who had come to live in Luoland. Nobody in the family can recall how old Onyango was when he left, but he must only have been in his early teens – old enough to wander away from home alone, but young enough to return before the outbreak of the 1914 war.

So at the age of perhaps fourteen or fifteen, Onyango took off and nobody in his family knew what had happened to him; for all they knew, he could have been taken by a leopard or bitten by a deadly snake. During Onyango's absence, life in Kendu Bay carried on as it had done for generations; the older girls slept together in the *siwindhe* and learned from their grandmother, the boys tended the livestock and joined their father in his *simba* to talk long into the night about heroic deeds of past warriors. It was Luo life as it always had been for hundreds of years. Then, after several months' absence, Onyango returned to his father's compound wearing long trousers and a white shirt. In a household where everybody else was wearing nothing more than a piece of animal skin to cover their genitals, a young black boy dressed like a white man was deeply shocking. Onyango's father was convinced that his son had broken a strict tribal taboo and had been circumcised; after all, why would anyone wear trousers if it was not to cover this humiliation? And his shirt? He surely wore this to cover an illness or sores on his body – after all, venereal disease was not uncommon among the white people, or perhaps he had caught smallpox and was contagious. Sarah claims that Onyango's father Obama turned to his other sons and said, 'Don't go near this brother of yours. He is unclean.' His brothers laughed at Onyango and had nothing more to do with him; at the age of a young teenager, Onyango was rejected by his family, and he became a social outcast. The young man turned his back on village life in Kendu Bay and returned to Kisumu; Onyango would remain estranged from his father for many years.

By 1914 it was generally acknowledged that Nyanza was the most successful and prosperous of the provinces in British East Africa. In the financial year 1909–10, tonnage shipped to Mombasa on the railway showed a 90 per cent increase over the previous year, and this grew by an additional 45 per cent the following year.[43] Exports and taxes were bringing money into the region, and what few roads and other transportation systems there were in Nyanza were considered to be the best in the region.

But change had come very quickly to the Luo, and there was now a growing resentment building among some of the people living in the lake region. There was still bitterness over the punitive wars fought against them at the turn of the century, at the imposition of the iniquitous hut tax, the forced labour on road construction and on the settlers' farms, all compounded by the paternalistic attitude of the missionaries. In central Nyanza, a uniquely local religious cult had grown in popularity, one that had its roots in traditional religion and which helped to focus the African's opposition to the white man – 'Mumboism'. At its worst, it was a brutal movement which threatened to sever the arms of those found wearing European clothes, and to transform whites and their allies into monkeys.[44]

According to the religion's followers, the Mumbo spirit serpent used Onyango Dunde of the Seje clan in Alego as a Luo prophet. In a story which has echoes of Jonah and the whale, Onyango claimed to have been swallowed by the serpent which, after a short time, spat him out unhurt.[45] The giant snake then gave Onyango a message to pass on to his people:

I am the god Mumbo whose two homes are the Sun and in the Lake. I have chosen you to be my mouth-piece. Go out and tell all Africans ... that from henceforth I am their God. Those of whom I choose personally and also those who acknowledge me will live forever in plenty ... The Christian religion is rotten and so is its practice of making its believers wear clothes. My followers must let their hair grow never cutting it. Their clothes shall be the skins of goats and cattle and they must never wash.[46]

John Ndalo, who was a Christian from birth and was never attracted to the cult, is nevertheless familiar with the effect that Mumboism had on the people of the region:

'Yes, I remember this very well – they were calling the white men *bogno* – something "fragile". Because they were white, they looked on you like a weak child. They were saying that the *bogno* were coming, and they will come with things like clothes and things like sweets – things to corrupt our culture. Maybe they had overheard these people in Kisumu, or they were somewhere in Mombasa. But they said they were told by their gods, so we believed these people. So when the missionaries came, the people realised that they were telling the truth – they believed their words. This inflicted fear among the Africans, by foretelling them that the *bogno* – the white men – were coming with their new religion. So they scared quite a lot of people, who ran away from the missionaries.

'The Mumbo became influential because here, they were calling it *rabudi*. Now the Mumbo thing was a religion to us. The *rabudi* diviners were telling us of the things which were coming, so they would say, "Next year, there will be rain or there will be famine, or there will be peace." They were like foretellers to us, so the religion was like more of a place where we were told things which were going to take place in our lives, and they explained what the gods had told them in the morning or at night.'

One of the Mumbo predictions was that all Europeans would disappear from their country, and this seemed to be prophetic, for in 1914, German troops crossed the border from German East Africa and attacked the British garrison at Kisii. The Africans took this to be a sign that Mumbo's forecast was correct and they rose up and plundered administrative and missionary centres throughout the region – although this particular response came primarily from the Gusii tribe, rather than the Luo. The British were harsh in their suppression of the rebellion, killing over 150 Africans.

John Ndalo recalls that many of the Mumbo leaders were also exiled: 'These people, the cult leaders who were inflicting fears in the people, were then rounded up and arrested and taken to an island off Kismayo [in the Indian Ocean, now in southern Somalia]. Some of them came back, but some of them also died there.' However, this did not deter Mumbo's most devout followers, and despite frequent arrests and deportation of their leaders by the British authorities, they continued their insurrection throughout the inter-war years.

The border with the German protectorate was only 120km from Nairobi, and the outbreak of war brought panic to the white settlers. Many planters left their farms and flocked to the city, carrying any weapon they could lay their hands on; elephant guns, shotguns and sporting rifles. Twelve hundred men were enrolled into the East African Mounted Rifles (EAMR) and the rest were asked to return to their farms. There were no uniforms available; instead, recruits handed over their shirts and volunteer women sewed the letters EAMR on their shoulders.[47] Horses were commandeered from farmers, martial law was declared, and 'enemy aliens' rounded up and incarcerated.

British East Africa was going to war.

An African soldier from the King's African Rifles. During the first twelve months of the First World War, 4,572 Africans were recruited into the KAR from central Nyanza alone.

6

FIVE WIVES
AND TWO WORLD
WARS

Pand nyaluo dhoge ariyo
An old knife has two edges

**The first half of the twentieth century; the rise of
African nationalism; Hussein Onyango's adult life**

As the clouds of war began to roll in over the fields of Flanders in the summer
of 1914, there was a consensus in East Africa between colonial Britain and
Germany that war on the continent was pointless. People argued that the
two colonial nations faced such similar problems in trying to administer large
African populations that open hostility was not in anybody's interest. By 1914
a quarter of the African continent was ruled by Britain, and the German
colonies were five times larger than the Fatherland. It was a comfortable
alliance, and Dr W. S. Solf, the German Secretary of State for the Colonies,
willingly accepted that his nation's ambitions in Africa would best be served
by being 'England's junior partner'.[1] Despite the scepticism voiced by both
Bismarck and Gladstone in the 1880s about the wisdom of colonising Africa,
by the beginning of the twentieth century both nations were beginning to
profit from their overseas ventures, and so the perceived wisdom was that
nothing would be gained by opening up a second front in the colonies.

Prior to the outbreak of war in 1914, most of the operations by the King's
African Rifles (KAR) were little more than 'large scale cattle raids'.[2] Besides,
the military forces in the two colonies in East Africa were not ready for

war, and their numbers were finely balanced; in the summer of 1914, Britain had 2,383 officers and *askaris* (African soldiers) in the KAR; Germany had 2,756 troops. One resident of Nairobi wrote that British East Africa 'was not prepared. Why should it have been, with a German colony cheek-by-jowl across the border? . . . German East Africa was much too near to be dangerous.'[3] However, this comfortable alliance was not to last, and it is ironic that the first shots discharged in anger during the First World War were fired not in Europe, but in Africa.

On 5 August 1914, the day after Britain declared war on Germany, British troops from the Uganda protectorate attacked a German river outpost near Lake Victoria. On 15 August troops in German East Africa retaliated and were ordered to take the small port of Taveta on the coast, a dozen miles inside British East Africa. By doing so, a German volunteer soldier called Bröker became the first casualty of war on foreign soil. In south Nyanza in western Kenya, there was near panic in September 1914 when Captain Wilhelm Bock von Wülfingen led a detachment of German troops and took the undefended British post at Kisii. The town was reclaimed by KAR troops after fierce fighting and several deaths, but the British now worried that the strategic railhead and port at Kisumu was vulnerable to attack.

By the autumn of 1914 there was open war between German and British forces in East Africa, which lasted until after the armistice in Europe. For the first time, ordinary Africans were dragged into a war between European nations. In financial terms, the cost to the British Treasury of the African war was unofficially estimated to be £70 million (about £2.8 billion today).[4] However, this did not include the contributions made by India, South Africa and Britain's other colonies in Africa. On 3 February 1919 the *Cape Times* claimed that the real figure was 'said to exceed £300 million', or about £12 billion in today's prices. As always, though, the real cost of the war was in human life, and in East Africa – by far the largest and bloodiest of the African campaigns – the Africans themselves paid a high price. The soldiers of the KAR were often required to march 30km or more a day in the jungle, sometimes for weeks and months on end, in tropical conditions of intense heat and often torrential rain. They survived on meagre rations and minimal medical support.

Of the 165,000 African porters who were employed in British East Africa during the war, more than 50,000 died – a much higher percentage of casualties than on the Western Front. This extraordinary figure represented one in eight of the adult male population in Kenya and Uganda. War devastated large areas, laid waste farming land, and brought hunger, disease and death to ordinary African civilians; thousands more perished in the global influenza pandemic which followed the war. The Afro-American writer and civil rights activist William DuBois wrote in his seminal essay, 'The African Roots of War', that 'a great cloud swept over sea and settled on Africa . . . twenty centuries after Christ, black Africa, prostrate, raped and shamed, lies at the feet of the conquering Philistines of Europe'.[5]

By 1914 all local insurrections in British East Africa had been suppressed, including the Mumbo rebellion in south Nyanza, and the British had established an effective and comprehensive administration across their region of control. The Africans had 'buckled under' colonial rule, and they demonstrated remarkable stoicism in coping with the outbreak of a European war in their country. Despite the occasional brutality shown by the colonials towards the local people, there were plenty of Africans who admired and respected the organisation and stability that British rule brought to the region. In fact, some of the fiercest opponents to British rule in the 1890s contributed many combatants to the KAR, and some historians have argued that this enthusiasm for fighting arose because the KAR offered an opportunity for young Africans to maintain their warrior status in a society increasingly dominated and controlled by the British. One young African summed up the situation by claiming that the army 'was a suitable job for a warrior . . . It showed that we were men.'[6] This was particularly the case with the Nandi, who had fought long and hard against the construction of the Uganda Railway, yet they contributed a greater percentage of their male population to the KAR than any other tribe in Kenya.[7]

War not only brings death and devastation, but also adventure and opportunity. In Nyanza, the Luo were mixed in their response to the conflict. Initially, finding volunteers in south Nyanza was relatively easy as there was high unemployment among the Africans because of the disruption in the region caused by the attacks on Kisii and the mission stations from the Mumbo cult. However, the British soon ran out of willing recruits as young African men began to volunteer to work on white farms as a way of avoiding the Carrier Corps, and their colonial masters resorted to more persuasive means. Young men were rounded up at public gatherings such as sporting events or whilst out herding their livestock; the local chiefs were given a quota to meet and sometimes unwilling recruits were even seized from their homes at night. John Ndalo told me that nobody in the Kendu Bay area wanted to fight, and they were all forcibly conscripted:

'In the First World War, they were taking people by force and they picked a lot of Africans, and very many of them didn't come back. They were using the local chiefs to identify the homes with the young men who were capable of fighting.

'So the chiefs would come into the locality and say, at such and such a home, we want one young man, or two or three. So the chiefs identified them with the village elders. In the First World War, there were no volunteers – they used to pick young men and take them by force.'

It was a modern equivalent of the 'press gang' method used by the British Royal Navy during the eighteenth century. However, even these drastic measures did not fulfil the quota demanded by the British and the colonial government was obliged to introduce legislation to allow the conscription of Africans. In the first twelve months of the war, 4,572 Africans were recruited into the KAR from central Nyanza alone, and their numbers continued to increase as the war progressed.

The conscription was effective and thousands of young Luo men joined the army, and their tribe eventually dominated the battalions of the KAR.[8] Of all the major tribes in Kenya, it was only the semi-nomadic Maasai who declined to enlist, although they did provide valuable military intelligence along the border with German East Africa (as indeed did the Maasai living on the other side of the border for the Germans). Hans Poeschel, the editor of *Deutsch-Ostafrika Zeitung*, damned the tribe with faint praise when he wrote that their reluctance to take up arms on behalf of the the British was because the Maasai 'had grown to know the English ... as still greater cattle-thieves than they themselves'.[9]

For several years in the run-up to the outbreak of war, Onyango Obama had been living with the whites in and around Kisumu, and he was part of the first generation of young Luo boys to benefit from an education in a mission school. Onyango was clever and ambitious, and by 1914 he could read and write both English and Swahili; Sarah Obama claims that he also learned about administration from the British, and was familiar with paper records and land titles.[10] So it was inevitable that he was drafted into the King's African Rifles, although like many young Luo men it was against his will. Here, the Africans worked mostly as porters, scouts, cooks, guards and wagon drivers. Onyango's grasp of administration, as well as his ability to speak Dholuo, Swahili and English, made him an ideal recruit for the KAR. The biggest task for the British in 1914 was to enlist enough young Africans for the Carrier Corps and other related military duties, and then have translators on hand to pass down commands from the white officers; for this job, Onyango's language skills were extremely valuable.

The Carrier Corps was essential for warfare in East Africa. There were very few roads on which mechanised vehicles could be used, and it was not possible to use draught animals because of the prevalence of the tsetse fly. So human porters were the only viable option to move military equipment around the region. Sir Philip Mitchell, who later became Governor of Kenya in 1944 and fought in Togoland, Cameroon and East Africa, claims that it took three porters to support a single armed soldier on the front line in East Africa.[11] He also regretted the terrible loss of life sustained by the Africans in the KAR Carrier Corps: 'The heaviest sufferers were the porters, among whom loss of life was greatest and lamentable; faithful men, who did what they had to do with little complaint and great endurance; but who ought never to have been asked to do it, and who suffered much which should have been prevented.'

With virtually no roads in East Africa at the outbreak of the First World War, all the equipment had to be carried by the KAR Carrier Corps.

John Ndalo too remembers that the conditions were tough and the casualties high: 'During that time, there was no organised form of transport, so the soldiers were walking and many died on the road. So we lost quite a lot of Luo young men. They were working as porters as well as fighting.'

Sarah Obama claims that Onyango's first job in the KAR was to be in charge of African teams who were building roads as part of the war effort. Later in the war, when the German forces began to retreat south, Onyango was sent into German East Africa, and towards the end of the war he also spent time in British-controlled Zanzibar.

To the African, the war that the Europeans were fighting was incomprehensible. The missionaries and colonial administrators had spent years condemning inter-tribal wars as sinful and uncivilised, but now the Africans were being recruited for what they saw as just another inter-tribal war – but on a much larger scale. They could not understand why they were marched for days into a strange and inhospitable country, only to fight an enemy from whom they took little or nothing; why not fight a quick campaign, seize their cattle and women, and then go home? Sir Philip Mitchell understood the bewilderment the African faced:

> The White Men, hitherto seen by the native people in small numbers of superior, almost fabulous, people, all apparently of one tribe, with similar habits and common interests were suddenly found to belong to different tribes which were fighting each other and required African help to do it. Not only was it no longer a shocking and dangerous thing to offer violence to a *Mzungu*; on the contrary, if he was on the other side, it was a soldier's duty to attack him, and kill him if possible or to take him prisoner, and even Chiefs and villages could earn rewards from the other side for what was in fact treason and rebellion against their lawful Government.[12]

John Ainsworth was one of the ablest British administrators in British East Africa, and he was impressed with the Luo porters during the war:

> As the campaign progressed the Civil Administration was very largely employed in finding porters for transport ... A very large portion of the responsibility for producing porters fell on the Nyanza Province. It can be said with truth that they helped to win the war. The Kavirondo porter became a very well-known feature in 'German East' during the war. He was usually referred to as '*omera*' (a Luo word meaning 'brother').[13]

As well as supplying recruits to the Carrier Corps, the inhabitants of Nyanza were required to contribute to the war effort in other ways. In the last year of the First World War the people of central Nyanza provided over 2,000 head of cattle as well as 3,000 goats. In addition, the dreaded hut tax was further increased.

Throughout the war in Africa, the German colonies fought their European neighbours with varying degrees of success; Togoland, Kamerun (Cameroon), and German South West Africa (Namibia) fell to Allied forces by the early

months of 1915, with the exception of the German stronghold of Mora in
Kamerun, which held out until February 1916. However, it was a very different
story in German East Africa (comprising today's Tanzania, Burundi and
Rwanda). The German commander, Colonel (later General) Paul von Lettow-
Vorbeck, led a brilliant campaign with the support of well-trained *askaris*. Von
Lettow-Vorbeck understood the special demands of fighting a war on African
soil, and he also spoke fluent Swahili – this alone helped to earn him the
respect and admiration of his African troops. Unlike the British, he also
recruited black officers. Von Lettow-Vorbeck also understood that, strategically, East Africa would never be anything other than a sideshow during the
First World War. His instructions from Berlin were to maintain the defence
of the colony at all costs, but with no real hope of winning the campaign he
was determined to tie down as many British troops as possible, thereby denying
them a place on the Western Front.[14] Through a combination of pre-emptive
strikes on towns such as Kisii and brazen attacks on the Uganda Railway, he
not only captured badly needed weapons and supplies but also kept more
than 150,000 Allied troops fighting in East Africa throughout the war.

In March 1916 the British launched a formidable offensive against the
Germans under the command of General Jan Christian Smuts, who had
more than 45,000 troops at his immediate disposal – four times the number
of Germans. Von Lettow-Vorbeck was hopelessly outnumbered and the British
progressively forced him to yield territory. The German commander fought
an effective rearguard action as he moved his forces south through German
East Africa. It was during this campaign that Onyango Obama was moved
from his road-building duties in British East Africa and transferred to German
East Africa to support the growing offensive. For almost a year the Germans
and their loyal African *askaris* lived off the land, and from what supplies they
could capture from the advancing Allied forces as they were pursued relent-
lessly across German East Africa, and south into Portuguese-controlled
Mozambique. Von Lettow-Vorbeck's army was so successful at acquiring
provisions and equipment from the enemy that by the end of the war the
German forces had more ammunition than they could carry.

By early November 1918 rumours were beginning to circulate among
the German forces that the war was nearly over, but von Lettow-Vorbeck
remained convinced that any end to the conflict would be favourable to
Germany. He and his army had been pursued around East Africa by British
forces and had little idea of the real situation in Europe, and he expressed
disbelief when the British Commissioner told him about what was happening
back home in the Fatherland:

The Commissioner told me that the German fleet had revolted, and that a revolution had also broken out in Germany; further, if he was to accept a report which was official but had not yet been confirmed, the Kaiser had abdicated on November 10th. All this news seemed to me improbable, and I did not believe it until it was confirmed on my way home months later.'[15]

As the commander of German forces in East Africa, von Lettow-Vorbeck had no choice but to offer his surrender to Brigadier-General W. F. S. Edwards. Hostilities ceased at 11 a.m. on 25 November 1918, under a storm-laden sky at Abercorn on the border between German East Africa and Northern Rhodesia. It was exactly two weeks after the armistice was signed in Europe; not only had the first shots of the war been fired in Africa, but so too were the last, and von Lettow-Vorbeck's army remained the only German forces to have occupied British soil during the Great War.

Among British imperialists there was an almost palpable excitement about the new opportunities in Africa – for the first time there was now the chance to paint Africa 'Empire Red' from south to north, and Cecil Rhodes' dream of a 'Cape to Cairo' route became a reality. It was now possible to travel from the extreme south of the continent to the Mediterranean Sea without ever leaving the British Empire; it was a journey which took fifty-three days, travelling 7,171 km by railway, 3,225 km on river and lake steamers, and just 584 km by road.[16]

The discussions in Versailles in 1919 about how to manage Africa in the aftermath of the war now assumed the same importance as they had done in Berlin in 1885, and once again the Africans were given no voice in their future. Granted, there were now missionaries who were tasked with canvassing African opinion and representing them at the conference in France, but like the politicians, the missionaries had their own vested interests and agenda. However, there was one significant concession made to 'African interests' at Versailles, and that was a realisation that Africans 'could no longer be bandied about like so many sheep'.[17] At the insistence of the USA – who was now beginning to realise a much greater role in international politics – the ex-colonies of Germany were not to be handed over to the victorious allies en masse. Instead, they were to become 'mandates', to be administered under the auspices of the newly founded League of Nations. These mandates declared that:

To those colonies and territories which as a consequence of the late war have ceased to be under the sovereignty of the States which formerly governed them and which are inhabited by peoples not yet able to stand by themselves under the strenuous conditions of the modern world, there should be applied the principle that the well-being and development of such peoples form a sacred trust of civilization . . . [and that] . . . The best method of giving practical effect to this principle is that the tutelage of such people should be entrusted to advanced nations who, by reason of their resources, their experience or their geographical position, can best undertake this responsibility and who are willing to accept it . . .[18]

The so-called Class B mandates covered all of the former German colonies in Africa; in German East Africa specifically, the territory was split up, with Ruanda and Urundi joined in administrative union with the Belgian Congo and the rest of Deutsch-Ostafrika falling under British military rule, later to be known as Tanganyika.

Despite the grandiose ideals of the League of Nations, any ordinary African would be hard pressed the see the distinction between a 'colony' and a 'mandate'. As the historian Brian Digres explained, mandates were simply 'imperialism's new clothes'.[19] It would take another World War, when Africans again fought (and died) alongside their European masters, before the politicisation of Africa by Africans really took hold. But for the moment at least, the end of the First World War was a turning point in the history of East Africa, and the seeds of independence had been sown.

Between 1914 and 1918, Africans fought alongside their white masters, and the experience transformed the image that the black man had of the white. Previously, the European had been feared – he was a superhuman, capable of killing on a whim and curing at a stroke. Now, having spent four long and arduous years living, sleeping and dying alongside white officers, the Africans realised there was nothing omnipotent about their colonial masters – they had witnessed astonishing examples of both bravery and weakness, and they realised that the white man was fallible. During the hostilities, Africans warrant and non-commissioned officers often advised the European volunteers in the art of jungle warfare, and the Africans began to realise that the white man was, after all, only human.

For the Africans – as with everybody else involved in the war – their world would never be the same. Apart from their realisation that the white man had his limitations, they had been also been introduced to the new technology of the European, as one post-war reporter noted:

'Men who a few years ago had never seen a white man, to whom the
mechanism of a tap or a doorhandle is still an inscrutable mystery, have
been trained to carry into action on their heads the field wireless or the
latest quick-firing gun. Men of tribes which had never advanced so far in
civilisation as to use wheeled transport, who a few years ago would have
run shrieking from the sight of a train, have been steadied till they learned
to pull great motor lorries out of the mud, to plod patiently along hardly
stepping to one side while convoy after convoy of oxcarts, mule carts and
motor vehicles grazed by them, till they hardly turned their heads at the
whirr of passing aircraft.'[20]

For some young Luo warriors – as with many of the other African tribes –
the white man's war was traumatic. They had long known inter-tribal war
and death, but this European conflict was on a scale and magnitude far
beyond anything they could have imagined. The rules of the white man's
war were different from those of the African, and the traditional tribal taboos
had been broken. Now they had a deep-rooted anxiety about the events
they had witnessed which went far beyond mere death. Much of their work
during the war was not only unpleasant, but it brought with it a persistent,
lingering anxiety about the consequences; the African *askaris* had lived in
huts and camps which were obviously cursed with the deaths of others,
they had witnessed horrific injuries and diseases inflicted on their comrades,
who were then violated in death by being buried in mass graves with
strangers. These things could bring a curse, not only on an individual, but
also on his children and grandchildren; after death and without a proper
tribal burial, his spirit could return to become an evil force, roaming its
homeland for generations.

Some returning Africans could not face the future and took their own
lives – itself a rare occurrence in Africa. Others feared to talk about what
they had experienced in case they were banished from their community.
Military doctors diagnosed the condition among the Africans as a mental
illness similar to shell-shock, but they could do little to alleviate their problems, as the circumstances were different both between individuals and
between tribes. The Kikuyu in particular were badly affected and many young
men were classified as temporarily insane. With the Luo, there was always
that lingering fear that, because the bodies of their fallen comrades could
never be buried in Luoland, their spirits would become demons – *jachien* –
because their deaths had not been marked by the correct tribal protocol.
Onyango Obama was away from Nyanza for the whole of the war. After

road duties he joined the British force that was pursuing the Germans south out of German East Africa. He also spent some time in Zanzibar, which was a British protectorate throughout the war years, and it was here that he encountered Islam for the first time. As a young boy he was brought up to worship the Luo God Nyasaye, who was manifest in everyday things around him, including the sun, the moon, the lake, and in some wild animals such as the python. When he went to mission school he was introduced to Christianity; he was baptised and even took the very English name of Johnson for a short time. But for Onyango, like many Africans at the time, there was confusion over the teachings of Christ. They could not reconcile the Christian message of love and compassion towards all men with the white man's apparent willingness to go to war and kill his own kind. Onyango saw the Christian doctrine of showing mercy towards one's fellow man not only as ambiguous, but also as a sign of weakness. Nor could he accept the principle of forgiveness and absolution. To Onyango, this was nothing more than sentimental gibberish. So it is not surprising that Islam should appeal to Onyango, who appreciated the structure and discipline it brought to his life.

However, members of Onyango's family think there were other reasons why Islam should appeal to Onyango. John Ndalo thought that at least part of the appeal were the Muslim women: 'Onyango was an adventurous person and he went to many places, including during the First World War. He met many different people, including Muslims. He even married Muslim wives. So, he had a liking of the Muslim people and he had a liking of the Muslim ladies.'

Charles Oluoch thought similarly:

'I think there was something he may have admired about the Muslims. These Muslim ladies, they know how to treat men. Onyango was attracted to these Muslim ladies because they are different from our women. They are more submissive.

'The Christians, when they came, they believed that polygamy was wrong. But Muslims, they gave you the assurance that you can have even five wives. And you know, Onyango was a polygamous person. So I think he found it to be more comfortable in Islam than Christianity. I think that is what must have driven him to be a Muslim.'

As part of his conversion, Onyango took the Arab name Hussein, which he later passed on to his eldest son, who in turn gave it to Onyango's grandson, President Barack Hussein Obama. However, Onyango's conversion to Islam was an anathema to his family back home, who were adopting Christianity under the teachings of the evangelical Seventh Day Adventists. But for a young man who had decided to walk his own pathway through life, it seems that Onyango took satisfaction in being different, and no doubt he relished his independence.

Life in East Africa was not easy for any tribesman after demobilisation, and the young men returned home to find a society in turmoil. For more than four years the normal, supportive African village life had been in limbo; families were dislocated, ageing parents neglected, farms abandoned. Young men returned – some of them ill, traumatised or disabled – to find that their traditional way of life had gone. Instead, they watched as their chiefs were rewarded for their loyalty to the British for recruiting young men in the first place, and then for returning those who had opted to desert. Not surprisingly, the Africans blamed their colonial masters for their post-war problems.

Onyango stayed in Zanzibar for a couple of years after the war, and did not return to Kendu Bay until 1920. By this time, his family had given up any hope of seeing him alive – after all, he had been away for six years without making any contact and when he returned he had to persuade them he was real: 'See, this is the real Onyango – it is me!' he is claimed to have said.

When Hussein Onyango returned to south Nyanza, he found a region in famine. He was still only twenty-five and under normal circumstances he would have moved back to his father's homestead and looked for a wife. But Onyango was too proud to return and, besides, he had taken the Islamic faith and this made him even more of an outsider in the eyes of his family. He had to retain his independence and establish a life for himself in Kendu Bay, away from his family. Fortunately there was still land available, so Onyango set about clearing an area some distance away from his father's homestead so that he could establish his own compound. Onyango always sought to be different, so he did not initially build himself a traditional *simba*, but chose instead to live in an ex-army tent. People thought that he was crazy, and this only added to his estrangement from his family.

Others demobilised from the KAR faced other post-war problems. In south Nyanza, the war had disrupted a profitable trade with the region bordering German East Africa, and the population was suffering the consequences. In 1918 the rains failed in western Kenya and this brought with it a famine in 1919. The Luo called it *kanga*, after the name of the returning soldiers, and an estimated 155,000 people in British East Africa died from starvation that year. John Ndalo remembers the locust swarms which exacerbated the food shortages in Nyanza:

'The locusts used to invade this place. They came over the trees and they ate all the leaves and everything, and just left the trees as sticks. So there was another invasion which caused a famine. The locusts came and ate everything green, and it left people out of food – there was no food for cattle and there was no food for people. This was after the war.

'We devised a method, because they were eating all our food. We said that we must eat them. Before they fly away, we'd come very early in the morning and collect them, and then we'd have to boil them for food, and they were very nutritious. Even now, we still eat the locusts – it's called *ongogo* here. You put salt on them so they are tastier.'

If famine and locust swarms were not enough, East Africa was also struck by the Spanish influenza pandemic which swept the world in the aftermath of war. In the two years between 1918 and 1920 it caused many times more deaths worldwide than four years of fighting in the Great War. The Scottish medical missionary Dr Horace Philp estimated that in south Nyanza district alone 5,000 people died from flu, and many more from smallpox and plague.[21] Yet in the aftermath of the war, there was not a single trained medical doctor or pharmacist to help the debilitated population of south Nyanza.

The families of the war veterans were also poorly treated by the authorities. Many parents and widows had lost their men, and they hoped for compensation; however nothing was forthcoming. The British authorities announced that if the men were not registered, then it would be impossible to trace the relatives of any victims of war, and no payment would be made.

There were other changes to come after the war. In 1915 the government had accepted the white settlers' demand for greater security of land tenure and the lease on their farms in the White Highlands was extended from 99 to 999 years. Then, in 1916, the British increased the hut and poll taxes on the Africans to help pay for the war. Now that the hostilities were over, the British government formally annexed British East Africa, declared it to be a crown colony, and renamed it Kenya after the mountain in its centre. The government also introduced new, onerous demands on the African population: labourer's wages were reduced by a third, a certificate of identification – the *kipande* – was introduced to catch those who ran away from their employers, every male over sixteen was fingerprinted, direct taxation was increased to sixteen shillings a head, and women and girls were compelled to work on European farms. Harry Thuku was a Kikuyu leader who founded the Young Kikuyu Association in 1921 to oppose colonial rule, and in his autobiography he explained how the women were recruited to work on the new farms:

> A settler who wanted labour for his farm would write to the DC [District Commissioner] . . . The DC sent a letter to the chief or headman to supply such and such a number, and the chief in turn had his tribal retainers to carry out this business. They would simply go to people's houses – very often where there were beautiful women and daughters – and point out which were to come and work. Sometimes they had to work a distance from home and the number of girls who got pregnant in this way was very great.[22]

There were also changes for the white population too, but these were much more favourably received. A new Soldier Settlement Scheme was introduced, designed to double the European farming population in Kenya. In order to accommodate the anticipated influx of white farmers, the government claimed a further 12,810 square kilometres of the highlands – land taken mainly from the Kikuyu.

By the early 1920s Hussein Onyango had established his independence by building a proper homestead in Kendu Bay. He built a fine hut which was admired by everybody, which he kept scrupulously clean. He had also unpacked some of the things that he had brought back with him from the war. He only added to the overall impression of mystery about him when he produced a small wooden box which could speak like a human. The whole community congregated to witness this miracle. One of the elders, his great-uncle Aguk, suggested they should destroy it as it was obviously their ancestors who had come back to life – they could only be the much feared *jachien*. Onyango's older brother Ndalo suggested that, instead, they should take the box apart so that they could see the small people talking inside. Onyango patiently explained that the box was called a 'radio', and it allowed people to talk to each other across long distances. Some of the villagers were not convinced, and they insisted that he cleanse his house of the spirits with an animal sacrifice, otherwise they would never return.

On a later occasion, Onyango only increased his aura of mystique when he told the villagers that he could go to an office in Kisumu and talk to people in Nairobi. James Otieno, who is now a very old man living in K'ogelo, was a young boy at the time; he remembers people blowing horns and beating drums to call everyone together. Some of the men were heard murmuring that Onyango had gone completely mad, whilst others claimed that he had been turned into a witch. Some even accused him of using the occasion to call Africans together so that they could be tricked into being sold to the white man. The bravest of the group left Kendu Bay early one morning and accompanied Onyango to the Kisumu railway station. Once there, he went into the telegraph office, and just as he had promised, a message came through from his white employers in Nairobi.

Once Onyango had built his house in K'obama, there was little more that the impoverished countryside of Nyanza could offer. He returned to Nairobi, where he began to build up a reputation among the white colonialists as a reliable house servant and cook. In this respect Onyango was like a lot of Africans at this time who were obliged to work for cash to pay the government taxes. Besides, rural life was hard in Luoland after the war, and Onyango was better off in Nairobi, learning the white man's ways. Sarah Obama claims that among his many employers during this time, Onyango worked for Hugh Cholmondeley, the third Baron Delaware, de facto leader of the white community in Kenya and founding member of what became known as the 'Happy Valley' set – a clique of wealthy British colonials whose pleasure-seeking habits led to riotous parties, drug-taking and wife-swapping.

Around the time that Hussein Onyango decided to work in Nairobi, his older brother, Ndalo Raburu, left Kendu Bay and returned to the ancestral home in K'ogelo, which his great-grandfather Obong'o left in the 1830s. It was a big step for Ndalo – he had two wives and young children, and all his immediate family were in Kendu Bay. The circumstances surrounding his departure comprise a typical Luo story of squabbling and infighting. His grandson, Charles Oluoch, explained to me what happened:

> 'Ndalo was a very proud man. There were three sons, but Ndalo and Onyango were similar in character. Oguta – their youngest brother – was somebody very polite. But Ndalo was always aggressive and he was very boastful. He was told he was *jadak* [a foreigner] – "You are disturbing us!" [they said] He got annoyed, so he decided to come and tell his brothers, "I've decided to go to Alego. He was a very proud man. So he took his two wives and his cattle – he took everything – and he walked from here up to Alego [a distance of 130km].'

In 1920 Ndalo moved onto the land his great-grandfather Obong'o had vacated nearly a hundred years previously. He cleared the land, planted his crops, and built huts for himself and his two wives. He also took to riding a bull around the village, looking very regal; this earned him the nickname King George, after the reigning British monarch. Here in K'ogelo at least, nobody could call him *jadak*.

Two years later Ndalo's senior wife Odero gave birth to their second son, Peter Oluoch, who became father to Charles and his older brother, Wilson. However when Peter was three, Ndalo and his two wives died unexpectedly, leaving their oldest son Gerishon Odero, Peter Oluoch, and their young daughter Judy orphaned. People say that the three adults died very suddenly, within a couple of days of becoming ill. The people in K'ogelo were convinced that a curse had been placed on the family and their homestead was bewitched. In practice, the cause of their deaths was almost certainly smallpox. However, the disfigurement and pustules which form on the bodies of smallpox victims could only have added to the horror their neighbours felt at such a family catastrophe, and reinforced the belief that witchcraft was the cause of their deaths. But Charles Oluoch explained that a second tragedy was about to befall the family within days of their deaths: 'When they died, my father was three years old, so it was around 1925. When people were wailing [at the funeral], he fell into the fire and he was burnt. And it was my aunt, who was called Drusilla, who was the one who rescued him from that fire. At the time he could not walk fully.' Peter Oluoch was scarred for the rest of his life.

After the funeral, distant relatives of Ndalo offered to take care of the three young children, as is the Luo custom. But Hussein Onyango would have none of it, and despite not being married, he insisted on taking his two nephews and his niece with him back to Kendu Bay:

'Onyango took them and brought them back here [to Kendu Bay], to their grandmothers. When my father [Peter] was at school age, Onyango adopted him. So where he worked – all these whites – they knew him as the son of Onyango. They never knew this was his brother's son. He also converted him to be a Muslim – even these Muslims in Kendu Bay – they thought my father was the first son of Onyango.

'He used to like my father. Odero [the eldest boy] stayed behind here with his grandmother, but Onyango took my father. There was something he admired about him. I think it was the way my father used to behave that he liked. You know, Onyango was a very harsh person – he'd call you and he'd like you to run. I think my father knew how to work Onyango.'

Onyango decided that Peter Oluoch should join him in Nairobi, where he would receive a better education than in Kendu Bay. However, the rest of the family were unanimously against the idea. After all, Onyango was considered to be a madman – or at best, very odd. How could he possibly look after a young boy when he didn't even have a wife? But Hussein Onyango had made up his mind, and together they left to take the ferry from Kendu Bay to Kisumu. The women of K'obama followed him down to the jetty distraught, and one – who was more hysterical than most – threw herself into the waters of Winam Gulf as the boat left for Kisumu, in a last-minute attempt to rescue Peter.

The early 1920s saw the beginnings of a grass-roots rebellion against the colonial government, both in Nyanza and in the Kikuyu lands. In 1921 Harry Thuku founded the Young Kikuyu Association as a political protest against unreasonable taxation and the much reviled *kipande* system. A literal translation of the word in Swahili is 'a piece' – in practice, it was a millstone around the necks of African workers, a small steel cylinder containing identity papers which every African labourer had to wear constantly, and without which he could not find employment. The following year, Thuku founded the East African Association, which also campaigned against the forced labour of women and girls, but that too was short lived. Thuku was arrested for his political activities on 12 March 1922 and exiled, without charge, to the remote Northern Frontier province. He remained there for the next nine years.

In Nyanza province, the more politicised Luos convened a secret meeting to decide what they should do as a protest against direct governance. The main protagonists were the young 'mission boys' – the first generation of Luo boys who had been educated by the missionaries. The mission boys decided to organise a strike and a boycott of classes at Maseno school – the top mission school outside of Kisumu, which later became the alma mater of President Obama's father. The missionaries at Maseno were generally sympathetic to the principles of the boycott, because they too had lost some of their autonomy under the new colonial regulations. The secret meetings continued and a public gathering was organised to call for the Kenya protectorate to become a colony. The meeting was held on 23 December 1921, at Luanda in Gem (north-west of Kisumu), and nine thousand people attended – a remarkable number at a time when the ordinary African had no access to the telegraph, telephones or any mechanised transport. The main demand of the meeting was for the Luo to have local autonomy under an elected president – a *ker*. The people also voted to form a new association – the Young Kavirondo Association, following the lead of Harry Thuku, who had formed the Young Kikuyu Association only months before. The Young Kavirondo Association was the first attempt by the Luo to mobilise the people of Nyanza into a militant, political force. This was the beginning of one of the first African political movements in Kenya, which not only challenged the British colonial rule, but would firmly establish tribal politics in an independent Kenya more than forty years later. But in 1923, in order to avoid being banned by the British, the Young Kavirondo Association rewrote its constitution and changed its name to the Kavirondo Taxpayers' Welfare Association; the YKA had lost its teeth.

Politics, however, was not really what interested Hussein Onyango. By the mid-1920s he was an accomplished and successful cook, working for the British in Nairobi and in the Rift Valley. Onyango had come to admire the British, especially their discipline and organisation. In this respect, Onyango was not alone among the Luo. It was the Kikuyu who had lost huge areas of their land to the white farmers, and they were now forced onto tribal reserves with poor farming land. The Luo were not subject to such draconian measures; the British recognised that the Luo had a reputation for intelligence – something the Luo put down to their high-protein diet of fish and meat – and they had encouraged the education of the young 'mission boys', hoping they would form the foundation of an Africanised administration in East Africa. Meanwhile, it suited the British to 'divide and rule' the different Kenyan tribes, and many Luo found well-paid jobs working for white families or for the colonial administration.

By African standards, Onyango prospered. He was earning good money in Nairobi, and this allowed him to acquire more cattle back in Kendu Bay. He replaced his tent with a proper hut, which he kept spotlessly clean, and he insisted that people take off their shoes and wash their feet before entering. But his family and neighbours in Kendu Bay still thought he was odd – Onyango lived like a white man, even when he was home in Luoland. He ate at a wooden table with a knife and fork, and he wore European clothes, which were always scrupulously neat and tidy. People thought he was peculiar, something of an oddball, and they would laugh at him behind his back. Inevitably, Onyango, the misfit, became the focus of village gossip,

especially as he had not married. According to President Obama's autobiography, *Dreams from My Father*, Onyango is said to have married three
women. However, in talking to several elders in Kendu Bay, I found the
reality was much more complicated than that. So I tried to unravel Onyango's
tangled love life by first asking Charles Oluoch about his uncle's complex
relationships with women:

'I know Onyango liked the ladies, so even in Zanzibar, he might have kept
maybe another woman there. But he never brought the woman back here.
You know, we recognise that you are married when you give the bride
price. But if you stay in a town there [with a woman] for sometimes two
years, we don't say that you are married.

'Onyango was his own man, and he knew how to find women. He had
so many friends, and if they liked him, they would say, "I have a sister
here...", because he had so many friends, and he used to travel a lot.
Onyango had the spirit of adventure. [But] it took him time to settle, to
have his own family, whilst his other brothers overtook him [with a family]
when they were younger.'

I hoped that John Ndalo might be less discreet:

'There was a lady from Kawango in Mumias [in central Nyanza], and he
even took cattle to Mumias and paid a bride price. Then there was Halima,
and then Sofia Odera from Karungu, beyond Homa Bay in south Nyanza.
Then Habiba Akumu, then Sarah.'

Onyango was already up to his Islamic limit of five wives, and they were
only the ones he had actually married, but John Ndalo tried to clarify the
situation:

'In Africa, if you don't have a child with your wife, it is very easy to marry
another one. In our culture, we only recognise somebody as your wife if
you take the cattle. But we cannot rule out if there were some who were
"good friends", because you can stay with them for one or two years, but
we do not recognise them [as a wife], because you have not taken the
cattle.'

Nobody can remember the name of Onyango's first wife from Kawango,
but they do remember that he paid her family twenty head of cattle as

a bride price. When she did not produce a child, Onyango divorced her, but he never went back for his cows. Onyango had very high standards of cleanliness and behaviour, and he also had a violent temper. Even by the harsh standards of Luo husbands in those days, Onyango was cruel towards his women; one by one they left him, but John Ndalo explained that he was always too proud to ever ask for the bride cows to be returned:

> 'Onyango loved to welcome visitors. If his women did not behave well in front of them, then he would beat them there, right in front of the visitors. He would not wait.
>
> 'He was a very funny person. If he divorced you, then he would not go back and claim those cows. He sent twenty cows to Kawango [for his first wife], but he never claimed them back.'

By the late 1920s, Onyango found a respectful and gentle woman who tolerated his outbursts and beatings. Halima came from Ugenya, a region in central Nyanza, north of Siaya, and he met her when he was working for a white man in the area. Onyango was now in his early thirties, and like any Luo husband in that situation, he looked forward to his new wife producing a son and heir quickly. Unfortunately their union was not blessed with children; clearly Onyango was not infertile, as he went on to father eight children with his later wives, so the problem must have been with Halima. However, a married man without children soon becomes the subject of gossip in Kenya.

Sarah Obama tells the story of a confrontation that Onyango once had in a dance hall in Nairobi, when a drunk confronted him: 'Onyango, you are already an older man [he was in his mid-thirties at the time]. You have cattle, and you have a wife, and yet you have no children. Tell me, is something the matter between your legs?'[23] Onyango was furious, but the cruel words found their mark and he returned home to Kendu Bay, determined to find another wife who could give him children.

I asked Charles Oluoch about Halima; he was adamant that she was never a 'proper' wife: 'I am trying to tell you that Halima was not recognised in our place. She came briefly and then she went. You only recognise a woman who gives you children, so we never saw Halima.'

By tradition in Luoland, infertility in a woman constitutes grounds for divorce, so Onyango married again, this time a young girl called Sophia Odera from Homa Bay – a fishing village on the south side of Winam

Gulf, about 20km west of Kendu Bay. John Ndalo recalls that Onyango paid fifteen head of cattle this time as the bride price, but when Sophia and Onyango parted company, childless, Onyango again was too proud to reclaim his cows.

It was around 1930 that Onyango's father Obama died. Although they had been estranged when Onyango was young, father and son had been reconciled and Obama had contributed cattle to Onyango's bride prices. Obama was a successful, traditional Luo tribesman and he left five widows – Nyaoke (who was the mother of Onyango and great-grandmother to the President), Auma, Mwanda, Odera and Augo. Between them they bore him eight sons and several daughters (although nobody in the family can recall exactly how many, let alone all their names). However after his death, Obama's hut was not destroyed in the Luo tradition; instead, his wives stayed living there, although they were inherited by other men.

In the small village of Kanyadhiang I met a close relative of Onyango called Laban Opiyo – his father's sister was Nyaoke, Obama's first wife; this makes Laban a first cousin to Onyango. Laban is a small, thin, frail man who has spent his whole life working in the sun, and he looked every one of his eighty-seven years. Born in 1922, Laban was only about eight when Onyango's father died, but he still has a razor-sharp recollection of the event:

'I knew him very well. Obama was a tall man, a huge man, and well built. He married three girls just from our village here. There was Nyaoke and Mwanda, and then Auma, all from the same clan. But Nyaoke and Auma were real sisters. He kept working until he was very old – he loved farming. He didn't go to school. When he was an old man, he went to his *simba*, his hut, to attend to his garden and he sat there on a small stool, gardening. I know he was very, very old when he died.

'Onyango was in Nairobi [at the time]. He brought a gun – a rifle. He said that by 9 p.m., everyone had to be at his father's home. When he reached the compound, he fired into the air. At the first gunshot, everybody ran into the houses because they had never heard anything like this before. I counted six gunshots. He fired up into the air and I kept asking him, "What is this that is sending fire into heaven?" And we were very much afraid, because we had never heard a gun before, never. That is one thing that I can really remember about Hussein Onyango. He used that gun to send off his father in a dignified way.

'Obama had a traditional burial. Before he died, he slaughtered his biggest bull and its skin was used as his shroud. He was buried the next day – his body could not be preserved like today. He was buried mid-morning – that is the traditional way. He was probably in his seventies when he died. When they buried him, they had a ceremony called *tero buru* – it is "taking the dust" – to scare away the dead spirits. They used to run here and there, sing songs and had mock fights. They also slaughtered a big cockerel.'

By 1926 there were 22,000 Africans working in domestic service in the protectorate – about one in every seven men in gainful employment.[24] After the Great War, all Kenyans had to be registered with the colonial authorities. Onyango was issued with a small red book; on its cover was printed DOMESTIC SERVANT'S POCKET REGISTER, followed in smaller type by: ISSUED UNDER THE AUTHORITY OF THE REGISTRATION OF DOMESTIC SERVANT'S ORDINANCE, 1928, COLONY AND PROTECTORATE OF KENYA. During his first visit to Kenya in 1988, Barack Obama Jnr's half-sister Auma showed him Onyango's registration document, which Sarah keeps in her hut in K'ogelo.[25] The booklet is faded now and the spine is broken, but it gives a fascinating insight into Onyango's life at the time.

Inside the cover are Onyango's two thumbprints – a standard identification mark at the time, even though Onyango could sign his own name as well as read and write English proficiently. The introduction inside the document explains its purpose:

> The object of this Ordinance is to provide every person employed in a domestic capacity with a record of such employment, and to safeguard his or her interests as well as to protect employers against the employment of persons who have rendered themselves unsuitable for such work.

The term servant was defined as: 'Cook, house servant, waiter, butler, nurse, valet, bar boy, footman, or chauffeur, or washermen.'

The British took their official documents very seriously, and if anyone was found defacing the booklet, they were 'liable to a fine not exceeding one hundred shillings or imprisonment not exceeding six months or to both'. This was more than a month's earnings for a Kenyan house servant.

Further into the book are Onyango's full registration details:

Name:	*Hussein II Onyango*
Native Registration Ordnance No.:	*RWL A NBI 0976717*
Race or Tribe:	*Ja'Luo*
Usual Place of Residence When Not Employed:	*Kisumu*
Sex:	*M*
Age:	*35*
Height and Build:	*6'0" Medium*
Complexion:	*Dark*
Nose:	*Flat*
Mouth:	*Large*
Hair:	*Curly*
Teeth:	*Six Missing*
Scars, Tribal Marks, or Other Peculiarities:	*None*

The back of the book is reserved for notes, mainly references from previous employers; this is obviously why the authorities took any deface-ment or alteration of the booklet so seriously. From the citations, it is clear that Onyango was highly thought of by most of his white employers; Captain C. Harford, who gives his address as Government House in Nairobi, wrote that Onyango 'performed his duties as personal boy with admirable diligence'. Mr A. G. Dickson noted that 'he can read and write English and follows any recipes . . . apart from other things his pastries are excellent'. Dr H. H. Sherry was equally flattering and commented that Onyango 'is a capable cook but the job is not big enough for him'.

However, Onyango was not always the model employee, and a certain Mr Arthur Cole of the East Africa Survey Group noted that after a week on the job, Onyango was 'found to be unsuitable and certainly not worth 60 shillings per month'. (The East African shilling was introduced in 1921 and was equivalent to one shilling sterling; Onyango's monthly wage would now be worth about £135 ($220), much the same that a Kenyan would earn today in a similar position.) The registration document also gives a fascinating insight into the short-term employment that Onyango experienced in the 1920s; Mr Dickson no longer required Onyango's services, because, he wrote, 'I am no longer on Safari', and it is unlikely that Onyango would have worked much longer for Arthur Cole either, after such a poor reference.

By the early 1930s, Onyango was approaching his fortieth birthday, but still he had no children. He soon found a beautiful young girl called Akumu Njoga in the most unusual circumstances. The events surrounding their elopement are one of the most unexpected and extraordinary stories that I ever heard about Onyango.

Throughout his marriage to Halima and Sophia, Onyango continued to work in Nairobi, and this allowed him to buy many head of cattle. By Luo standards, he was now a wealthy man. In 1933 he was back in Kendu Bay on one of his regular visits when he saw a young girl walking along the road to market. She would eventually become the paternal grandmother of the President of the United States of America.

Akumu was from the village of Simbi Kolonde, just a short distance outside Kendu Bay; she was tall, young and very beautiful, and Onyango was smitten. Akumu's youngest daughter Auma (aunt to President Obama) told me how they met: 'My mother was taking fish into the market and she was carrying one of the traditional baskets [on her head]. And when my father saw my mother, she was very beautiful. My father forced my mother to leave the fish and then grabbed her and put her into the car and sped off.'

It was a foolish, impulsive thing for Onyango to have done; he literally snatched the young girl away from her mother and ran off with her – her family claim that she was abducted in broad daylight. Nobody knew where Onyango had hidden Akumu and her family was distraught. Auma continued the story:

> 'My mother could not agree to this because she did not know him at all, and she was crying a lot. Now my father had taken my mother forcefully, and he was cautioned by the local leadership. Then he was questioned and they arrested him.
>
> 'Now this is what my father said: "I can't leave this woman because I love her and I did not rape her. I want her and I love her and I will pay everything that the people want." My father went and untied thirty-five cattle just to come and pay for this girl. And all these thirty-five cows were taken because he loved her so much.'

Thirty-five head of cattle was a very large bride price for Onyango to pay:

> 'Having paid this, the authorities allowed him to take Akumu back to Nairobi. At first, my mother did not like my father, because she had not known him at all. This was a forceful marriage. But now, having taken

her, he showed her a lot of respect and love, then she loved him and she agreed to stay with Onyango. This was about 1933.'

It was a typical, impetuous act by Onyango – he was nearly forty and Akumu was only sixteen or seventeen years old. Such an age difference was not unusual in African marriages at the time, and when Onyango married his fifth wife several years later, Sarah too was in her teens. Akumu came from a Christian family, but Hussein Onyango insisted that she convert to Islam, and she took the Muslim name Habiba. It is normal for Luo women to become pregnant soon after they marry, and with several barren relationships behind him, Onyango was keen to have children. Their union quickly brought a result, and Habiba Akumu's first child, Sarah Nyaoke, was born in 1934, followed by Barack Snr (father to the President) two years later. Their third child, Hawa Auma, was born in 1942, and a fourth child, Rashidi, was born in 1944, but Auma explained to me that he died from a fever when he was about ten. All of Hussein Onyango's children were raised as Muslims.

Throughout the 1930s Onyango continued to work in Nairobi as a cook whilst Akumu and her two young children lived in Kendu Bay; it is a pattern of married life which is still common in Kenya even today. After several years of married life, passion began to wane and Akumu and Onyango began having heated arguments. Although Akumu had agreed to become a Muslim when she married Onyango and had taken an Islamic name, she had been born a Christian; indeed, she was the only Christian-born woman that Onyango ever married. By all accounts the President's grandmother was a strong and determined woman, and she was not prepared to tolerate what she saw as Onyango's unrealistic expectations of discipline and spotless cleanliness around the compound.

As the marriage began to fade, so Onyango took a fifth wife. Sarah Ogwel was born in 1922 in Kendu Bay, and she told me that she married in 1941, when Onyango was forty-six. Sarah was born into a Muslim family and she shared the faith with Onyango. Sarah's youngest brother, Abdo Omar Okech, is seventy-six and he still lives in the Muslim quarter of Kendu Bay, a stone's throw from where he was born. He explained that his father, Omar Okech, had been a good friend of Onyango's, and the family had strong ties going back years:

'At that time I was only a small kid, but I overheard that my sister Sarah was to be given to Hussein. They were very good friends and my father said, "Will you marry my daughter?" According to our African customs, Sarah could not go against my father's will.

'It is possible that she would even have been given freely, but because Onyango loved my father, Hussein gave many cows to my family for her bride price.'

Sarah remained married to Onyango for more years than all his other wives combined, and I asked Abdo what was Sarah's secret:

'Onyango would not allow a woman to talk whilst he was talking, or to go against his wishes. So the difference between Mama Sarah and these other women was that Sarah would not talk back to him. He loved Sarah because whatever he said, Sarah complied.'

Abdo also knew all about Hussein Onyango's reputation as a ladies' man, and he explained why he thought Obama was so successful with women:

'Onyango was a medicine man and he knew a lot about herbs which could cure people. Because of this, many women liked him. In our African culture, we don't really count the numbers of women unless you take the dowry and become a real wife.

'Most of these ladies were not married, but when they looked at him, I think because of his build, they just loved him. They just fell for him. He must have been a very attractive man because of all these women. A woman would come and stay with him for a month or two, then he would kick them out and take another one.'

Sarah and Onyango married when Onyango returned from a brief spell of service in the King's African Rifles during the Second World War, and they spent their first years of married life together living in Nairobi, whilst Akumu tended the farm back in Kendu Bay, and brought up her two young children.

Onyango was well respected within the community, but he had a reputation for being a strict disciplinarian, and he certainly had a fiery temper. But he was also generous, and he gave members of the family a lot of support. The Luo have a saying, *pand nyaluo dhoge ariyo* – an old knife has two edges. I was beginning to realise that this certainly applied to Onyango; he was a complex man with more than one side to him. On the one hand, he could be violent and cruel; on the other, he was generous and always ready to help people. As a young man, John Ndalo knew Onyango well:

'I was born in 1924 – I can't remember the month or the day. They didn't keep records in those days, but I have known Onyango since I was very young. He was a very interesting man. He did not want any friends – everybody had to be under him, not above him. He had a very strict set of rules about where you would sit. He would even whip you – friends and visitors – if you did not do what he said. He had a lot of influence. He was well known all around the area – he was known even fifty miles away!

'I have lived here [in Kendu Bay] all my life, but I worked in Nairobi for the whites in big hotels, and also at the airport. Hussein Onyango taught us how to work. He prepared us for these jobs and he moved me to Nairobi in 1941 and found me a job. He did not want us to be lazy. He always said, "If you do a good job for the white man, then he will always pay you well." Many whites loved him because he was a good worker. But he was harsh, a strict man, a disciplinarian. Onyango never allowed a young person to speak in front of the elders.'

I spoke to a lot of people about Onyango and a clear picture was beginning to emerge of this proud, complicated man. Everyone said much the same thing; Onyango was strongly opinionated and did not suffer fools gladly. Without exception, everybody used the same words to describe Onyango: harsh, strict and severe. His youngest daughter with Akumu, Hawa Auma, told me that when they were children, he would call them over to his side, and if they did not respond immediately and run to him, then he would hit them. I assume it helped him to maintain a strong sense of authority, which was important to him. He was a man who certainly commanded respect, but he was admired rather than liked. The more I came to understand Onyango, the more I think this is exactly how he wanted it to be.

There is no doubt that Onyango was a hard worker and throughout the 1920s and 1930s he spent much of his time in Nairobi, where he was employed as a manservant and cook. It was during this time in the capital that he developed a deep respect for the British – his youngest wife Sarah told me that he loved the British. But I think it was more a reverence for the power, organisation and discipline that they brought to Africa rather than any real emotional attachment.

By the end of the 1930s Hussein Onyango was a committed Anglophile; he dressed like a white man, he behaved like a white man, and he even had dentures fitted to fill the gap left by his six missing teeth which had been removed during his initiation into adulthood. I once asked Charles

Oluoch if he thought that Hussein Onyango, deep down inside, might have
wanted to be British, but Charles was adamant:

> 'No! He was proud to be a black man. But he admired the British because
> of their openness, and that is why he did their things. Onyango never liked
> somebody who lies. If you lied to him, then you cannot be his friend. He
> liked people who were truthful to him, and that is why he was very close
> to my father, because my father would always tell him the truth. If he asks
> you, "Where have you been?" you tell him exactly where you were. The
> British liked people who were truthful, and if you were truthful, then they
> would promote you and give you things. So Onyango admired them.'

Charles also told me a story about how his father, Peter Oluoch, and Onyango
fell out. Onyango had adopted Peter and wanted him to have the best education he could find. So he enrolled Peter in a top school in Kisii, where
Onyango was working at the time. Peter was twelve or fourteen, so this must
have been in the mid-1930s. One day Peter was sent out on an errand, but
he dropped the coins which Onyango had given him. When he got home,
rather than lie and tell Onyango that the money had been stolen, Peter
admitted that he had lost the coins somewhere. Onyango was furious and
beat Peter until his back bled. Peter was shocked at the injustice – after all,
he had owned up to a small mistake, so why was he being beaten? Disillusioned, Peter ran away back to Kendu Bay. Onyango followed him to bring
him back, but by the time he arrived at the family compound, Peter had
already left for Kisumu and would have nothing more to do with Onyango.

On 1 September 1939, the world was plunged into another global conflict.
The Second World War was fought on a larger scale even than the Great
War, and over 100 million military personnel were mobilised around the world.
The British used conscription to recruit 323,483 East African troops into the
King's African Rifles. This time, however, the KAR fought not in East Africa
but against Italian forces in Ethiopia and against the Japanese in Burma.[26]
Even though he was now in his mid-forties, Hussein Onyango joined the KAR
for a second time in 1940. Sarah told me that he saw service in both theatres:

> 'The white man he was working for was called Major Batson ... They
> went to Addis Ababa, they went to India and Burma and everywhere. He

was old, but he was a man who could cook very well and they liked him. He was a cook, but when the enemies came, he had to put on all the uniform and he was ready for combat. This was in 1940 and he came back in 1941 and didn't go back again.'

It was when Onyango was on active service in Burma that he met and claims to have married another wife. Onyango might have had a rather casual attitude to what exactly constituted a marriage, but he returned from overseas with a framed photograph of the woman, which Sarah Obama still keeps in her hut in K'ogelo.

This second European conflict was a final turning point for the Africans; when they went to war for the British, they were told that they were fighting for liberty and freedom from repression. When hostilities ended, they came home with high expectations. They looked forward to being granted freedom in their own country, and an end to British rule. The reality was very different; Hussein Onyango, Peter Oluoch and hundreds of thousands of other Kenyan soldiers returned to a country which offered little hope and even less opportunity. They had their savings from the war years, but they were thwarted in their efforts to start small businesses by the imposition of petty colonial rules and regulations. The ex-soldiers became disillusioned, and that made them dangerous.

For the British, the war marked the end of Empire and the beginning of the end of colonial rule in Kenya. But their disengagement would take another eighteen years, and once again Onyango Obama would be drawn into a conflict of interests between the white men he admired and his own people.

Onyango returned from the war early, in 1941, to his homestead in Kendu Bay and that year he married Sarah. I had been told that shortly after his return from the war, Onyango moved his family back across the Winam Gulf to his family's ancestral home in Alego. I had always been puzzled why the Obama family was divided, living as they still do on opposite sides of Winam Gulf. I knew that Onyango's great-grandfather Obong'o left their village in K'ogelo and moved south to Kendu Bay because of the pressure on land and the constant fighting between the sub-clans. I also knew that Onyango's older brother, Ndalo Raburu, returned to K'ogelo after the Great War, only to die suddenly from smallpox, together with his two wives, leaving three young children orphaned. But I never understood why Onyango took the big step and left Kendu Bay to return to his ancestral village with his two wives and young children. Only when I was talking with John Ndalo in Kendu Bay did I discover the extraordinary story about why Onyango left Kendu Bay.

By 1943 Hussein Onyango was nearly fifty years old, a wealthy middle-aged man, well respected within the community by all accounts, with two wives, three young children and with his extended family living around him. The problem started, apparently, with a football trophy. At the time, Onyango was working for the local British District Commissioner, a man called William – nobody can remember his second name. DC William knew that the local boys were passionate about playing soccer, so he gave Onyango a trophy – it was really more of a bell than a cup – and suggested that Onyango should organise the local soccer teams to play in a tournament, with the winning side being presented with the trophy.

John Ndalo then explained to me how things suddenly went so terribly wrong: 'Onyango was very proud of the trophy and he wanted to call it the "Onyango Cup". The local chief, Paul Mboya, did not like this and he insisted on renaming it the "Karachuonyo Cup", after the name of the local district. Onyango was furious – he could not be told what to do by another African. He thought he was better than other Africans.'

Being a local chief gave any individual a lot of power, and Onyango and Mboya had crossed swords several times before, including over the recruitment of forced labour, and also over the abduction of Akumu – it was Mboya who had had him arrested over that episode. Now Onyango was challenging the chief's position again. It is easy to imagine the insults that must have been exchanged between Chief Mboya, who was trying to impose his authority on the situation, and the fiercely proud and argumentative Hussein Onyango. They must have been like two old bulls fighting in a field – and neither one of them was prepared to back down:

'Mboya became very angry and he accused Onyango of being *jadak* – a settler [because his family had moved to the area three generations previously]. Onyango was furious! "I know my roots," he said, and he immediately went back home and told his family that they were leaving. Samuel Dola was one of Onyango's best friends – he was the previous chief before Mboya – and when Dola heard what had happened, he ran to Onyango's house and beseeched him to stay. But Onyango had made up his mind and he would not change it, so he packed up and left. He gave away all his possessions and left the village and went back to K'ogelo.'

It was exactly the same argument over being called an outsider that Onyango's brother Ndalo had had more than twenty years previously – and Onyango's response was the same. Not surprisingly, neither of Onyango's two wives wanted to leave Kendu Bay, especially because of a ridiculous argument about the name of a football trophy. Sarah claims she was young and adaptable and was prepared to move – one family friend indelicately told me there was 'hot love' there – and Onyango had little trouble in persuading her to go. However Akumu was strongly against the idea of moving, and this only made her frequent arguments with Onyango even worse. However, her family intervened and they eventually persuaded her to go for the sake of her children. They needed their mother, and Onyango was going to take them to K'ogelo whether Akumu went or not.

Knowing Onyango's hot-headed temperament, it is easy to understand how this split occurred with the sub-clan in Kendu Bay. But Onyango's move to K'ogelo created a rift in the Obama family which still exists today, made worse because the family in K'ogelo are all Muslim because of Onyango's faith, and the Obamas who stayed behind in Kendu Bay remain Seventh Day Adventists. At least the story explains why Onyango lived out the last of his days in K'ogelo, and why both he and his only son Barack Snr are buried there today, and not in Kendu Bay.

Nobody is quite sure exactly when Onyango moved to K'ogelo with Akumu and Sarah, but local people remember Paul Mboya stepping down in 1946, so the argument over the trophy between the Mboya and Onyango must have happened before then. Sarah's first child Omar was born in K'ogelo in June 1944, so the family probably moved in late 1943, after the birth of Hawa Auma. The first thing that Onyango did when he arrived in K'ogelo was to claim his brother's old compound, which had been left empty for over twenty years. Even though Ndalo and his two wives had died there in 1925, the local people still thought the homestead was bewitched and they would have nothing to do with it – for that reason, it had been left untouched for a generation. This did not deter Onyango, and I think secretly he relished the chance to prove everybody wrong, and show that he was stronger than the curse of any local witch doctor.

Any new family moving into a tightly knit community can upset the natural balance of village life, and Onyango's difficult temperament meant that he soon made his mark. Word spread quickly that the family had moved into Ndalo's bewitched compound, yet Onyango and his family were living there with no adverse effects. This was seen as a bad omen and a threat to the well-being of the village. The local witch doctor – the *uyoma* – was summoned by the local people to finish him off. I have no doubt that the locals genuinely believed that their *uyoma* was responsible for the deaths of Ndalo and his two wives, and they believed that the shaman was clearly not a man to be crossed. I am equally sure that the shaman would have made the most of his 'success' for years, by claiming responsibility for the death of these three adults, and his reputation as a powerful man would have been enhanced by their demise.

It was a confrontation between the most powerful medicine man in the community, and a headstrong disbeliever. The *uyoma* arrived with his super-natural paraphernalia and cast his spells over the family compound, whilst Onyango looked on, unimpressed. When the witch doctor had finished, Onyango walked up to him, took away his magical tools of the trade, beat him up and threw him out of his compound. The neighbours were appalled at Onyango's audacity, and they waited patiently for the most horrible curse to befall the family. But nothing happened, and Onyango's reputation went from strength to strength.

Nor was this the only time that Onyango confronted an *uyoma*. On another occasion a local witch doctor was sent from outside the area to kill one of the neighbours in K'ogelo following a dispute over a girl. Onyango's reputation was now rock solid in the community, and he was asked to inter-vene; he picked up his whip and his *panga* – a broad-bladed machete – and waited on the roadside for the *uyoma* to arrive.

Sarah Obama recalls that Onyango confronted the shaman: 'If you are as powerful as you claim, you must strike me now with lightning. If not, you should run, for unless you leave this village now, I will have to beat you.'[27] No lightning strike was forthcoming, so Onyango did as he threatened and beat up the witch doctor, then took away his case of medicines. The shaman had never been confronted like this before and he was taken by surprise, so he turned to the elders and threatened to bring a curse down on the whole village unless his medicine case was returned. Onyango stood his ground: 'If this man has strong magic, let him curse me now and strike me dead.'

Once again, nothing happened and the neighbour kept his girl. But this time Onyango made a very clever move; he befriended the *uyoma* and took him back to his hut, where Sarah fed him boiled chicken. He then insisted that the witch doctor explain to him how all his potions worked, before sending him on his way. Onyango was already an experienced herbalist, but now he was learning new techniques from another expert. It was typical Onyango, who had always stressed the importance of learning. He had befriended the British and learned how they worked, and he used this to his own advantage; now he did the same with his own people, learning new things about the power of plants.

There was one other story that I had heard about Onyango, which says much about his temperament. It was told to Barack Obama on his first visit to Kenya in 1987 by his step-aunt, Zeituni, and I wanted to know from John Ndalo if it had really happened.[28] According to Zeituni (who was a young girl at the time), a neighbour started to walk across Onyango's land with his goat on a leash – it was a short cut that he frequently took. Onyango stopped the man and said, 'When you're alone, you are always free to pass through my land. But today you can't pass, because your goat will eat my plants.' The man insisted that because his goat was on a leash, he would control it and that he would not allow it to eat any vegetation. The two men argued and Onyango called Zeituni to bring 'Alego' – his pet name for one of his *pangas*: 'I will make a bargain with you. You can pass with your goat. But if even one leaf is harmed – if even *one half* of one leaf of my plants is harmed – then I will cut down your goat also.'

The man decided to take a chance and he walked across Onyango's land, closely followed by the old man and his young daughter. Zeituni recalls that they had taken barely twenty steps before the inevitable happened, and the goat started to nibble a plant. With one swift stroke, Onyango decapitated the goat: 'If I say I will do something, I must do it,' said Onyango, 'otherwise how will people know that my word is true?' The neighbour was furious, and he took his complaint to the village elders to arbitrate. Although they were sympathetic to the owner of the goat, they had to agree that Onyango was in the right, because the neighbour had been warned about the consequences of his action if he allowed his goat to eat the vegetation.

It was a fascinating story which said a lot about the way that Onyango saw things simply in black and white. I related the tale to John Ndalo and asked him if it was true; he looked at me slightly bewildered at first before shrugging his shoulders: 'That sort of thing happened all the time with Onyango!'

The town of Oyugis in south Nyanza claims to have some of the best coffin-makers in western Kenya.

7

A STATE OF EMERGENCY

Kudho chuoyo ng'ama onyone
A thorn only pricks the one who steps on it

**Hussein Onyango moves to K'ogelo; Barack Snr goes to school;
and the Mau Mau insurrection creates turmoil throughout Kenya**

The township of Oyugis lies to the south of Kendu Bay and straddles the
main A1 trucking route from Kisumu to Kisii. It is a typical ramshackle
Kenyan town, and to the first-time visitor it is total chaos. Dangerously overloaded minibuses – the ubiquitous *matatus* – screech to a halt every few
minutes to squeeze even more passengers inside; pedestrians risk life and
limb every time they cross the road, first dodging a fuel tanker from one
direction, then a pair of speeding *matatus* jostling for position from the other.
You can buy almost anything on the high street: beautiful ripe fruit, a second-
hand T-shirt, a bottle of warm beer, or a woman for the afternoon. Oyugis
has a reputation for having one of the highest HIV/AIDS mortality rates in
East Africa, and it is also well known as the home of some of the best coffin-
makers in western Kenya. It is best not to dwell too long on the connection.

Down the side streets leading off the main road, life is a little safer, as
the pot-holed dirt roads force even the most reckless drivers to slow down.
This is where you find the smaller businesses – dressmakers, food stalls and
corner shops selling telephone credit. On most days you will find an old
woman here selling charcoal by the side of the road; on a good day, she

makes $2 profit. Her name is Hawa Auma Hussein Onyango Obama, wife of the late David Magak and the closest living blood relative to the President of the United States:

'I am the daughter of Hussein Onyango Obama and the sister of Barack Obama Snr and the aunt of the President. His first child was Sarah Nyaoke, the second was Barack, and the third is me. I was born in 1942 in the Kendu Bay area. We migrated to K'ogelo when I was still young. I was still being fed on the breast.'

I first met Auma at the Obama inauguration party in Kendu Bay in January 2009, when she introduced herself in a torrent of incomprehensible Dholuo. She told me in no uncertain terms that it was my duty to write about the forgotten Obamas of Kendu Bay. She has one of the biggest toothless smiles in the world, and she instantly became one of my favourite Kenyan 'aunts'. The day after the inauguration party, I went to see her in her small hut, a half-hour walk from the centre of Oyugis. She told me that she was too young to remember living in Kendu Bay, but she remembers life in the family compound in K'ogelo, which she shared with Hussein Onyango's two wives, Akumu and Sarah, and her two older siblings:

'When my father left the army [in 1941], he came back and became a professional cook. He used to work for the whites in Nairobi until he came back to K'ogelo to retire. My father was a friend towards the British, and they would come and visit us on motorcycles and using cars. They were very good friends. He loved all the whites and they loved him.

'We had a very big home, a typical African home, with all the family there. There used to be so many. Many cousins have since died, which has reduced the number. There were five houses there, five huts, for the first mother, the second mother, the girls, Barack's house and Baba's [Father's].

'In those days there was no water in the compound as there is today. We had to fetch water down by the river. We would have to walk about two miles for the water. So when I went, I could not go alone because of the animals. There were *crocuta* [spotted hyena] – these were very common. In the evening you could not walk anywhere. Even if you went out with two or three others, they would come and attack you. They always went for your buttocks. So we could not go out by ourselves.

'At the time there were also lots of leopards – leopards were everywhere.

They even came to our home, because my father had cultivated lots of fruits – all types of fruit that you can imagine: mangos, lots of passion fruit, lemons, oranges. Baba also had a lot of poultry – he had all the chickens and all the turkeys and other small animals in our home. But then the leopards would come and eat them. One day I was sitting next to our cat – a big fat cat, our family pet. A leopard came and took the cat. I cried so much, I was very little.'

Hawa Auma is aunt to President Obama and his closest living relative; on a good day she can earn $2 selling charcoal at the roadside in Oyugis.

Soon after moving to their new home in K'ogelo, Sarah Obama gave birth to her first child, Omar, in June 1944. Hussein Onyango went on to father three more children with Sarah: Zeituni Onyango in 1952, and two more sons, Yusuf and Sayid. For much of the time, Onyango was still working as a cook in Nairobi, but when he came back to K'ogelo he worked hard on his smallholding, which is home to Sarah Obama to this day. The land had been left derelict since his brother Ndalo died in the early 1920s and bush had taken over. Yet within a year Onyango had cleared the undergrowth and started to apply modern farming ideas which he had learned from people in Nairobi. Soon he had enough of a surplus to sell at the local market.

Today his wife Sarah holds court in K'ogelo, sitting under one of the mango trees which Onyango planted soon after he moved to the village. On one of my visits there, Sarah waved her arm across the compound: 'Look at all these fruit trees that he left here – he planted these. He wanted all this to be beautiful. He had lots of paw-paw plants, and oranges, all these mangoes, everything here.'

Life in K'ogelo however, was not a bed of roses. Onyango's oldest wife, Habiba Akumu, had never wanted to leave Kendu Bay, and she did so only because her parents pressured her into going with her children. Now life was as she feared: she was lonely, she was away from her family, and she had the indignity of being displaced by Sarah as her husband's favourite wife. According to Hawa Auma, Akumu and Sarah did not get along well, and this only exacerbated Akumu's loneliness. But Akumu was proud and stubborn, and she continued to stand up to Onyango's excessive demands for cleanliness and tidiness, and this led to their arguments becoming more frequent and more violent.

Auma told me that one day there was a furious row between Onyango and Akumu, and things came to a head: 'My father then went out to dig a very big grave, to go and kill my mother.' I was startled by the revelation, but Auma was tired from sitting in the hot sun selling charcoal all day, and she told me that she did not want to talk any more, because thinking of her mother upset her too much. So I let the matter rest for the moment.

Onyango was a farmer and he must have spent a lot of time in those early days in K'ogelo, digging over the soil, so perhaps Auma had misunderstood the situation. The story, however, was too intriguing to pass up. I knew that Akumu came from a village close to Kendu Bay, so I decided to try my luck at tracing her family. Like many of the small villages in the area, Simbi Kolonde lies some distance off the main road along a bone-rattling dirt road. The track runs around the edge of Simbi lake – a deep volcanic lake which I was told was steeped in myth. One story claims that an old woman was denied hospitality by the locals and in a fit of wrath she created a massive flood which swamped the village, drowned all the people, and created the lake.

Fortunately, my own experience was the exact opposite, and not for the first time during my research I arrived unannounced at a home, only to be welcomed with warmth and kindness. Here I found Charles Odonei Ojuka and Joseph Nyabondo, both brothers of Akumu. We spent a couple of hours or so chatting about life in the past, then I casually asked Charles if he knew why Akumu left K'ogelo in such a hurry back in 1945:

'Onyango used to love cleanliness, and he being a clean man, he never wanted his face to be touched by dirt. He didn't like anything that is called dirt to be around him. So that is the number one cause which brought the disagreement with Akumu. There was a fight between Akumu and Onyango in K'ogelo – a quarrel. He dug a grave and he was going to cut her up and bury her there. An old man [a neighbour] came and helped Akumu, otherwise she would have been killed – she was being slaughtered!

'The old man came and wrestled with Onyango, then Akumu escaped and walked all the way to Kisumu by foot [64km]. I think there was some problem because having married the other wife Sarah, it might have put a lot of pressure on Akumu. When Akumu came back [to Kendu Bay], Onyango never followed her, to look for her or to be reconciled with her. He just left her.

'When Akumu came over to this side [of the gulf], the man who came to marry Akumu was called Salmon Orinda, and she gave birth to another five children. She was buried here when she died in 2006.'

In her desperation to get away from Onyango, Akumu had abandoned her children, and it is for this reason that Sarah Obama raised President Obama's father. Sarah told me that Barack Snr was nine years old when Akumu left, so this must have happened in late 1944 or early 1945, shortly after the family moved to K'ogelo.

Akumu's three children – Sarah, Barack and young Auma – were not happy in K'ogelo. Auma claims they were not looked after, and often went hungry:

'Sarah was very bad to us and she really inflicted a lot of pain on us. She never wanted us in any way when we were young children. She treated us very, very badly. This woman, she mistreated us because she didn't want us to have food. Then every time and again she kept on beating us. She forced Sarah Nyaoke and Barack to work on the farm. If they could not work when they were very young, then nobody would eat, so [sometimes] we did not eat for many days.'

Akumu's three young children decided to run away. Sarah Nyaoke was only eleven at the time, Barack Snr was nine, and Auma was still a toddler. Together, they set out on the 120km trek back to their mother in Kendu Bay. Little Auma was too young to walk far, and her brother and sister tried to carry her, but she became too much of a burden:

> 'They were walking all the way to Lake Victoria, and this was very difficult for them. They left me behind. Peter, you need to know this, that Barack and Sarah left me because I was heavy, and they could not carry me. I was left alone, crying by the sisal plantation.
>
> 'Now, there were leopards near me, looking at me. I think they were sympathetic towards me. They never wanted to interfere with me. Then women from the community came and picked me up and took me home. I was still very young, but I can't remember how old. I was still a toddler.'

In fact, Auma must have been three years old at the time. Eventually, Sarah Nyaoke and Barack were found by a local chief, walking near the lake at a place called Nyakach. The two children had managed to walk almost all the way back to Kendu Bay, before being returned to Onyango and Sarah in K'ogelo.

Not surprisingly, Sarah Obama has a very different recollection of these dramatic events back in 1945. When I first asked Sarah about Akumu, she asked, 'Who is Akumu?' I got the impression that she was being dismissive about Onyango's previous wife, rather than forgetful. But her memory soon returned: 'She left when the father of the President was nine years old. And by that time, he had never started schooling. So it was me – Mama Sarah – who protected and took care of them!'

I asked Sarah why she thought Akumu left K'ogelo: 'She went, even leaving the children. She never liked this place, saying that people would kill her here. So she went, and left me to take care of Barack Senior. She didn't like K'ogelo. I couldn't abandon the children, because she had left them! I had to take care of Barack and the rest of the children and look after them. She left when I had given birth to one child [Sarah's first son, Omar.]'

Hussein Onyango always made education a high priority. He had enrolled Peter Oluoch into Kisii High School in the 1930s, and now it was time for his own son to go to school. Barack Snr started at the Gendia SDA Primary School near Kendu Bay, but Sarah recalls that he found the schooling to be too easy: 'He came back after the first day and told his father that he

Sarah Obama is Hussein Onyango's fifth wife and step-grandmother to President Obama; she raised the president's father from a young age.

could not study there because his class was taught by a woman and he knew everything she had to teach him. This attitude he had learned from his father, so Onyango could say nothing."

Once they were settled into their new homestead in K'ogelo, Barack went to another school in nearby Ng'iya – a small village on the main road from Kisumo to Siaya, and an 8km walk from his new home.

I had been told that Barack's primary school teacher from Ng'iya, Samson Chilo Were, was still alive and living in retirement in a village called Malumboa. So we left Kisumu early one morning to see if we could track him down. Malumboa is in a very remote part of Nyanza, close to Got Ramogi, where the first Luo settled in Kenya five hundred years ago. It was the rainy season, and even a four-wheel-drive vehicle could not make it all the way to Samson's house, so the last kilometre was on foot, wading ankle-deep in mud and water. Samson was delighted to have unexpected visitors; he told me that he was born in April 1922, which made him eighty-seven years old, and apart from a slight deafness he showed little evidence of his advanced years – certainly his memory seemed as good as ever:

'I taught [Barack] Obama in standard five when I was teaching in Ng'iya primary school for boys. From K'ogelo it is something like five miles. He was a smart boy, very clever in class. Very keen at hearing what we were telling him. Every time he learned well – English, Swahili – he did it properly. He liked sports and he liked singing as well. He was a very good singer and a very good dancer. We started before eight in the morning and school finished after games around 5 p.m.

'There were only six classrooms, just mud huts – there were no permanent huts then. We used to make iron sheets out of old oil drums for the roof.

'At that time, the whole school was about two hundred [students], because many parents didn't like school. They thought it was a waste of time. The parents liked their children to look after their cows. School was a white man's thing. The school fees were three [Kenyan] shillings [£3 or $5 at today's prices] a year, at most. His father used to pay for his uniform – it was a white shirt and brown shorts. Even at secondary school there were no long trousers at that time. They were all walking barefoot.'

Samson also knew Hussein Onyango, and he was often invited to his compound for a meal. Like everybody else I had met, Samson stressed Onyango's priority on education, obedience and cleanliness:

'Onyango used to prepare a meal for me at [his] home. He was very keen on education, on [Barack] Obama getting an education. Onyango was keen like a white man; he knew how to be organised like a white man. He was working for the whites in Nairobi, so when he came back here, he was calling himself a white man. And he wanted his son to go to school and get a good education.

'He was a very harsh man as well. He would not allow Obama to joke with school. He wanted Obama to study and become a good man in the future. Sometimes Obama would hang around because he didn't want to go to school, so Onyango would bang everything! "You've not gone to school yet and you are still here! Wake up and go to school." And he would chase him to school.

'Mr Onyango was a "British man", a British-African man. His working style and his wearing style, he wanted to imitate the British, and speak like the British. Mr Onyango had his six lower teeth removed like any other Luo man. But he wanted to impress, so he went and had artificial teeth, so that he could smile.

'He was a very clean man. Even his home – he was a very clean man.
He wanted things to be organised. I know Onyango was a very harsh person.
If you did not do things properly, he became hot and very angry!'

Even though Hussein Onyango was keen on educating his sons, he was a
traditional African at heart and he put less emphasis on the education of
girls. After all, so the reasoning went, why spend good money on educating
your daughters if they were only going to leave home and become part of
another family? So neither Sarah Nyaoke nor Hawa Auma went to school,
and to this day Auma cannot read or write. In 1948 Onyango donated land
adjacent to his compound to build the first primary school in K'ogelo, and
a secondary school was later built there in 1968, with money partly donated
by Barack Snr.

Some African families however, were more progressive about schooling
girls, and their daughters had the benefit of at least a primary education.
One such local girl was Magdalene Otin, who went to school with Barack
Obama. I met her purely by chance, when I was looking to find somebody
who was still living in a traditional Luo roundhouse. There were several
museum examples in both Kisumu and Nairobi, but I was keen to see a
real, working example. However, because the modern trend is to build
square huts in brick a genuine traditional mud-walled roundhouse was
something of a rarity – their fragile construction means that they seldom
last more than thirty years. After many enquiries in and around K'ogelo, I
was eventually directed to Magdalene's hut, which was a short walk from
the dirt road that led into the village; eventually, after some searching, I
found her house hidden among trees and fields of tall maize.

Magdalene couldn't remember how long she had lived there, but she
told me it was 'a very long time'; her hut must have been at least fifty years
old. Inside there was a thick inner mud wall running like a doughnut; in
the centre of the hut – the 'hole' in the doughnut – there was a small table
and several chairs where she entertained her guests. Between the interior
doughnut walls and the outer walls of the hut was a small, private space
which provided a tiny sleeping area, plus dry storage for grain in one area,
and a place for her chickens in another. The birds obviously felt comfort-
ably at home, as they wandered in and out all the time, constantly in search
of something to peck; despite the birds, Magdalene's home was spotless.
She had few other personal possessions, except for a dozen framed family
portraits – her husband was long dead, as were seven of her eight children.

Magdalene was tiny, frail and shy. She didn't know how old she was, but she did remember when Barack Obama Snr went to school in Ng'iya, so she was probably in her mid-seventies, although a lifetime in the fields had made her look very much older. The first three times I visited Magdalene she was reluctant to open up; she seemed overwhelmed by the attention of a *mzungu*, and she was unsure of herself, not wanting to speak out of turn or inappropriately. On my second visit she insisted on cooking me a meal of boiled chicken and *ugali*, a traditional dish of maize flour cooked to a thick dough. In the way of Luo women, Magdalene served her guests (all of them men), but did not eat herself. Instead she gently berated us for not eating enough, and kept piling more food on our plates; she then sat opposite with the other womenfolk from the compound, and watched us eat.

It was on my fourth visit that Magdalene finally opened up, and she started to talk about her past:

'I grew up with Obama. Barack loved school – he attended school regularly, and this was because his father was very strict and would not allow him to stay at home. Obama liked football – most African children like football. But he would come home early, not like the other children who did not come back until late. He had to put the cows back in the pen – they couldn't be left out late. If they are rained on badly they get sick, and we didn't have the drugs for them that we have today.'

I asked her what life was like in K'ogelo back in the late 1940s:

'In those days the population was very small, and the trees were very tall and bushy. We had to meander through the trees to go anywhere. There were leopards and hyenas and all the other animals you talk about. And many snakes. I was very much afraid of the hyenas in those days. They are gluttons – I think they're worse than leopards. We could only fetch water in the mornings because they chased us later in the day. They go for the buttocks of humans, as this is the bit that's fat and soft. Even recently, what hyenas do is incredible. The drunken men fall down at night, and they come home without a face or any buttocks! So our children are very much afraid of going outside.'

I asked her if the animals were still dangerous today:

'It's the leopards which have killed most of our children. They took two children here just a couple of years ago. They go up in trees, and jump

on them when they're going to school. They twist your neck and you're
dead. If the hyenas kill you, they will eat you right there, but the leopards
will always drag you away to a safe distance.'

After his primary schooling in Ng'iya, in 1950 Barack Snr sat for what was
then called the Kenya African Preliminary Examination. This was a selection exam based on the British education system, which was designed to
identify the brightest African students for admission to secondary school.
Barack Snr passed the exam, and he easily exceeded the standard required
to gain admission to the prestigious Maseno High School, which was, and
still is, one of the top boarding schools in Kenya. The Maseno school lies
almost equidistant between K'ogelo and the main town, Kisumu; the school
was established in 1906 by the Church Mission Society (CMS), and it is
the second oldest secondary school in Kenya. Presumably Onyango had
no religious objection to sending Barack to a Christian school, even though
he was raising his son as a Muslim. Maseno was primarily founded by the
CMS as part of the initiative by the British to tutor the sons of local chiefs,
thereby creating an educated elite to work for the colonial administration.
Today, the school looks much like any provincial English boarding school
from the 1930s, except for the *tumbili* (vervet monkeys) playing around the
roofs of the classrooms, and the simple black-and-white painted sign on
the main driveway which tells visitors that they are about to cross the
equator from the southern hemisphere to the north.

The cost of sending Barack to Maseno was substantially more than
Onyango had to pay at Ng'iya primary school, but education was always
one of his main priorities; like parents the world over, Onyango and Sarah
struggled to find the money for their son to go to a fee-paying school.
Despite being a practising Muslim, Sarah decided the best way to earn
some much-needed extra cash was to brew *chang'aa* for sale to the neighbours. It was a nice little earner until Onyango came home one afternoon
and discovered her fermentation vats. He was furious – he tipped them
over and refused to allow Sarah to continue her home brewing; instead,
she resorted to the less profitable trade of making chapattis for sale to her
neighbours to support Barack's schooling.

In 1951, Barack's second year at Maseno, the headmaster, an Englishman
by the name of A. W. Mayor, was replaced by B. L. Bowers. Bowers stayed
at the school until 1969 – the longest serving principal in the history of Maseno.
Even by the standards of the early 1950s, Bowers had a reputation for
strictness, and he would ultimately prove to be the young Barack's nemesis.

However, for the first couple of years, Barack excelled. The journalist Leo
Odera was one of Barack Snr's old friends and drinking companions, and
he recalled Barack's achievements at school:

> 'Barack had a very excellent record in form one, form two and form three.
> He was top in mathematics, English, and almost every subject. But his
> personal conduct from the end of form three was not so excellent; academ-
> ically he was OK, but he became difficult. From being the person at the
> top of the class, he became arrogant and rude to the teachers.'

The student records at Maseno go back to 1906, and the administrators
retain the reports of every boy who has passed through the school since it
opened. Barack Obama Snr's records are kept securely in a safe in the principal's office, rather than in the school archives. The documents are concise
to the point of pithiness – the principals of the day were certainly not guilty
of verbosity in their annual reports. Obama Snr's fading brown card, index
number 3422, explains that Barack was a bright boy and had been promoted
from Class B to A. In graceful handwriting, Bowers notes that the young
Obama was: 'very keen, steady, trustworthy and friendly. Concentrates, reliable and out-going.' It was a good report, but things started to go downhill
soon after that.

By the time Obama reached form three at Maseno, he was seventeen
years old and his attitude towards the staff and discipline at the school
began to change. Sarah Obama recalls that he was rebellious – he began
to sneak girls into the dormitories and he would raid the nearby farms with
his friends, stealing chickens and yams because the school food was not
very appetising. However, Leo Odera maintains that there was a much
more complicated story about what happened in Barack Snr's final year at
the school, which ultimately led to his downfall:

> 'As he was moving to senior classes, he became rude and arrogant. He did
> not like to do the manual work, like when the boys were clearing the bush
> or working the plough. He hated this work, and this developed friction
> between him and the principal. Because at the school, the work was done
> communally and collectively. The teacher may assign you [the task] to go
> and clear an area of the school where grass was overgrown, but Barack
> didn't like doing these things.
>
> 'At Maseno, when Obama Snr was in form three and progressing well
> as one of the top students, something strange happened. Some of the senior

boys wrote a nasty letter, accusing and outlining some serious grievances the students had about the school administration. The letter was anonymous and unsigned. But because Barack Obama Snr had been identified as the cleverest boy and politically minded, he became the prime suspect.

'The principal – a white Anglican missionary from the UK – was furious, and so was the board of governors. The school authority then threatened to invite the dreaded Special Branch Police – this is what the directorate of security intelligence was called.

'Obama Snr got wind that he was to be investigated, and that handwriting experts had been summoned to the school to come and examine the offensive letter. So Obama left the school voluntarily – he was never expelled as such – but opted out of his own volition, leaving behind the belief by the other students that he'd had a hand in the authorship of the offending letter.'

Barack would have been wise to have heeded the Luo proverb, *Kudho chwoyo ng'ama onyone* – A thorn only pricks the one who steps on it.

Hussein Onyango was furious with his son; after all, he and Sarah had saved every penny they had to give him the best education that was available to a black student in Kenya at the time, and he had thrown the opportunity away. Onyango's response was predictable – he beat Barack with a stick until his back bled; still angry, he effectively threw him out by sending him to work in Mombasa with the parting words, 'I will see how you enjoy yourself, earning your own meals.'[2] Barack had no choice but to obey his father and he left for Mombasa immediately.

Meanwhile, political and civil unrest had been brewing across the protectorate for several years, and Kenya was about to suffer one of the most deeply shocking and violent decades that any British colony has ever experienced. The 1950s were dominated by the Mau Mau insurgency – a brutal and violent grass-roots rebellion by Africans against white colonial rule. Like many such revolts in history, it started slowly. Ever since the 1920s there had been growing resentment among Africans over the way the white settlers had forced labour rates down, and over the much reviled *kipande* – the identity card which was introduced after the First World War, without which no African could gain employment. (The white settlers frequently punished badly behaved workers by tearing up their *kipande*, thereby denying them the opportunity to find work elsewhere.)

The early 1920s had also seen the emergence of African political groups such as the Young Kikuyu Association led by Harry Thuku, and the Young Kavirondo Association, founded by the Luos of Nyanza. However, the colonial government soon became concerned about what they considered to be 'seditious' activities by the leaders of these organisations. On 14 March 1922 Harry Thuku was arrested in Nairobi and exiled for eight years, without charge or trial. Within two days of Thuku's arrest, between seven and eight thousand of his supporters protested outside the police station in Nairobi where he was detained. The police, armed with rifles and fixed bayonets, attempted to control the crowd; stones were thrown, shots were fired, and the crowd panicked. The official report into the incident claimed that twenty-one Africans were killed, including four women. Unofficial reports from staff at the mortuary suggest that fifty-six bodies were brought in. It was the first violent political protest in Kenya's history, but it was only a foretaste of worse things to come, and the killings only added to the growing resentment among Africans that they had no representation in the governance of their own country.

In Luoland, the Young Kavirondo Association was set up by a teacher called Jonathan Okwiri in the same year. Among other things, they also called for the abolition of the infamous *kipande*, a reduction in hut and poll tax, an increase in wages, and the abolition of forced labour.[3] The colonial administration was alarmed at the demands of the group, but they used less confrontational means to control the movement. They persuaded the Young Kavirondo Association to make W. E. Owen, the Anglican Archdeacon of Kavirondo, their president; the authorities claimed that he would make an excellent intermediary to negotiate with the colonial government. Instead, Owen subverted their political initiatives and persuaded the group to focus on non-political issues such as better housing, food and hygiene. He even convinced the group to change its name to the Kavirondo Taxpayers Welfare Association; it was a master stroke, succeeding in making what was once a grass-roots activist movement utterly impotent.

In the 1930s the issue of land ownership became an even bigger problem. The seeds of resentment were sown in 1902, when the first white settlers claimed the most fertile hills around Nairobi. Within three decades the settler farms had grown in size and fences were beginning to enclose them. This exacerbated the land shortage problem for the Africans, and especially for the Kikuyu of central Kenya. The historian Professor David Anderson claims that by the 1930s the issue of land had become *the* crucial political grievance.[4] Anderson calls it 'the tyranny of property', and this only fuelled

the Africans' sense of injustice. Attempts by the Kikuyu to organise themselves politically continued to be thwarted. The banned Young Kikuyu
Association was replaced by a new political organisation called the Kikuyu
Central Association, but this too was banned in 1941 when the colonial
government clamped down on African dissent during the Second World War.

Between 1939 and 1945 the colony was put on a war footing and Kenya's
northern border with Ethiopia and Somaliland was threatened by the presence of Italian troops; it was this campaign that took Hussein Onyango
briefly to Addis Ababa. As the war came to a close, so the colonial government turned its attention to improving political representation for Africans,
and in 1944 Kenya became the first East African territory to include an
African on its Legislative Council. The government progressively increased
the number of local representatives to eight by 1951, although none of them
was elected; instead, they were appointed by the governor from a list of
names submitted by the local authorities. Not surprisingly, this did not
satisfy African demands for either political equality or democracy. Nor was
the injustice of land ownership being addressed: in 1948, 1.25 million Kikuyu
were restricted to living on just 5,200 square kilometres of farmland, whereas
30,000 white settlers occupied six times as much space.[5] Inevitably, the
most fertile land was almost entirely in the hands of the colonists.

The Kikuyu's political leader was Jomo Kenyatta. Kenyatta had lived in
Britain throughout most of the 1930s, studying anthropology at London
University and also travelling to other European countries as well as the Soviet
Union. During his time abroad, he married an English woman called Edna
Clarke, who became his second wife. In September 1946 he returned to Kenya,
shortly to become president of the newly formed Kenya African Union (KAU)
and the leading advocate for a peaceful transition to African majority rule.
The KAU had been established in 1944 to articulate local grievances against
the colonial administration, but it attempted to be more politically inclusive
than the banned Kikuyu Central Association (KCA) by trying to avoid tribal
politics. Nevertheless, the KAU progressively fell under Kikuyu domination
and it was generally regarded as little more than a reincarnation of the outlawed
KCA. Kenyatta had a powerful, domineering personality, and this was resented
by some of the political leaders, and especially by the Luo from Nyanza.[6] This
was just the beginning of the deep-rooted problem of tribalism in Kenyan
politics which would eventually plunge the country into turmoil.

There were others, however, especially among the Kikuyu, who thought
that Kenyatta's approach was not producing results quickly enough. The
land issue had resulted in thousands of Kikuyu migrating into towns

and cities in search of work; as a consequence, Nairobi's population doubled between 1938 and 1952. The result was increasing poverty, rising unemployment, and a growing problem of urban overpopulation.

During the late 1940s the general council of the banned KCA began a campaign of civil disobedience in protest over the land issue. Members of the secret group took traditional ritual oaths, which had the effect of strengthening their commitment to the group; the militants believed that if they broke their oaths, they would be killed by supernatural forces. These oathing rituals often included the sacrifice of animals or drinking animal blood. By 1950, what had begun as a peaceful movement to organise civil disobedience was getting out of hand. Rumours circulated that members of the group indulged in cannibalism, bestiality with goats, and wild orgies, and that the ritual oaths included a commitment to kill, dismember and burn white settlers. (Whilst many of these stories were either untrue or greatly exaggerated, they helped to convince the British government to send troops out to Kenya in 1952 to support the colonists.)

By 1950, Nairobi had become a fertile recruiting ground for the militants. The genteel colonial city of whitewashed government offices and luxury hotels was gradually becoming surrounded by squalid shanties and seedy slums as more and more landless Africans moved into the city. With few jobs and fewer opportunities, the temptation to drift into petty crime was irresistible for many; in the absence of an effective police force, criminal gangs began to control the poor estates and street crime, robbery, smuggling and protection rackets increased alarmingly. As is so often the case, though, it was the impoverished African who was most likely to be the victim of crime, rather than the wealthy white colonials. It was the Kikuyu gangs who controlled the slums, and by early 1950 the Nairobi-based urban militants known as the Muhimu started to organise mass oathings throughout central Kenya. There were plenty of guns and ammunition in the colony, brought back by the 75,000 Africans who served in the King's African Rifles during the war, and the Muhimu set about collecting whatever weapons they could find, in preparation for what they saw as an inevitable armed struggle to free themselves from colonial rule.

Nobody is really quite sure how the name Mau Mau came to be used to describe the insurgents who set themselves on a course of violence to achieve independence from the British. The Kikuyu never used the name to describe themselves, and some argue that the moniker was invented by the white settlers themselves to ridicule the rebellion; some maintain the name refers to the mountains in the Rift Valley where the rebellious

Kikuyu took refuge during the hostilities; whilst others claim it is an acronym for *Mzungu aende ulaya – mwafrica apate uhuru*, which loosely translated from Swahili means 'The white man should return to Europe – the African should gain freedom.'[7]

Mau Mau was a conflict both between the Kikuyu and the white colonists, and among the Kikuyu themselves. It was the Kikuyu who had suffered most from the confiscation of their land by the white settlers, and most of the violence occurred in the 'White Highlands' and the Rift Valley, the traditional home of the Kikuyu. However, the general state of unrest in the late 1940s and early 50s had an unsettling effect throughout the colony, and in Nyanza the repercussions of the violence had a knock-on effect which involved even Hussein Onyango.

In *Dreams from My Father*, President Obama relates the story told to him by his step-grandmother Sarah, of how Hussein Onyango was arrested during the early years of the Mau Mau insurrection. Like many Luo in Nyanza, Onyango went to political meetings where there was much talk of independence. Although he believed *in principle* that independence was a good thing for the colony, he was sceptical whether it was really possible. Onyango warned his son, Barack Snr, that it was unlikely that anything would come of the initiative:

> 'How can the African defeat the white man when he cannot even make his own bicycle?' he would say to Barack. 'The white man alone is like an ant. He can easily be crushed. But like an ant, the white man works together. His nation, his business – these things are more important to him than himself. He will follow the leadership and not question orders. Black men are not like this. Even the most foolish black man thinks he knows better than the wise man. That is why the black man will always lose.'[8]

Onyango was not particularly strongly motivated politically and in many ways he was a great admirer of the British. Yet despite his loyalty and long service to the British going back thirty years, he was arrested and interned during the early years of the troubles. In 1949 Onyango was accused of being a subversive by a local chief who harboured a long-standing grudge against him. This was before Mau Mau really became a serious threat to the colonial government, but the first rumblings of dissent were beginning to be heard from underground groups. Onyango's accuser, so Sarah Obama claims, had been cheating people by charging them excessive taxes and then pocketing the surplus for himself. This was not an unusual practice, as these local chiefs wielded wide-ranging powers once they were put in a position of authority by the British. According to Sarah, Onyango had challenged the man over his embezzlement, and the chief waited for a chance to take his revenge. Sarah maintains that he accused Onyango of being a supporter of the rebels, and her husband was arrested and taken away to a detention camp. The penal regime set up in the camps to deal with those suspected of supporting the Mau Mau was brutal, and Sarah claims that Onyango sustained regular beatings at the hands of his keepers:

> 'The African warders were instructed by the white soldiers to whip him every morning and evening until he confessed . . . He said they would sometimes squeeze his testicles with parallel metallic rods. They also pierced his nails and buttocks with a sharp pin, with his hands and legs tied together with his head facing down . . . That was the time we realised that the British were actually not friends but, instead, enemies. My husband had worked so diligently for them, only to be arrested and detained.'[9]

Nobody can be absolutely sure who it was that accused Hussein Onyango of supporting Mau Mau, and Sarah Obama does not name him. However, the finger points most likely to Chief Paul Mboya from Kendu Bay. Onyango had been at loggerheads with Mboya ever since Mboya had been appointed chief in central Karachunyo around 1935, and Obama had certainly taken him to task over recruiting forced labour, so there was no love lost between the two men. Perhaps Mboya thought that he had at last extracted his revenge on Onyango for constantly challenging his authority in Kendu Bay.

Whoever was responsible, it was a traumatic period for Onyango. He was held in custody for over six months, and he would certainly have been interrogated by the British Special Branch, which in those early years were desperate to find out as much as they could about the emerging Mau Mau movement. Onyango was, however, ultimately cleared of all charges and released. He returned home a broken man – thin, dirty, with a head full of lice, and permanently scarred from his beatings in the detention centre. From that day, Sarah Obama claims, Onyango became an old man.

By the middle of 1951 information was beginning to filter back to the colonial government that secret Mau Mau meetings were being held in the forests outside Nairobi. In early 1952 there were arson attacks against white farmers in Nanyuki and also against government chiefs in Nyeri, both important towns in the White Highlands. However, attacks on the white settlers were rare, and the main violence was directed against other Africans who were seen as being 'loyal' to the whites. In this respect, the Mau Mau insurrection was as much an internal conflict – a civil war where African turned on his fellow African – as it was a struggle for independence against the colonial powers. Certainly, it was the black African who suffered infinitely more than the white colonials.

In one example, Mutuaro Onsoti, a Luo from the Kisii area of south Nyanza, was murdered by Mau Mau.[10] Onsoti had been employed by a white farmer, James Kean, to help him control the disruption caused on his farm by his Kikuyu squatter labourers. In May 1952, Onsoti told his employer that he suspected that Mau Mau activists were plotting to take over his farm. Kean was concerned about the safety of his foreman after this revelation, but to no avail; on 25 August Onsoti was brutally attacked by four Kikuyu squatters. His decapitated body was exhumed from the woods on the following day, but his head was never recovered.

In October 1952 Governor-General Sir Evelyn Baring cabled London to request that a state of emergency be declared in the colony. This would allow the governor special powers to detain suspects, to deploy the military, and to impose other laws without further reference to London. The Colonial Office was loath to devolve such power to the Kenyan government, which had a reputation for being reactionary and unpredictable. However, Whitehall reluctantly granted his request on 14 October and Baring began his preparations to declare a state of emergency, which involved rounding up KAU activists and suspected Mau Mau leaders in an operation code-named Operation Jock Scott. Many senior officials in the KAU had no association with Mau Mau at all, but Baring was convinced this would stop the insurrection in its tracks.

Not everybody was quite so confident that Baring's plan for the screening and internment of suspected Mau Mau sympathisers would be successful. One of the more thoughtful and insightful white highlanders drafted a memorandum to the Govenor:

It is obviously illogical that any person of European extraction could, by
looking at an African and examining his papers, know whether or not he has
Mau Mau inclinations ... The methods adopted so far usually culminate
in a parade of Kikuyu, and any that can produce a current hut-tax receipt
and an employment card, or appear to be unaggressive, are released. Others

who cannot produce these documents are frequently detained, and more often than not a proportion of these quite decent people are forced into close association with criminals and taken off to some detention camp. These decent people, or any of them who are in a state of indecision, immediately build up the utmost contempt for the methods of law and order, and are ripe for Mau Mau allegiance, either now or when released from detention.[11]

A week after the state of emergency was declared, the Lancashire Fusiliers were flown in from Egypt to supplement three battalions of the King's African Rifles who were recalled from abroad. The authorities were still lacking in any good-quality intelligence about the militants, so when hostilities began in earnest in 1952 the colonial forces struck out blindly to suppress the violence. It was the beginning of a brutal period of repression which would permanently change the image of Kenya as a paradise for the white colonials. In the words of the historian David Anderson:

> Before Mau Mau, Kenya had an entirely different image. In the iconography of the British imperial endeavour, it was the land of sunshine, gin slings and smiling, obedient servants, where the industrious white colonizer could enjoy a temperate life of peace and plenty in a tropical land. This was 'white man's country', with its rolling, fertile highlands. Sturdy settler farmers had made their homes here, building a little piece of England in a foreign field . . . Mau Mau shattered this patronizing pretence in the most poignant, disturbing manner, as trusted servants turned on their masters and slaughtered them.[12]

News of the intended arrests under the emergency powers leaked out; this allowed time for the real revolutionaries to flee to their forest refuges in the Aberdare Mountains, whilst the moderates stayed put and awaited their fate. Jomo Kenyatta was considered by many Africans to be a moderate leader, but he failed to unambiguously denounce Mau Mau violence to the satisfaction of the colonial government. Kenyatta knew exactly what to expect; he was arrested on 18 November 1952 and flown to a remote district station in Kapenguria, which reportedly had no telephone or rail communications with the rest of Kenya. He was charged, together with five other Kikuyu leaders, with 'managing and being a member' of Mau Mau. They became known as the 'Kapenguria Six', and their trial lasted for fifty-nine days – the longest and most sensational trial in British colonial history. The main prosecution witness, a Kikuyu called Rawson Mbugua Macharia, claimed that he had taken a Mau Mau oath in the presence of Kenyatta. (Macharia was the only witness at the trial to give evidence that linked Kenyatta with Mau Mau directly, yet in 1958 he swore an affidavit that he and six others had perjured themselves, and that some of them had been rewarded with land for their testimony.) For security reasons there was no jury at the trial, and the British judge was paid £20,000 (£700,000 adjusted for 2010 prices) to come out from Britain to put Kenyatta behind bars – many claim it was a bribe to gain Kenyatta's conviction. In April 1953 Kenyatta was found guilty and sentenced to seven years' imprisonment with hard labour, and indefinite restriction thereafter; his subsequent appeal the following year was refused by the British Privy Council.

The consequences that the emergency brought to the ordinary Kikuyu are almost impossible to conceive. Large bands of Mau Mau fighters freely moved around their bases in the highland forests of the Aberdare Mountains and Mount Kenya, attacking isolated police posts and terrorising and killing Africans loyal to the white settlers. A typical group of insurgents numbered about a hundred; they operated mainly at night and took refuge in the forest during the day. Some of them had learned the art of guerrilla fighting during the war, when they fought with the British army against the Japanese in the Burmese jungle, and this made them very effective combatants.

On 24 January 1953 two British settlers, Roger and Esme Ruck, together with their six-year-old son Michael, were hacked to death by Mau Mau fighters on their isolated farm in Kinangop, together with one of their farm workers who came to their assistance. The Rucks were a hard-working and respected farming couple in their early thirties, and they played an active role in the community. Esme Ruck ran a clinic on their farm, where she treated squatters in the area free of charge; her husband was a member of the Kenya Police Reserve. They were the embodiment of everything that white settlers held dear in post-war Kenya.

Panic immediately spread among the white community and the Rucks' murder became a turning point in the war for the colonials, who demanded that the government should toughen its response to the crisis. The day after the murders, white Kenyans massed outside Government House, calling for the cordon of 'nigger police' who were holding the crowd at bay to be taken away. Some demonstrators even stubbed their cigarettes out on the arms of the black constables in an attempt to break through the police line. Sir Michael Blundell was the acknowledged leader of the settler community in Kenya at the time, and he was in a crisis meeting inside Government House with the governor-general. Blundell came out to try and pacify the crowd, and was shocked by their mood:

> This was my first experience of men and women who had momentarily lost all control of themselves and had become merged together as an insensate unthinking mass. I can see now individual pictures of the scene – a man with a beard and a strong foreign accent clutching his pistol as he shouted and raved; another with a quiet scholarly intellectual face, whom I knew to be a musician and a scientist, was crouched down by the terrace, twitching all over and swirling with a cascade of remarkable and blistering words, while an occasional fleck of foam came from his mouth.[13]

The white settlers inevitably reacted strongly to the security situation. It was only some days after the Rucks' murder that it became clear that their killers had been employed by them for several years – loyal workers who had suddenly turned and butchered them without warning. The outcome was that long-standing relationships and friendships between black and white could no longer be trusted. White settlers, including women, armed themselves with any weapon they could lay their hands on, and they fortified their farms as best as they could. Some of the farmers dismissed their Kikuyu staff because nobody could tell Mau Mau sympathisers from loyal servants.

Only a week before the brutal murders in Kinangop, Governor-General Sir Evelyn Baring had sanctioned the death penalty for anyone caught administering the Mau Mau oath. (The oath, however, was often forced upon Kikuyu tribesmen at the point of a knife, and they were threatened with death if they failed to kill a European farmer when ordered.) Now, these first few months of 1953 saw a new offensive by the authorities on Mau Mau; hundreds of suspects were killed and thousands arrested on suspicion of being members of the insurgency. At the height of the crisis over 70,000 Mau Mau supporters were held in British detention camps, and throughout the eight years of conflict at least 150,000 Africans, perhaps more, spent some time in detention, including Hussein Onyango and his son Barack Snr. (In her controversial book on Mau Mau, historian Caroline Elkins claims the number of Africans detained was much greater than the official British figures, anywhere between 160,000 and 320,000.)[14]

On 26 March 1953, Mau Mau demonstrated that they were a force with which to be reckoned. In response to the declaration of emergency and the mass round-up of KAU officials and Mau Mau suspects, the insurgents sought revenge – not on the whites, but on the Kikuyu themselves. That evening, a patrol in the town of Lari was called to investigate a body; they found the mutilated remains of a local man nailed to a tree – he was known to be loyal to the British. His body had obviously been left there with the intention of being found; it was a trap, and the Home Guard had been lured away from the town. When they returned, they found that nearly a thousand Mau Mau fighters had attacked the settlement.

The Mau Mau insurgents were well prepared, and they were organised into four or five gangs numbering over a hundred men each. The gangs had systematically moved through the unprotected homesteads of Lari, killing and mutilating as they went. They tied ropes around the huts to prevent the occupants from opening their doors, before setting fire to the thatched roofs. As the occupants struggled to escape through the windows, they were butchered from outside. The Home Guard patrol reached Lari at 10 p.m., just as the attackers had finished their gruesome work; over 120 people were killed or seriously injured – mostly women and children. No other attack by the Mau Mau during the emergency had the same terrifying impact on public opinion.

At first, the killings were thought to be random, but it soon became clear that the heads of those households which were attacked were loyal to the British – members of the Home Guard, local chiefs, councillors, and those who were outspoken critics of Mau Mau. The following night a police outpost near Naivasha in the Rift Valley was also attacked; three black policemen were killed and the Mau Mau rebels released 173 suspects and captured 50 rifles and 25 machine guns, together with a large quantity of ammunition. The attacks changed the way Africans viewed the conflict, and it became clear to the ordinary Kikuyu that they were now embroiled in a civil war as Mau Mau inflicted a reign of terror on their own people.

As with the murder of Mutuaro Onsoti, the Luo foreman from Kisii, these murders by Mau Mau were often particularly brutal, and intended to terrorise the population. One district officer reported that: 'There was one murder of an old man at Ruathia; he was chopped in two halves because he had given evidence against the Mau Mau in court . . . and down by the river below Gituge we found the corpse of an African Court Process Server who had likewise been strangled for informing against the Mau Mau.'[15] Many Christian Kikuyu refused to take the Mau Mau oath, because they believed that taking the blood of a goat was blasphemous;

this left them vulnerable to attack. One Mau Mau fighter recalled that: 'We generally left the Christians alone. But if they informed on us, we would kill them and sometimes cut out their tongue. We had no choice.'[16]

During the emergency, over 1,800 Kenyan civilians are known to have been murdered by Mau Mau; hundreds more disappeared and their bodies were never found.[17]

History so often shows that brutality begets brutality, and the British authorities were also guilty of carnage, especially during the 'screening' process that was designed to isolate the hard-core Mau Mau supporters from innocent Kikuyus rounded up in error. The interrogation process was designed to terrorise the Mau Mau supporters, first by breaking the spirit of the detainees, and then by making them confess. Onyango had endured a similar procedure when he was arrested in 1949, but the techniques now used by some of the colonial authorities were very much more brutal. In her book on the insurrection, Elkins assembled damning evidence of extensive human rights abuses:

> Teams made up of settlers, British district officers, members of the Kenya police force, African loyalists, and even soldiers from the British military forces demanded confessions and intelligence, and used torture to get them ... electric shock was widely used, as well as cigarettes and fire. Bottles (often broken), gun barrels, knives, snakes, vermin and hot eggs were thrust up men's rectums and women's vaginas. The screening teams whipped, shot, burned and mutilated Mau Mau suspects, ostensibly to gather intelligence for military operations and as court evidence.[18]

At least one detainee had his testicles cut off and was then made to eat them. 'Things got a little out of hand,' one witness told Elkins when referring to another incident. 'By the time we cut his balls off he had no ears, and his eyeball, the right one, I think, was hanging out of its socket. Too bad, he died before we got much out of him.'[19] Another British officer described, with remarkable openness, his exasperation with an uncooperative suspect during an interrogation:

> 'They wouldn't say a thing, of course, and one of them, a tall coal-black bastard, kept grinning at me, real insolent. I slapped him hard, but he kept right on grinning at me, so I kicked him in the balls as hard as I could. He went down in a heap but when he finally got up on his feet he grinned at me again and I snapped, I really did. I stuck my revolver right in his

grinning mouth and I said something, I don't remember what, and I pulled the trigger. His brains went all over the side of the police station. The other two Mickeys [Mau Mau] were standing there looking blank. I said to them that if they didn't tell me where to find the rest of the gang I'd kill them too. They didn't say a word so I shot them both. One wasn't dead so I shot him in the ear. When the sub-inspector drove up, I told him that the Mickeys tried to escape. He didn't believe me but all he said was, "Bury them and see the wall is cleared up."[20]

In the early hours of the morning of 21 October 1956, four years to the day after a state of emergency was declared in Kenya, the insurgent leader Dedan Kimathi Waciuri was shot and captured as he tried to break out of his forest hideout near the town of Nyeri – a Mau Mau hotspot. Kimathi's capture and subsequent execution by hanging marked the end of the forest war against the Mau Mau.

The official number of casualties among the European settlers during Mau Mau was 32 dead and 26 wounded, and British records claim that 11,503 Kenyans were killed. However, David Anderson maintains the real number was likely to be more than 20,000. Caroline Elkins has controversially estimated that at least 70,000 Kikuyu died, and argues that the number could run to hundreds of thousands, although this figure has been challenged as being based on unsound statistics. The demographer John Blacker has more recently estimated the total number of African deaths to be around 50,000, half of whom were children under the age of ten.[21] The real figure will never be known with any certainty, but it must surely run into tens of thousands of Kenyans – most of them innocent civilians.

There is little doubt that the very worst of the atrocities committed by the British and white Kenyans were limited to a small number of people, as indeed was the case within the Kikuyu population. For the most part, the white community struggled to maintain law and order during a very difficult, violent and uncertain period in Kenya's history. Nevertheless, many people in a position of power were guilty of turning a blind eye to the many acts of violence by members of the white community against black Kenyans during the Mau Mau rebellion, making the decade one of the most shameful and inglorious episodes in British colonial history.

A rare photograph of Barack Obama Snr with his ten-year-old son. It was probably taken at Honolulu airport in December 1971.

8

MR 'DOUBLE-DOUBLE'

Kapod in epi to kik iyany nyang'
Don't abuse the crocodile when you're still in the
water

**From 1953, when Barack Obama Snr left Maseno school,
to 1982, when he died in a road accident in Nairobi,
including his four marriages**

The world changed in 1953.

On 7 January President Truman ushered in the New Year by announcing that the United States had developed a hydrogen bomb. When Dwight D. Eisenhower took presidential office later that month, he kept up the pressure on the Soviet Union by making nuclear weapons a higher priority. In June, Julius and Ethel Rosenberg were executed in New York's Sing Sing Correction Facility, having been found guilty of spying for the USSR. The Cold War was about to get a lot cooler.

In the Soviet Union, Joseph Stalin collapsed and died from a haemorrhagic stroke, and he was replaced as First Secretary of the Soviet Communist Party by Nikita Khrushchev. On 8 August Soviet Prime Minister Georgy Malenkov announced that the USSR had also developed an H-bomb, and four days later they carried out their first test. Code-named RDS-6, it was thirty times more powerful than the crude atomic bomb dropped by the Americans on Hiroshima.

In the United Kingdom, Elizabeth walked up the aisle of Westminster

Abbey on 2 June a princess, and walked out a queen. Britain was, at last, emerging from the privation of the Second World War; Everest had been conquered by a British-led climbing team, the country was experiencing full employment, and its citizens were enjoying the benefits of their new National Health Service. But the country would never regain the global status it had enjoyed before the war, and over the next two decades the UK started to come to terms with its lost empire as it moved into a new era during which its colonies would gain their independence.

One of Britain's colonies in particular – Kenya – was in turmoil by mid-1953, as the government there tried to suppress the Mau Mau rebellion. A state of emergency had been declared the previous year, and on 25 March 1953, over 120 innocent Kikuyu civilians were slaughtered in the town of Lari. The rift between the white colonial community in Kenya and the Home Office in London would inexorably lead to Kenyan independence within a decade.

It was into this maelstrom of events, both at home and abroad, that Barack Obama Snr launched himself into the real world. He had decided that he must leave Maseno school, fearing that he might be linked to the anonymous letter sent to the principal. In his fury and disappointment with his son, Hussein Onyango banished him to work in Mombasa, where he was initially placed with an Arab trader and expected to make his own way in the world. However, the relationship did not flourish, and Barack left his employer without even asking to be paid. After working briefly as a clerk in another office in Mombasa, Barack moved to Nairobi. This was a period of real tension between Barack and his father; Onyango had suffered the indignity and pain of internment, and now he watched as his son seemed to fritter his life away – he had told Barack to leave his house, as he had brought shame to his father.

When Barack arrived in Nairobi in 1955, he was nineteen years old, and he found a temporary job working for the Kenya Railway. This was still at the height of the Mau Mau emergency, and Nairobi was a hotbed of polit-ical action. Barack began to take an interest in politics, and one evening the following year he was attending a Kenya African Union meeting that was raided by the police. He was among those arrested and charged with violating the meeting law – the KAU had been declared illegal in 1953 as part of the emergency powers granted to the colonial government. Onyango was again furious with his son, and refused to pay his bail. According to his friend Leo Odera, Barack was briefly detained by the British colonial police, but he was later released after his white employer in Nairobi gave the authorities reassurance that his social and political activities were unconnected with Mau Mau.

It was when he was living in Nairobi that Barack Obama Snr became a regular visitor to Kendu Bay. After all, his father was angry with him and thought he was a failure, so it was best not to be around the homestead too much. Besides, even today, K'ogelo is a quiet and remote village – in the mid-1950s, it must have seemed like the end of the world for a restless teenager with an eye for the girls. So Barack preferred to spend time in Kendu Bay, rather than with his family in K'ogelo.

Leo Odera recalled how Barack Snr met his first wife: 'In Nairobi, Barack Obama Snr became a frequent visitor to his Kanyadhiang' roots, and here is when he came into contact with two young girls, whom he had known whilst learning at Gendia SDA Mission [primary school]. One of the girls was called Mical Anyango, daughter of Mr Joram Osano, a local pastor. The other girl was the seventeen-year-old Kezia Nyandega.'

Today, Kezia is a sixty-eight-year-old grandmother living in a modest semi-detached house in Bracknell, a commuter town 25km west of central London. She remembers clearly the place and day of her first dance with Obama Snr – it was in the local hall in the Obamas' family compound in Kendu Bay, and the date was Christmas Day 1956: 'It was at a dance in Kendu Bay, my home town. Barack was there on holiday with his family. I went to the dance hall with my cousin William and I saw Barack enter the room. I thought, "Ohhh, wow!" He was so lovely with his dancing. So handsome and so smart. We danced together and then the next day my cousin came to our house and told me that Barack liked me."

When I was in the town one afternoon, I tracked down Kezia's older sister, Mwanaisha Atieno Amani, and she confirmed the story of their meeting: 'Barack was a very good dancer. It was at Onyango's [old] home, there was a dance there. Yes, that is where they met. He took Kezia dancing, they were number one. Number one!'

What the family will not tell you (but Leo Odera will), is that Kezia and her rival Mical fought at the dance over the attentions of Barack Obama Snr: 'Kezia was very young at the time. Kezia fought with the other girlfriend, who gave up after fighting on the dance floor in Onyango's small hall. That is where they fought, and Kezia became the winner.'

Even though Kezia and Barack had known each other at primary school in the SDA Gendia Mission in Kendu Bay, Barack had moved to K'ogelo with his family when he was seven and they had inevitably lost contact. Now, as normal hormonal teenagers, their attraction was instantaneous.

Barack, however, was proving to be just as impetuous as his father when attracted to a pretty young girl. Throughout late December and into early January, Barack and Kezia's cousin William stopped by her house to talk to her, to try to convince her to run off to Nairobi with Barack. Kezia's sister still remembers just how persistent Barack Snr was in pursuit of Kezia: 'Barack came back again and again. And in their meetings, the relationship began, and they informed his father. Then Barack said, "my dad Onyango will go and talk to Nehemia" [Nehemia Nyandega was Kezia's father].

When Barack Snr went to the railway station in Kisumu to catch the train back to Nairobi in early January 1957, Kezia went with her cousin William to see him off – except that Barack's smooth talking persuaded Kezia to stay with him, and the two lovers eloped together to Nairobi. Kezia moved into Barack's apartment in Jericho, a suburb of Nairobi specially created for government employees, but she recalls that her father was furious over what had happened: 'He did not like Obama. My father and brothers came to Nairobi to bring me back. They said I had to go back to school. When I wouldn't, they said they would never speak to me again.'[2]

Barack too was worried about what Hussein Onyango's reaction would be. Certainly, his relationship with his father had not been good recently. In the previous four years Barack had left Maseno school under a cloud, had walked out of two jobs in Mombasa, had been arrested and jailed by the authorities on suspicion of being a political activist, and now he had eloped with a young girl to Nairobi, where he had only a menial job as a clerk working for the railway company. This was not the life that Hussein Onyango had planned for his son, whom he knew was fiercely intelligent and capable of greater things.

Nevertheless, Barack spoke to his father about Kezia, and according to her sister Mwanasha, Onyango agreed to the wedding: 'So Hussein met with my father, who told Hussein, "I want sixteen head of cattle. That is when you can take her as Barack's wife." Then Onyango said, "I am willing to pay anything, even if you want twenty of them. This is my eldest son, and if he wants a woman, and that is the woman he wants, I will not stand in his way.'

There are three different forms of marriage in Kenya, and all of them are recognised as being legally binding. A couple can choose to have a civil wedding, a church wedding or a traditional tribal wedding – this was the case in 1957, just as it is today. Civil and church weddings are very similar to marriages in Europe and North America, but a traditional wedding is significantly different, and even today it is normal for the groom's family to pay a bride price, which usually comprises several animals plus other goods; the wealthier the family, the greater is the expected contribution. In Kezia's case, Onyango paid her family sixteen cows. The marriage was not to last, and Barack Obama Snr went on to marry another three women, including two young white Americans, but he never divorced Kezia. In Kenya, polygamy was (and still is) legal, and there is no limit to the number of wives a man can have. Muslims usually consider five wives to be a maximum, but there are many instances where a Kenyan – Muslim or Christian – takes many more. (In nearby Homa Bay there is an infamous 90-year-old Luo called Ancentus Akuku, known locally as 'Akuku Danger', who has 130 wives, although he now jokes that, 'I am still very strong, though I am now worn out.')

While Barack Snr was living in Nairobi and becoming more involved in African politics he met Tom Mboya. Mboya, who was no relation to Chief Paul Mboya from Kendu Bay, was six years older than Obama Snr and a typical Luo: charming, charismatic, intelligent and ambitious; Mboya was also a good dancer, and Barack became his friend and protégé. He was also a leading trade unionist and a rising political star in Kenya. When Kenyatta was arrested in 1952 during the Mau Mau emergency, it was Mboya who stepped into the political vacuum by accepting the position of treasurer in Kenyatta's party, the KAU. In 1953, with support from the British Labour Party, Mboya brought Kenya's five most prominent labour unions together to form the Kenya Federation of Labour (KFL). When the KAU was banned later that year, the KFL became the largest 'officially' recognised African political organisation in Kenya. This made Mboya, at the age of twenty-three, one of the most powerful and influential Africans in the country. He used his position to organise protests against the detention camps and secret trials of the emergency, but managed to stay free of arrest himself. In 1955 the British Labour Party arranged a year's scholarship for him at Ruskin College in Oxford, to study industrial management. By the time he returned to Kenya a year later, the Mau Mau rebellion had been effectively quashed. By the late 1950s, Mboya had become a leading Luo politician, and he was seen as a figurehead for national unity. He campaigned for Kenyatta's liberation, and when the Kikuyu leader was released on 21 August 1961, Kenyatta effectively took over the leadership of Kenya's struggle for independence.

Tom Mboya was a visionary who was looking ahead at how Kenya could manage its own affairs once it gained independence from Britain. During

the 1950s, university education for Africans remained highly elitist, and
Mboya was determined to change the system. In the middle of 1959 he
returned from an extensive tour to the USA to announce that he had secured
scores of scholarships for young Kenyans to study on American campuses.
Some of Mboya's early supporters in America included the African-
American baseball legend Jackie Robinson and the actors Harry Belafonte
and Sidney Poitier. Mboya's initiative became known as the 'Airlift Africa'
project, and initially it gave eighty-one Kenyan students the opportunity to
study at top universities in the USA. Mboya's initiative was seen as a way
to help Kenya prepare for independence by educating some of the brightest
and best students in the country. The late 1950s was the height of the Cold
War, and the airlift was also a reaction to what the USA saw as an alarming
number of Kenyan students being offered much better scholarships in the
Soviet Union.

It has frequently been reported that Barack Obama Snr was part of this
first wave of Kenyan students to come to the USA. Even President Obama
himself suggested in a 2007 campaign speech that his 'very existence' was
due to the generosity of the Kennedy family, and implied that his father
was part of the airlift that was partially funded by the Kennedys. The 'Camelot
connection' became part of the mythology surrounding Obama's bid for
the nomination. At his address to civil rights activists in Selma, Alabama,
on 4 March 2007 Senator Obama said:

'What happened in Selma, Alabama and Birmingham also stirred the
conscience of the nation. It worried folks in the White House who said,
"You know, we're battling Communism. How are we going to win hearts
and minds all across the world? If right here in our own country, John,
we're not observing the ideals set forth in our Constitution, we might be
accused of being hypocrites." So the Kennedys decided we're going to do
an air lift. We're going to go to Africa and start bringing young Africans
over to this country and give them scholarships to study so they can learn
what a wonderful country America is. This young man named Barack
Obama [Snr] got one of those tickets and came over to this country.'[3]

The Kennedy family was not, in fact, involved in the first airlift in 1959,
although the Kennedy Foundation did contribute $100,000 towards the
second airlift in 1960. The American scholarships were offered annually
through to the mid-1960s, by which time over 800 African students had
been given the opportunity to study at some of America's most prestigious

universities.[4] Neither was Barack Snr part of that first Mboya initiative in 1959. It was a simple assumption to make, as Obama Snr and Mboya were good friends in Nairobi, but the true story of how Barack Snr got to the University of Hawaii is much more interesting– and very much reflects the 'Obama way' of using a combination of charm and charisma.

During his time in Nairobi during the mid-1950s, Obama watched as his old school friends from Maseno graduated and went on to study at university in Uganda and even London. Barack considered these students to be less gifted then he was, and he became depressed – Sarah Obama says even desperate – at the thought of becoming trapped in a menial administrative job. Sarah claims that two American women befriended him and helped him take a correspondence course, which would give him the school certificate he needed to move on. Obama was motivated, and for several months he used every opportunity to study for his Cambridge A-Level examinations – the recognised British high-school certificate. He took his exams at the US embassy in Nairobi, but it still took several months of nervous waiting before he received word that he had passed with excellent scores.

John Ndalo Aguk is an eighty-five-year-old Obama relative who still lives in K'obama, close to Hussein Onyango's old compound. As a young man in his early twenties, John Ndalo was taken to Nairobi by Onyango, who helped him find work in some of the city's big hotels. He was living in Nairobi in the late 1950s when Barack Snr made his breakthrough:

'Onyango taught us to work. Many whites loved Hussein because he was a good worker. At the time, Hussein worked for the US ambassador in Nairobi – this was around 1956 or 1957. I remember Onyango got involved with these people who got Barack a scholarship abroad. One woman at the embassy liked Barack a lot – I can't remember her name. Barack loved education, he was hard working and presentable. Barack was charming, and he caught the eye of these people, and they supported Barack going to the US. They said, "This young man has the potential to become a leader."'

One of the women instrumental in Barack's successful application for a scholarship was Helen Roberts from California, who was living in Nairobi at the time; another was Jane Kiano, the American wife of Dr Julius Gikonyo Kiano. Dr Kiano was the first Kenyan to gain a US doctorate (from Stanford University) and he played an important political role in the years running up to Kenyan independence, and also in higher education for Kenyans. Kiano later became closely involved with Mboya in organising the student airlifts to the USA.

It was during 1958 and 1959 that Barack Obama Snr used his engaging personality to his advantage and impressed Jane Kiano and other American women at the US Embassy in Nairobi. These women helped Obama to submit applications for scholarships, and he applied to more than thirty colleges in the USA, before being accepted at the University of Hawaii. There were 140 serious applications from East African students for places on Mboya's 1959 chartered aircraft but only 81 seats, and Obama did not make the final selection. The records of Barack's move to the USA are incomplete, but it seems that he did receive some funding from the former baseball star, Jackie Robinson. In addition, Mrs Roberts and another American woman, Miss Mooney, paid for his flight to Honolulu and also gave him a partial scholarship. It was an exciting opportunity for an ambitious young Kenyan.

When the President's father left Nairobi in 1959, it took several days to make the long flight to Honolulu. Kezia was three months pregnant with her second child Auma, and she came to the airport for a tearful parting. Meanwhile, on the opposite side of the world, Hawaii became the fiftieth state of the Union on 21 August amid an explosion of cannon fire, marching bands and parades. When Barack arrived at the University at Mānoa in the summer of 1959 he was just twenty-three years old; he was the first black African student at the university, and inevitably he became the focus of great curiosity on campus. His relatives claim that he was already a slick womaniser, and within a short period he had gathered a group of supportive friends around him. He had long renounced Islam and now declared himself to be an atheist. As he started his classes in mathematics and economics in September, he must have reflected how far he had come from a mud hut in K'ogelo.

It was not until the following year that Barack met Ann, the eighteen-year-old freshman student who would become the mother of the 44th President of the United States of America. Ann Dunham had only started attending classes at the university in September 1960, and she and Obama enrolled on the same Russian-language class. Ann was born on 29 November 1942, in Wichita, Kansas, the only child of Madelyn Payne and Stanley Armour Dunham. Her birth names were Stanley Ann, after her father who had really wanted a boy, and she was constantly teased about it at school. After the war, her parents moved regularly in search of work and a more prosperous life – first to Ponca City, Oklahoma, then to Vernon, Texas, and then back to Kansas, to El Dorado. In 1955 the family resettled in

Seattle, Washington, and then a year later to Mercer Island, a suburb of Seattle, because her parents wanted her to attend the new high school there. Finally, Ann's parents moved to Hawaii, hoping to cash in on new business opportunities in the fledgling state. Her father was a furniture salesman, and judging by the family's frequent moves, he was a restless man – a characteristic which Ann seems to have inherited.

In many ways, Ann Dunham was an enigma. When she graduated from high school in June 1960 she was accepted by the University of Chicago. Her father, however, refused to allow her to go because he thought she was too young to live away from home – she would not turn eighteen until the November. So instead, the young, naïve teenager enrolled at the University of Hawaii, where, for the first time, she began calling herself 'Ann' rather than Stanley. Yet despite her innocence, her high school teacher, Jim Wichterman, recalls that she had a sharp, inquisitive mind: 'As much as a high-school student can, she'd question anything: What's so good about democracy? What's so good about capitalism? What's wrong with communism? What's good about communism? She had what I call an inquiring mind.'[5]

President Obama, too, recalls that his mother was a woman who always seemed to challenge orthodoxy: 'When I think about my mother, I think that there was a certain combination of being very grounded in who she was, what she believed in. But also a certain recklessness. I think she was always searching for something. She wasn't comfortable seeing her life confined to a certain box.'[6]

Within a very short time of meeting Ann in September 1960, Obama Snr was dating her – although he did not tell her about Kezia back in Nairobi, nor about his son and newborn daughter. Around this time, Barack wrote to his friend Leo Odera. Leo claims that Obama Snr had been getting reports that Kezia had been seen out and about, partying in a manner which did not suit a married woman and mother. Odera also claims that Kezia herself had become pregnant by another man, and it was this which finally finished the relationship:

> 'When he went to the US, he was still writing back home until some friends of Obama's wrote to him telling that Kezia had been seen in public, at dancing places and whatever, as well as having two children. And later on she conceived a third one. He wrote [to me] that he was disappointed . . . He said, "She has disappointed me because she is expecting a child." . . . It is this that put the final nail in the marriage, and he decided now to look for another.'

Even though Hawaii was a racial melting pot in the early sixties, the mix was mostly white Americans and Asians – mainly Chinese. A black man dating a white girl was still something unusual, though interracial marriage was at least legal, unlike in most southern states of the Union. By November 1960, within weeks of meeting Obama Snr, Ann was pregnant and the couple were married on the island of Maui three months later, on 2 February 1961. Even by the easygoing standards of Hawaii in the early sixties, Ann was very young to be married, and their relationship raised alarm on both sides of the family. Onyango thought his son was behaving irresponsibly and wrote to Barack to try to persuade him to change his mind, and he even threatened to have his student visa revoked. Ann's parents also had their reservations but they both supported her in her decision none the less. The only people present at the ceremony, apart from Barack and Ann, were her parents, Stanley and Madelyn. Later that semester Ann dropped out of college. Their son, Barack Hussein Obama Jnr, was born at 7.24 p.m. on 4 August 1961, at the Kapi'olani Medical Center for Women and Children in Honolulu. At the time, Obama Snr was still legally married to Kezia in Kenya, and still he had not told his new wife. Under US law polygamy is illegal so Obama Snr was in principle a bigamist, and their son, therefore, technically illegitimate.

In *Dreams from My Father*, President Obama recalls the stories he was told of the three years his father spent in Hawaii, related to him by his mother and grandparents, '. . . seamless, burnished smooth from repeated use'. He recalls his mother saying that Obama Snr was a terrible driver, 'He'd end up on the left-hand side, the way the British drive, and if you said something he'd just huff about silly American rules.'[7] But Barack Jnr found these stories to be generally inadequate to help him understand his father – he wrote that they were 'compact, apocryphal, told in rapid succession in the course of an evening, then packed away for months, sometimes years, in my family's memory'. As a result, his father became a distant, mythical figure to Barack Jnr.

When Obama Snr graduated from the University of Hawaii in the summer of 1962, he was interviewed for an article published in the *Honolulu Star-Bulletin*; the piece gives a fascinating insight into the character of the 26-year-old student:

> He appears guarded and responsible, the model student, the ambassador for his continent. He mildly scolds the university for herding visiting students into dormitories and forcing them to attend programs designed to promote cultural understanding – a distraction, he says, from the practical training

he seeks. Although he hasn't experienced any problems himself, he detects self-segregation and overt discrimination taking place between the various ethnic groups and expresses wry amusement at the fact that "Caucasians" in Hawaii are occasionally at the receiving end of prejudice. But if his assessment is relatively clear-eyed, he is careful to end on a happy note: One thing other nations can learn from Hawaii, he says, is the willingness of races to work together toward common development, something he has found whites elsewhere too often unwilling to do.

Obama was clearly a model student and he was offered two scholarships to work towards a doctorate – a full scholarship from the New School in New York City, and a partial one from Harvard. He chose to go to Harvard, but the scholarship was not enough for him to take his family to Massachusetts. Ann stayed behind in Honolulu with their young son and resumed her studies at the university, and Barack flew to Boston in the fall and a new life at Harvard. It proved to be the beginning of the end of their short relationship.

By 1962 Mboya's airlift was into its third year and Harvard was now home to some of Kenya's brightest and most ambitious students. One of them was James Odhiambo Ochieng', a twenty-one-year-old student who arrived in that year:

'I went to the States in 1962. I was part of Tom Mboya's airlift. Tom Mboya was a very good friend of mine – I [later] came to work under him. I met Obama Snr in 1963 in Boston, after he had left the lady. At that time, Obama was also staying in Cambridge [Massachusetts]; we were all brothers. But we were staying more or less in the same place, and we liked parties and drinks.

'In America, it is very interesting. America, you see, you go to the grocery store and then you go and buy meat there, and you come and cook it the African way. Lots of ladies in America used to like that. That dish was so good for them, they liked it. We used our hands [to eat], we didn't use a fork.

'So when I met Obama at that time, Obama used to dance, seriously, and he used to know how to seduce. The women liked this man. Barry had lots of girlfriends.'

Barack Obama Snr rented a room in an apartment block just off Central Square in Cambridge and settled down to a bachelor lifestyle. Tom Mboya had heard that Obama had married again, and he wrote to his old friend, warning him not to abandon his new wife and son; Barack stayed true to his word – at least at first. In his book, *Dreams from My Father*, President Obama remembers only one visit from his father, just before Christmas in 1971, when the young Barack was ten years old. However, James Odhiambo claims that Obama Snr went back several times to see his son in Hawaii between 1962 and 1964: 'He told me that he had a brilliant young boy. Even when he was in Boston, he was going [back] to Hawaii. Why do I say so? Because he would talk to us about the boy all that time. He went [to Hawaii] more than once. I am sure, I am certain – three times that I know of.'

During the four years Barack Obama Snr spent in Hawaii, there were dramatic changes back home in Kenya as the country moved towards independence. The year that Barack left for America, 1959, marked a relaxation of British governance in the colony; the Mau Mau emergency was effectively over, and Jomo Kenyatta was transferred from jail to house arrest. In 1960 Tom Mboya's People's Congress Party joined forces with two other political unions in Kenya, the Kenya African Union and the Kenya Independent Movement, to form a new party – the Kenya African National Union (KANU). It was hoped that KANU would transcend tribal politics and create a united front in preparation for negotiations in London with the British Colonial Office. These discussions, which became known as the Lancaster House conferences after the grand neo-classical building in London in which they were held, were intended to create an effective constitutional framework for the country, and a transition to independence. As Secretary General of KANU, Mboya headed the Kenyan delegation to the three conferences in Lancaster House.

The other leading African politician of the day was another Luo, Jaramogi Ajuma Oginga Odinga, who was born in Bondo, a village close to K'ogelo in central Nyanza. He was revered by the Luo as *Ker* – their spiritual leader – a position previously held by that fabled ancestral chief Ramogi Ajwang', who first brought the Luo to Kenya five centuries previously. As a mark of respect, Odinga became known as *Jaramogi*, meaning 'son of Ramogi'. However, according to Luo tradition, a *Ker* cannot hold a political position, so Odinga relinquished his regal status in 1957 and was elected a member of the newly formed Legislative Council, representing the central Nyanza constituency. This made him, de facto, the political spokesman for the Luo in Kenya's embryonic government. He further consolidated his political position in 1960, when he formed KANU with Mboya. Although they had fundamental political differences – Oginga was much further to the left than Mboya – together they gave the Luo a powerful voice in the new Kenyan administration.

The following year, in February 1961, the very month that Barack Obama Snr and Ann Dunham were married in Honolulu, Kenya held its first general election in preparation for its forthcoming independence. The two main parties fighting the contest were Jomo Kenyatta's KANU and the Kenya African Democratic Union. KADU was founded in 1960 with the express aim of defending the interests of other Kenyan tribes against the domination of the Luo and Kikuyu, which accounted for the majority of KANU's membership. The most dramatically contested seat of the election was in Nairobi East, which was considered to be a weather vane in the leadership struggle for KANU. Over 60 per cent of the registered electors in the constituency were Kikuyu or allied tribal partners. The next largest ethnic group were the Luo, with just over 10 per cent of the vote. Five candidates contested the seat, but the fight was clearly between two KANU representatives, Tom Mboya and Dr Munyua Waiyaki, a Kikuyu.[8] On the first day of the election, a Sunday, 75 per cent of the electorate turned out to vote, with the overwhelming majority sporting Mboya badges. However, rumours were rife that whilst the Kikuyu might wear Mboya's image in public, when it came to the secrecy of the ballot box, they would vote strictly along tribal lines and elect Waiyaki.

Mboya defied all expectations and won 90 per cent of the vote, with all the other candidates losing their 1,000-shilling deposits, and there is nothing to suggest that these figures are anything but accurate. It was a remarkable demonstration of the popularity of the young Luo politician, and for the power of national democracy over tribalism. During the nine days of voting across the country, 84 per cent of the electorate voted; although some of the campaigns were marred by bribery, corruption and intimidation, KANU easily emerged the dominant party, winning about two-thirds of the vote over KADU. In March 1961 nominees from both political parties visited Kenyatta in Lodwar, the small town in northern Kenya where he was being held under house arrest. Kenyatta urged the politicians to unite and work together for full independence; he was released later that year and called for the two parties to form an interim coalition government, and to hold elections before independence.

The national election of what would be Kenya's first autonomous government were held in May 1963, with Kenyatta's KANU party, which called
for Kenya to be a unitary state, running against KADU, which advocated
majimbo – a Swahili word meaning 'group of regions' or regional governments. This system was seen as a way of minimising the problem of tribalism, by creating three autonomous self-governing regions (Rift Valley,
Western and Coast). This would give the Kikuyu and the Luo their own
ethnic regional governments, but prevent them from dominating the
national government. However, the concept of *majimbo* was rejected by
the electorate, and KANU won the election with 83 of the 124 seats. On
1 June 1963 Jomo Kenyatta became Kenya's prime minister; the Luos were
represented by Tom Mboya, who became Minister of Justice and Constitutional Affairs, and Oginga Odinga, who was Minister for Home Affairs.
It was an exciting time for the Africans, as they debated and argued about
what sort of nation Kenya should become.

For the 60,000 Kenya Europeans, however, this rapid transition from
Mau Mau rebellion to independent status in no more than four years

*1 June 1963: from left to right Tom Mboya, Oginga Odinga, Jome Kenyatta and
Minister of Finance James Gichuru.*

came as a huge psychological shock, for they had long considered themselves to be the last bastion of European rule in British Africa. In a very
public demonstration of their sense of abandonment by the government
in London, one settler threw thirty pieces of silver in front of Michael
Blundell, the de facto political leader of the white community, on his return
to Nairobi from Lancaster House; the white farmers felt that sixty years of
labour in the White Highlands had been betrayed by the politicians in
London.

On 12 December 1963, Kenya became a fully independent nation; one
year later to the day, the country became a republic – Jamhuri ya Kenya
– with Jomo Kenyatta as president and Jaramogi Oginga Odinga as vice
president. KADU was dissolved and integrated with KANU, leaving
Kenyatta's first government effectively without an opposition. This inevitably
led to a centralisation of political and economic power around the president,
and sowed the seeds of government corruption.

In January 1964, Ann Dunham filed for divorce from Barack Obama Snr
citing abandonment by her husband. It was clear that the marriage never
really had much chance of success; Obama Snr had been partying hard
in Boston, and now he had met a young school teacher in her early
twenties, Ruth Nidesand. Obama Snr soon moved in with Ruth, and they
started a serious relationship. But the talk over beers among the young
Kenyan students at Harvard was about what was happening back home.
Since they had come out to study their country had become an
independent nation, and there were exciting, new opportunities on offer
in Nairobi.

The following year, in 1965, Obama Snr gave up his studies for a PhD
and returned home. This was partly from financial hardship, but also
because of the new jobs to be had in Kenya. Following independence,
many students who were studying overseas returned home to join the
scamble for the top government positions in Nairobi – many of which had
been vacated by white administrators who had decided to leave Kenya.
Such was the demand for young, well-educated Kenyans that the
government even sent recruitment teams to the USA to persuade the
brightest and best to return and serve their country. Despite leaving his
studies early, Obama Snr was later awarded a master's degree, although he
frequently liked to refer to himself as 'Dr Obama' when wanting to make

an impression. Ruth too followed him out to Nairobi, and although Barack was reluctant at first, they soon married.

Obama Snr's first job in Kenya was as an economist with Shell, but he soon landed a job in the government, working for the Kenya Central Bank. It was a prize placement for a young man from a small village in Nyanza, and it should have been a springboard to greater things. But Obama Snr's tendency for self-destruction soon began to make itself felt. In July 1965, the summer he returned to Nairobi, he published an article in the *East Africa Journal* entitled 'Problems Facing Our Socialism'.[9] It was essentially a critique of 'Sessional Paper 10', an influential government paper, which argued for a model of government in Kenya based on African values. In his article, Obama chose to criticise the direction the new Kenyatta government was taking, and its lack of foresight in planning. He ended the paper by saying that planning would have been better: 'if the government were to look into priorities and see them clearly within their context so that their implementation could have had a basis on which to reply. Maybe it is better to have something perfunctorily done than none at all!'

His article might have gone down well with his tutors at Harvard, but it was certainly not a very wise thing to write when you are straight out of university, and with no experience in government. The paper did, however, impress Mboya (who gave Obama his government job) and it helped him to press Kenyatta and other members of the cabinet to address some of the inequalities of wealth in Kenya. However, it also marked Obama as a member of the Oginga/Mboya camp of left-wing Luo radicals. This outspokenness and highly opinionated attitude would ultimately lead to his catastrophic downfall.

Nevertheless, those early years back in Kenya were good for Obama Snr; he had a first-rate job at the Central Bank, he was paid well, and he was making friends at the very top of government. His old college friend from Boston, James Odhiambo Ochieng', remembers countless nights out on the town:

'Obama did one thing – he would order the drinks. He would say, "When I say drink, drink!" So everybody would drink. But if I say pay! What do you do? My goodness! But then Obama was actually a good rescue for us. He would go and call the waiter, and tell the waiter – "Take [the bill] to Mboya." And Mboya would take it very easily. He would not only do it to Mboya, he would do it to Odinga. Odinga was someone to reckon with.

He knew Obama very well. So then Obama tells the waiter, "Check it to this old friend of mine." And you know, the old man would be sitting here like this, and he would say "Yes?" and [the waiter] would say "Obama has given me this." Odinga would take it. He couldn't be angry about it. With Obama? Oh no, no, no. He wouldn't argue.'

At a personal level, however, Barack's life was not running so smoothly. Soon after he married Ruth, Onyango came to Nairobi to see his son. Onyango had opposed his marriage to Ann, and now Barack had returned home with yet another American wife. Onyango was, at heart, a traditionalist, and he wanted his son to have a Luo wife. So he tried to persuade Barack to set up a second home in Nairobi with Kezia – after all, a Luo always had separate huts for his wives in his compound, so why should the same idea not work in Nairobi?

Leo Odera explained to me what happened: 'When Obama Snr returned with Ruth, Hussein Onyango went to Nairobi physically to plead, because Kezia still had many children. So Hussein said, "You are now married to a white lady. Why don't you rent a house for this wife somewhere on another estate, so that you can visit your children there?" And Obama is saying, no!'

Ruth too put her foot down and refused to share Barack with another. However, despite Barack's problems with his father, those first few years together in Nairobi were happy, and Ruth bore him two sons, Mark and David, who were half-brothers to Barack Obama Jnr back in Honolulu.

At a national level, Kenyan politics was beginning to deteriorate. Oginga Odinga and Kenyatta had always been uncomfortable bedfellows, coming as they did from different tribes. Politically, the two men also disagreed over the direction the country should take, with Oginga Odinga advocating a socialist system whereas Kenyatta supported a mixed economy. In March 1966 Oginga quit KANU, resigned from Kenyatta's government and formed a new left-wing opposition party, the Kenya People's Union (KPU). In doing so, Barack Obama lost one of his most powerful mentors in government. Oginga Odinga claimed that Kenya was being run by an 'invisible government', and for the next three years the KPU insisted that KANU's policies of 'African socialism' were simply a cover for tribalism and capitalism. Kenyatta was not prepared to compromise, and if anything became even more entrenched in his own opinions; he believed that his opponents were 'paid agents of communism whose mission it was to dethrone him'.[10] Oginga Odinga – a senior Luo politician – had thrown down a gauntlet at the feet of his Kikuyu adversary. It was a confrontation which would eventually result in arrest, detention and assassination.

The first five years after independence saw some fundamentally important developments which defined what type of government Kenya would have for years to come. From the very beginning of its foundation, Oginga Odinga's KPU faced enmity from Kenyatta's government – Kenyatta was not prepared to countenance any opposition. By March 1968 – the third anniversary of the founding of the KPU – the government accused the political party of subversion. It was a very serious charge and members of the KPU were denied the right to address public meetings. The government's claim against the opposition party was: 'The record of KPU members must bring into anxious review the question of the stage at which free speech, as a tool of democracy, may also become a trap into which democracy must fall.'[1] Jomo Kenyatta and his close Kikuyu colleagues were determined to tighten their grip on their single-party government.

In May the following year KANU was dealt a severe blow in a parliamentary by-election in the Luo constituency of Gem, in central Nyanza. In the national election four years previously, KANU had a substantial victory there, but in May 1969 – less than a year after the KPU had been effectively silenced at public meetings – the KPU overturned that result and won the seat easily. Kenyatta realised that many of the Luo in Gem were voting for Oginga Odinga out of tribal loyalty, and he asked Tom Mboya – who by then had changed his portfolio to Minister for Economic Planning and Development – to reorganise KANU in preparation for the national elections, which were due the following year. The popular and charismatic Mboya was a possible successor – perhaps even a likely successor – to Kenyatta in those elections.

Two months later, on a hot, steamy July day in Nairobi, Barack Obama Snr found himself unwittingly drawn into one of the most momentous events in post-independent Kenya. Tom Mboya, his old friend and drinking companion, had returned the previous day from a meeting in Addis Ababa. As the July heat began to build up on the streets of Nairobi on the Saturday morning, Mboya arrived at his office at 9.30, in the Treasury Building on Harambee Avenue. At lunchtime he told his driver to go home for the weekend and took his own car to a pharmacy on Government Road (now called Moi Avenue) to buy some lotion for his dry skin. Just before 1 p.m., on his way into the shop, he bumped into Obama Snr, who casually joked with Mboya, saying that he should be careful as he had parked his car illegally.[12] Minutes after the two friends parted, Tom Mboya came out of the store having made his purchase and was confronted by a slight young man wearing a dark suit, holding a briefcase in his left hand. His right hand was in his pocket. Almost immediately, two shots were fired and Mboya fell to the pavement.

Mrs Mohini Sehmi, who was a family friend and who had just served him in the pharmacy, ran out to see what the sudden noise was about: 'He slumped against me and staggered back almost into the shop. Then he must have staggered again, and we were back in the shop. I saw blood on his shirt, which was red anyway, and I realised then what had happened. He never uttered a word. He fell into my arms and began to fall to the ground.'[13]

Dr Mohamed Rafique, another family friend, arrived soon after the shooting and gave Mboya mouth-to-mouth resuscitation, but the young politician was pronounced dead on arrival at Nairobi hospital. It had taken only one bullet to sever his aorta; the second bullet had struck Mboya's right shoulder.

Mboya's friends and colleagues could not believe what had happened. His bodyguard, Joseph Nisa, collapsed at the hospital, crying, 'It's not true, it's not true.' The publicity secretary of the KPU arrived in tears and announced, 'This is not a political assassination. There is no question of parties here. He belonged to us all.'[14] The citizens of Nairobi thought otherwise; within hours of Mboya's death, a highly charged crowd – mainly Luo – tried to force their way into the hospital against the police cordon that had quickly been thrown around the building. Doors and windows were broken and the police resorted to tear gas and clubs to disperse the angry crowd. The entire Kenyan police force was mobilised, roadblocks were set up and patrols were mounted throughout the city and into the suburbs.

News of Mboya's death soon reached Nyanza, where demonstrations soon degenerated into riots. In Kisumu, mobs of young men roamed the city, stoning shops owned by Kikuyu traders; in nearby Homa Bay, police were obliged to take Kikuyus into custody for their own protection. The following day Mboya's body was taken to his Nairobi home in Convent Drive; thousands of mourners lined the route and thousands more surrounded his house when the hearse arrived. Mboya's widow Pamela later told Mrs Sehmi: 'Tom would still have been alive today if he had had a streak of badness in him. They killed him because he was nothing but a good man. He died because they know he was good.'[15]

The death of Tom Mboya left a vacuum at the very heart of Kenya's government; the country had lost its most able government minister and its most astute political strategist. Now, as Kenyatta's government was trying to suppress the KPU, most Luos came to believe that the Kikuyu were determined to deny any Luo a senior position in the country. The government had already sidelined Oginga Odinga, and now, so they maintained, they had dealt permanently with Mboya.

On 10 July, five days after the murder, Luo suspicions seemed to be confirmed when a Kikuyu man, Isaac Njenga Njoroge, was arrested and charged with Mboya's assassination. Njenga was a one-time youth volunteer in KANU's Nairobi branch, and Mboya's death was widely seen as a politically motivated killing. Kenya had lost one of its brightest and most talented politicians – and Jomo Kenyatta had lost the one man who was most likely to succeed him in a popular vote.

Nor was Mboya's assassination the only death of a senior Luo. A few months before, in January 1969, Argwings Kodhek, the Foreign Minister in Kenyatta's government, died in what was initially thought to be a road accident. The subsequent exhumation of his body found evidence that he was actually killed by a single shot fired from a police rifle. Some people claim that this was Jomo Kenyatta's first political assassination.

By now Barack Obama Snr was well known as an outspoken critic of Kenyatta's government, and to his credit he was prepared to stand in the witness box and testify at the prosecution of Mboya's killer. It was a brave thing to do, and he later told a friend that, not long after the trial, he was hit by a car on a Nairobi street and left for dead. He was convinced that the occupants of the car were the same people who had killed Mboya.[16] On 10 September Njenga was found guilty in what people considered to be a tightly controlled showcase trial. But he almost ruined the carefully stage-managed event with a casual remark made just before his sentence was announced, when he asked: 'Why do you pick on me? Why not the big man?' Who exactly he was referring to has never been explained, but no Luo politician or historian I have spoken to has any doubt that it was Kenyatta who ordered Mboya's assassination. On 25 November 1969 the Kenya Prison Service announced that Njenga Njoroge had been hanged: 'The sentence imposed on Njenga has been carried out in accordance with the law, along with those other persons convicted of capital offences.' However, the trial records have since disappeared from the Kenya National Archives, and there have been persistent rumours that Njoroge was never actually hanged, but instead spirited

off to Ethiopia, where he lived the rest of his life under an assumed
identity.

Throughout the second half of 1969 the relationship between President
Kenyatta and Oginga Odinga – and effectively between the Kikuyu and
the Luo – continued to decline, and it was inevitable that the tensions
between the two politicians would come to a head. There is a famous saying
in Swahili: *Wapiganapo tembo nyasi huumia* – When elephants fight, the
grass gets hurt – and this is exactly what happened in Kisumu on 25 October
1969.

That month, Jomo Kenyatta decided to make a tour of the Rift Valley
and Nyanza in the run-up to the presidential elections scheduled for
6 December that year; it was his way of showing that he was back in control
of the country. On the 25th he paid a visit to Kisumu, ostensibly to open
the New Nyanza General Hospital – it was built by the Soviet Union, and
it is still frequently referred to as the 'Russian Hospital'. By visiting the Luo
heartland, however, Kenyatta found that he had strayed into hostile territory. It has been estimated that there were 5,000 people massed outside the
hospital that day, and the crowd started to chant the KPU slogan, *Dume,
Dume* (in this context, it meant brave man in Swahili, and referred to
Oginga Odinga). When the president rose to make his speech, the crowd
started heckling; perhaps unwisely, Kenyatta was in no mood to mince his
words. His attack on the Luo community in general, and the Luo political
leadership in particular, was extraordinary and unprecedented. Speaking
in Swahili, he opened his speech with the following diatribe:

'Now, I want, before opening this hospital, I want to say a few words; and
I will start with the Kiswahili proverb which states that "The thanks of a
donkey are its hind kick." We have come here to bring you luck, to bring
a hospital which is for treating the citizens, and now there are some writhing
little insects, little insects of the KPU, who have dared to come here to
speak dirty words, dirty words.

'I am very glad to be with my friend Odinga, who is the leader of these
people here. And I wish to say, if it were not for the respect I have for our
friendship, Odinga, I would have said that you get locked up today . . . so
that we see who rules over these citizens, whether it is KANU, or some
many little insects who rule over this country . . . On my part I do say this,

if these people are dirty, if they bring about nonsense, we shall show them
that Kenya has got its government. They dare not play around with us, and
you Bwana Odinga as an individual, you know that I do not play around.
I have left you free for a long time because you are my friend. Were it not
so, you yourself know what I would have done. It is not your business to
tell me where to throw you; I personally know where. Maybe you think I
cannot throw you into detention in Manyani [previously a British detention camp] because you are my special friend . . . And therefore today I
am speaking in a very harsh voice, and while I am looking at you directly,
and I am telling you the truth in front of all these people.

'Tell these people of yours to desist. If not, they are going to feel my
full wrath. And me, I do not play around at all . . . They are chanting
Dume, Dume – "Bull, Bull." Your mothers' c**ts! This *Dume, Dume* . . .
And me, I want to tell you Odinga, while you are looking at me with your
two eyes wide open; I have given my orders right now: those creeping
insects of yours are to be crushed like flour. They are to be crushed like
flour if they play with us. You over there, do not make noise there. I will
come over there and crush you myself.'[7]

It was an extraordinary speech for a nation's president to make; the threat
to the Luo people was crystal clear, and the insults explicit. Notwithstanding
the obscene remark, it is a great insult for Africans to be called 'writhing
little insects'. The crowd was furious, and there was soon a full-scale riot in
Kisumu against Kenyatta's security entourage; the police opened fire and
forty-three people were reported killed. Never again did Kenyatta set foot in
Nyanza, and the Luo province – like many other non-Kikuyu areas – was
denied virtually any further economic assistance or development for decades.
The effects of this rejection can still be seen in these parts of Kenya today.

The assassinations of Kodhek and Mboya, and the 'Kisumu massacre',
all occurred within just a few months of each other, and they created a
deep-rooted resentment of Kenyatta in particular, and the Kikuyu in general.
The entire Luo community now closed ranks around Odinga, and they
took on a markedly anti-Kikuyu stance which is still felt today. In that year,
1969, tribal politics won, and Kenyan nationalism died along with Mboya,
Kodhek and the forty-three ordinary citizens of Kisumu. Nor did Jaramogi
Oginga Odinga survive for long after Kenyatta's public tirade at the Kisumu
hospital; within a very short time the president did as he threatened, and
Odinga was arrested and detained for two years. After he was released, he
lived in political limbo until after Kenyatta's death in August 1978; then,

following a short period of political rehabilitation, he was again placed under house arrest by President Moi in 1982. In 1992, Oginga Odinga fought for a change in Kenya's constitution to allow multi-party democracy, and he won his challenge with the support of the British and US governments.

Oginga Odinga died two years later at the age of eighty-three, but he had created a political dynasty. His son, Raila Amollo Odinga, followed his father into politics; he won his first parliamentary seat in 1992, and after two failed attempts to run for the presidency against Mwai Kibaki, he challenged the incumbent again in 2007 in an election which he claimed was fraudulent. This led to the post-election violence in late 2007 and early 2008; in April 2008 Odinga was made Prime Minister of Kenya on a power-sharing basis with President Mwai Kibaki.

As the fortunes of the Luo fell during the late 1960s, so too did those of Barack Obama Snr. His outspokenness was beginning to cause problems at the Central Bank, and he was widely known to be a vociferous critic of Kenyatta. As a senior Luo civil servant within the Kenyatta government, he was particularly vulnerable; but now that his friend and mentor Tom Mboya was dead, he became even more exposed, as Leo Odera recalls:

'When Barry returned home [in 1965], Mboya was a government minister. When Mboya was assassinated, his protection was uncovered. Because you know, he liked drinking and sometimes not reporting to work. But whilst Mboya was there, nobody would do anything about him. Once Mboya died, he had no protector. It is a brave man who talked carelessly about the Kenyatta government in those days.'

Obama Snr did not heed the warning and he continued to speak openly against the government, even after Mboya's death. On one occasion, Odera claims, Kenyatta himself called Barack to his offices, to give him a personal warning:

'Barack was outspoken. After getting drunk, he would say the government killed the best brain. And then I think some intelligence men picked this up and I think this could have reached Kenyatta's ear. So he was ordered to Kenyatta's place. Kenyatta told him: "You'll be on the tarmac looking for another job." But still he did not shut his mouth.'

James Odhiambo, Barack's college friend in Boston, had also returned from America to work in Nairobi, and he was a regular visitor to the house that Ruth and Barack shared:

> 'They were very happy people when I came back. The problem that Obama Snr was having – despite the fact that Ruth was in the house – Obama was still enjoying himself with the ladies. He had a taste for the whites in Nairobi. This was in '67, '68. Obama was, I will use the word "arrogant". Because of his brightness, he actually felt that people like Duncan Ndegwa [the governor of the Central Bank of Kenya] were stupid, and he felt that he should be the governor! "Ndegwa? Who is Ndegwa? Ndegwa was not learned [educated]," according to him.'

On one occasion, according to Odhiambo, governors from several African banks met up in Nairobi for a banking summit: 'Obama had evidently spoken to these people who were coming from the Central Banks of other African countries. When he talked to them, he says, "You know, I'm the Governor *really*, you know." Oh Barry!'

The Luo have a proverb, *Kapod in epi to kik iyany nyang*'; it means: 'Don't abuse the crocodile when you're still in the water'. It certainly applied to Obama Snr, who was up to his neck in the murky waters of the Central Bank; the crocodile turned and attacked the young, outspoken economist, and Obama was fired – it is said that his dismissal was personally sanctioned by Kenyatta. Obama was devastated over the loss of this job, and his drinking became worse. He was always known as Mr 'Double-Double', for his habit of ordering two double whiskies at once – his preference was for Johnnie Walker Black Label and VAT 69. He was also very adept at getting others to pay for them, if at all possible.

Although Barack Snr was still living with Ruth at this time, he was also seeing his first wife Kezia, who was now living in Nairobi with Obama's two eldest children. Kezia had two more children in the late 60s; Abo was born in 1968 and Bernard in 1970. According to President Obama's account in *Dreams from My Father*, the family doubt whether either of them are the true biological sons of Barack Snr, as Kezia had other partners during this period. Nevertheless, this seemed to make little difference to Barack, who in traditional Luo style would say they were all his children, and welcomed them into a wide, extended family. However, by the early 70s, Barack was coming home very late at night on a regular basis, and very drunk. Inevitably, his relationship with Ruth began to deteriorate. Ruth has always kept a discreet silence about her marriage to Barack Obama Snr, but her eldest son, Mark Ndesandjo, claims that his father beat his mother and his young sons:

> 'It's something which I think affected me for a long time, and it's some-thing that I've just recently come to terms with. I remember situations when I was growing up, and there would be a light coming from our living room, and I could hear thuds. I could hear thuds and screams, and my father's voice and my mother shouting. I remember one night when she ran out into the street and she didn't know where to go.'[18]

Leo Odera also recalls this period of Obama Snr's life:

> 'He was becoming almost an alcoholic. Soon after, he began to have a problem with his American wife, Ruth. She went off with a Sikh – he took his wife. She was getting very frustrated with him getting drunk. At that time, I was told that he was even passing out on the bed. And Ruth was telling people that she was getting disappointed and she wanted to leave. So she eloped with this Asian. And she stayed with him for some time before eventually settling in with my former work colleague, Simeon Ndesandjo, who was to be the head of the Swahili service in the Kenyan Broadcasting Service. They are still together now.'

The relationship between Ruth and Obama Snr never recovered. In *Dreams from My Father*, President Obama writes of a very uncomfort-able meeting with Ruth and her oldest son Mark, when Obama visited them in Nairobi in 1987. By then, both of Obama Snr's sons had taken Ndesandjo as their surname. Ruth later had a third son in 1980 by her new husband, whom they called Joseph. Today, Ruth still lives with Simeon Ndesandjo in Nairobi, where she runs a kindergarten; Mark works in Shenzhen, China, and runs an internet company which helps Chinese companies export to the USA; David Ndesandjo, Ruth's second son and Obama Snr's fifth child, tragically died in a motorcycle accident in 1987; Joseph lives in San Antonio, Texas, and is president and owner of a security systems company.

Barack always had a reputation as a reckless driver; now that he had lost his wife, his two sons, and his job, his drinking became a serious problem. He had several serious motor accidents, including one in which Leo Odera was involved:

'He was a very bad driver. He was a drunkard. He had to have one for the
road. So [one evening] we took one or two beers and I was sleeping. The
first I knew, we were off the road and the dashboard hit my chest. After
taking a double – he would say "give me another double" – then he'd have
a blackout and would cause an accident. At that time I'd fear going near
him because he'd ask me for a beer.'

Leo Odera told me that Obama Snr had four major accidents, including
one in which his good friend Adede Odiero died.

'That was his first major accident. He doesn't remember [how it
happened]. They were drunk and they hit a pavement, and this boy had
a brain haemorrhage and he died. He was a very popular boy. That was
the first incident when the community in Karachuonyo [Kendu Bay]
and everybody started losing faith in him [Obama]. After the death of
that boy, people started talking ill of him. He was now becoming almost
an alcoholic.'

It was after one of his road accidents in 1971 that Obama Snr went back
to Hawaii to see his young son. It has frequently been reported that Obama
Snr had his legs amputated after one serious accident, but people who
knew him say this was not true, although he did, for a while, wear leg
irons. When he went to Hawaii just before Christmas in 1971, he was still
on crutches, and this was the only occasion that President Obama recalls
meeting his father. It was an uncomfortable visit; Obama Snr knew his
life was falling apart around him in Nairobi, and here in Honolulu he
found it very difficult to relate to a ten-year-old son he did not know. The
young Barack, too, found it impossible to form a relationship with this
big man with a deep, resonant voice who had suddenly appeared in his
life.

The last decade of Barack Obama Snr's life played out like a Greek
tragedy. After being sacked from his job at the Central Bank, his personal
connections back in Nyanza got him a new job. James Odhiambo still saw
Obama Snr regularly during this time:

'He had a lot of friends, very powerful friends. He had lost a job, and he
lost his lady friend, and because he did not have a job, he could not maintain a family. He could not make ends meet. He actually lost his lady to
somebody who was capable of actually maintaining her.

'Barry got another job. Somebody from Alego called Owuor – he was the managing director of the Kenya Tourist Development Corporation, the KTDC. I understand Obama was an Extension Officer – but an economist all right. He was pleased with the job.'

Unfortunately, Obama Snr did not learn his lesson, and it was not long before his inflated ego got the better of him. In his job at the KTDC, Obama Snr was in contact with influential people, many of whom were from overseas, and James Odhiambo recalls that Obama developed a habit of implying that he was rather more senior in the Corporation than was actually the case:

'Jerry Owuor was the managing director of KTDC. So Jerry would say, "Now Barry, what is all this again?" Because a letter comes in "For the attention of . . . What is all this? 'Barry Bwana?' [Swahili for 'boss']. What is all this now?"

'But you see Barry wanted to look big. He was much brighter than the other man. His intellect went far beyond. He complained about the amount of money he was being paid. He said he should be paid more money. Because of his generosity – he was not a millionaire – he became a drunkard more or less most of the time. So he would end up penniless. But in the interest of his friends, he entertained them to the maximum.

'That's Barry Obama. He had to be given his marching orders – that is all that I will say! Because he left. That is when this man really suffered; Barry now suffered a great deal for some time.'

Once again, Obama Snr found himself without a job, and his heavy drinking continued.

Then, in 1975, Obama suffered another blow. Onyango was now eighty years old and his health was beginning to deteriorate. Whenever Barack visited his father in K'ogelo, he could not bring himself to talk about his problems, although he did confide in Sarah on occasions; instead, Barack would behave as if nothing was wrong, bringing his customary gifts which he could ill-afford. Onyango could now only walk with the assistance of a stick, and he was almost totally blind – this made him more irascible than ever. He was so frail that Sarah even had to bathe him, something which this proud and self-righteous man found difficult to reconcile. He died later that year, and he was buried inside his compound, as is customary in Luoland. Barack came up from Nairobi to organise the funeral and he gave his father a Muslim burial, with his body wrapped in a simple cotton shroud, rather than a traditional Luo bull skin.

Meanwhile, the tragedy played out on a bigger stage. On 31 August 1978 Jomo Kenyatta died of a cardiac arrest during a visit to Mombasa. Although he had suffered a previous heart attack in 1966, his death was still unexpected. He was succeeded by his vice-president, Daniel arap Moi, popularly known as Nyayo – a Swahili word meaning 'footsteps', because Moi always claimed that he was following in the footsteps of Kenyatta. During the first few years of his presidency, Moi enjoyed widespread support throughout the country. In stark contrast to Kenyatta's imperious manner, Moi was a populist, and people liked him for it. However, his public approval did not last, and soon he was accused of nepotism, tribalism, political assassinations, torture, corruption, and presiding over a collapse of governance in the country.

Barack Obama Snr too had reached a crisis in his life, and once again his friends stepped in to help. James Odhiambo remembers that people were very concerned over the consequences if Obama was left unsupported: 'He was a man of substance, and they could not risk leaving him alone there, bickering and talking a lot of nonsense. They would rather absorb him. So they felt the gentleman must come and work in the Finance Ministry.'

It was here in the Finance Ministry that Obama Snr worked for Mwai Kibaki, who was then Minister of Finance and Economic Planning. (In 2006, when the then Senator Obama visited Kenya, Kibaki was keen to point out that he gave his father this position). Barack Obama Snr was lucky to get the job at the ministry; he was certainly recognised still as a highly intelligent man, but with a massive ego and a big mouth, both of which grew alarmingly when he started drinking.

Even his closest friends, such as journalist Leo Odera, are realistic about Obama Snr's failings during this period: 'You know what happened to Barack? Many of our people, especially those who are very bright at school, when they come out, they don't make a good life outside. There is too much brain, and when they have the whiskies, they go off the rails. Even in journalism, some of my contemporaries have drunk themselves to death.'

From the mid-1970s Barack continued to work at the Treasury. Ruth and her sons were long gone and Barack remained a bachelor for some time. By 1978 he had met a Luo girl called Jael Otieno, and they married in 1981. She became his fourth wife, although he still remained legally married to Kezia. In the summer of 1982 Jael gave birth to a son, George. Then, on the night of 24 November, Barack Obama Snr reached the end of the

road. He had been drinking all evening in a Nairobi bar, as was common
in those days. He left alone and drove home. Minutes later his car drove
off the road and hit a tree, but this time it was not just another road accident. Charles Oluoch, who is cousin to the President, happened to be
working just outside of Nairobi at the time:

> 'I was in Nairobi [at the time]. So Malik, his eldest son, told me his father
> had disappeared. So I rushed into Nairobi and we went up to the police
> station on my motorbike. We saw the vehicle which he was driving, and
> it seemed as if it had left the road and hit a tree. The impact seemed to
> have killed him. Anyway, we went into the city mortuary and we found
> him there. And from there we went back to his house and informed the
> people there. People were crying, and so we stayed throughout the night.
> The next day, we started making arrangements for the funeral.'

Habiba Akumu, paternal grandmother to President Obama, grieving by the
coffin of her son, Barack Obama Snr, K'ogelo, November 1982.

Obama Snr's body was taken from Nairobi back to K'ogelo for the funeral in a coffin. Although he had been raised a Muslim, by the time he went to Hawaii he was a confirmed atheist and considered religion to be nothing more than superstition.[19] Even so, his body was taken out of the coffin and wrapped in a white shroud before being buried, as is customary in an Islamic funeral. Several senior Luo leaders were present, including the Foreign Minister, the late Robert Ouko, and the Education Minister Oloo Aringo. His old drinking friend James Odhiamo was also there:

> 'It was a traditional Luo funeral, and there were a lot of people, three hundred vehicles I would say – cars, *matatus*, minibuses. Lots of people. Quite a number of friends and the elite who were available. Luos say that a funeral lasts for ever. According to the Luos, death will not diminish us.
>
> 'To be honest with you, he was the man I liked most. He was a man who loved almost everybody – no discrimination at all, at all, at all. Barry was one of the best people you could find – he was somebody who cared for the people.'

However, from the very beginning there was serious disquiet in the family over how Barack actually died. Charles Oluoch was at the scene of the accident, and he saw Obama Snr's body soon after:

> 'You might think it was an accident. But when our family saw how he was, it was very hard to realise how the accident killed him. So we were so confused. Because you know . . . Barack had [many other] accidents and they were [potentially] very fatal, but he didn't die. And this one . . . there was no way anything was broken. He was just the normal Barack. But he was dead. So now people were not sure what killed him. Although it looked like an accident, our family suspected that there must have been foul play. I am not a medical doctor. But the way we saw Barack lying there, he didn't look like somebody who was involved in an accident.
>
> 'You see, in these corridors of power, there're a lot of people here and there . . . maybe he'd made enemies. Because you know Barack was very outspoken, and he was very flamboyant, and he was very bright. So maybe some people thought they were threatened.
>
> 'So many people have died like that. So that's why we were worried when the accident didn't look like an accident. When you see somebody

who is said to have died in an accident, but doesn't have anything to show for it – you know, you become suspicious.

'We talked to the mortuary attendant. He had washed him, and when I went to the mortuary with Malik, he was already dressed in a suit. He was very clean and he was even sweating. In fact, I wondered if this man had really died. In fact, I wasn't sure. I was so much shocked.'

These were very serious accusations that Charles was making, and I wondered if perhaps he was a grieving relative who was unable to come to terms with the death of a man whom he loved and respected. Also, with Obama Snr's reputation as a reckless driver, it would seem to be an entirely plausible consequence of irresponsible behaviour on the roads. I raised the issue with Sarah Obama one afternoon, when we were talking in her compound in K'ogelo:

'It is God who arranges these plans. We found him sitting by the steering wheel. [The car] did not roll. So after it was said that he had hit the tree, we just had to believe it, because he could not talk back. We really didn't believe it was a real accident. Because his body was never broken, his vehicle was not badly crashed. He was just dead after the accident. How can you believe that? Not even much blood was seen.

'So why should we believe it was an accident? Even the policeman who was recording this – he was a very high-ranking officer, very big. But he could not say anything because the government was watching his lips. We think there was foul play there, and that is how he died, and they covered it up that he had an accident.

'I also do not believe it was an accident, but we just had to leave it like that because the government then was very harsh.'

Everybody that I spoke to in the family believed much the same thing, and his sister, Hawa Auma, is particularly bitter about the episode. But if Obama Snr's death was not an accident, then it would not be an isolated event, because the assassination of leading Luos has been a regular occurrence over the years. As we have seen, six months before Tom Mboya was killed in July 1969, the Kenyan Foreign Minister Argwings Kodhek was shot and his death made to look like a road accident. More recently, in 1990, the death of Dr Robert Ouko – the Minister of Foreign Affairs in President Moi's government – caused another outrage. Ouko was a leading Luo politician; on the night of 12 February, he was staying at his farm near Kisumu.

The following morning his body was found nearly three kilometres away from his homestead: his right leg was broken in two places, there was evidence that he had been tortured, and he had been killed by a single shot to his head and his body left partially burned. Items including a gun, a can of diesel, and a box of matches were found nearby. The initial police reports claimed that Ouku had committed suicide. Public pressure forced President Moi to request that Britain's Scotland Yard should send a team of detectives to investigate his death. They were unable to determine who had actually killed Dr Ouku, but there was no doubt from the evidence that he had been brutally murdered.

Roy Samo is a Luo local councillor, who lives and works in Kisumu, and he has taken a strong stand against corruption and poor governance. He understands from first-hand experience the risks of becoming involved with politics in Kenya; he has been beaten up on more than ten occasions, and has received many threats on his life. As recently as October 2009 a group of thugs raided his compound and stole his TV and other valuables. They left him a note in Swahili: *Roy wacha siasa, tumetumwa tukumalize, mamayako, baba, ndugu, mke wako sana sana wewe kwani unashinda Ouko or Mboya*. Loosely translated, it means: 'Roy leave politics, we've been sent to kill you, your mother, father, brothers, wife but especially you. We've warned you, do you think you are greater than Ouko or Mboya?' When they left, they decapitated his dog and left its body by the front gate to his compound. In the circumstances, I was not surprised that he too thought foul play was an entirely plausible explanation for Barack Obama Snr's death:

'If you want to talk about political death, it's common. We know of people like Tom Mboya, who was a son of this area. He was a powerful former minister – but he was killed. There have been other powerful cabinet ministers like Robert Ouko. He went abroad, and when he came back, he was killed the following week. People came and took him away, killed him and then his body was burnt. This is a very, very terrible story.

'Apart from Robert Ouko, there are so many Luos who died. Three years ago, a professor, Odhiambo Mbai, was helping us with the drafting of a new constitution. It was in 2006. Odhiambo Mbai was a very wise and influential man. He was killed, shot dead in his house. So many Luos have been killed because they have always been very outspoken. They're bright, they're the professionals – the professors and the doctors. So they are believed to be very wise. So many of them have been killed in cold blood. And it is not only Luos, but anybody who is viewed by the government of the day as anti-establishment.'

But could Barack Obama Snr's death have really been murder and the evidence covered up? Patrick Ngei is another of Obama's old friends. He is not a member of the Obama family, so I thought that he could, perhaps, look on the event dispassionately. Yet he too seemed to suspect the worst:

> 'There were serious allegations of foul play – Obama didn't die out of a pure accident. The Kikuyus were feeling that if we eliminate these bright Luos, then they can rule forever. That was the idea. It was possible. Bright Luos were eliminated by the Kenyatta government. They had this belief that if these people aren't there, then maybe one day they may stop us from going on with the leadership. Moi continued with it. Moi said that he was following in the footsteps of Kenyatta!'

Believing that Barack Obama Snr died at the hands of others is one thing, but proving it more than twenty-five years after his death would now be impossible. Yet in the back of my mind, there was still the question of how such a killing might have been orchestrated. Charles Oluoch had a theory: 'Let's say you are in a place where they put something in your drink and they know you will be driving. At a certain point, you will lose control. It will look as if it was an accident. But already they have poisoned you, so you lose control.'

Charles was making a very serious accusation and I wanted to be absolutely clear what he was implying: 'So you would die from the poisoning anyway?' I asked.

'It's very common,' he replied.

'So even if you had a small accident by driving off the road,' I suggested, 'you would still be dead.'

'You'd be dead.'

On the day that Barack Obama Snr died in Nairobi, a young twenty-one-year-old student at Columbia University in New York was making himself breakfast. The telephone rang, but the line was crackly and the caller indistinct:

'Barry? Barry, is that you?'

'Yes. . . . Who's this?'

'Yes, Barry . . . this is your Aunt Jane. In Nairobi. Can you hear me?'

'I'm sorry – who did you say you were?'[20]

With this briefest of calls from a complete stranger, albeit a relative, Barack Obama Jnr was told of the death of his father – a man whom he recalls only ever meeting once.

The young student went on to graduate the following summer with a degree in political science with a specialisation in international relations, before working briefly for a company that provided international business information to corporate clients. In 1985 he moved to Chicago, where he worked as a community organiser and also with a public housing development on the city's South Side. It was whilst he was in Chicago that Barack Obama Jnr decided to return to college, this time to Harvard – his father's alma mater – to study for a degree in law. But Barack Jnr had one piece of unfinished business before he could move on with the

The graves of Hussein Onyangango and Barack Obama Snr in Sarah Obama's compound in K'ogelo.

rest of his life. In the summer of 1987, he made his first visit to Kenya where he met his extended African family who, until that point, had only been faceless names from the past. He visited K'ogelo, where his step-grandmother still tills the soil made fertile by Onyango's hard labour. And he admits to sitting by the graves of his father and his paternal grandfather, and weeping. Afterwards he felt a calmness wash over him; the circle had finally closed around him. His five-week visit to the home of the Obamas had given him an insight into the person that he really was:

> I saw that my life in America – the black life, the white life, the sense of abandonment I'd felt as a boy, the frustration and hope I'd witnessed in Chicago – all of this was connected with this small plot of earth an ocean away, connected by more than the accident of a name or the color of my skin.[21]

Barack Obama Jnr made two more trips to his African homeland before he became president, and both visits represented key moments in his life. Ten years after the death of his father, he took a twenty-eight-year-old lawyer from Chicago called Michelle Robinson back to K'ogelo and introduced her to Mama Sarah as the woman he intended to marry. Then in 2006 he returned for a third time, this time in a professional capacity; as part of a broad sweep through Africa, Barack Obama – now a Senator for Illinois – made a brief visit to Nairobi and then to K'ogelo.

Now, with the chain of presidential office weighing heavy on his shoulders, never again will he have the opportunity to travel freely and unrecognised in the land of his forefathers.

Riots in Kisumu, December 2008. Anger over claims of vote rigging during the presidential election threw Kenya into turmoil and long-established tribal animosities bubbled to the surface once again.

EPILOGUE

Kinda e teko
Perseverance is strength

Corruption and tribalism in Kenya today;
President Obama and what he can do for the country

Every time I drove west out of Kisumu to visit K'ogelo, or south to Kendu
Bay, I would pass a police roadblock within a few kilometres. They are
spaced at regular intervals along every major road in Kenya, and they are
the bane of every road user in the country. It would be laudable if they were
genuinely checking the roadworthiness of the thousands of trucks which
pass though Kenya to Uganda, Congo and Tanzania, or the dangerously
overloaded *matatus* which have fatal accidents almost daily, or even for
drivers who are not properly licensed and insured to drive their vehicles. If
challenged, the police will claim that this is exactly what they are doing;
but if you sit discreetly two or three rows behind the driver of a *matatu* and
watch carefully, then you will see the real purpose of the police check. The
driver is flagged down and stops, a policeman will exchange a few words,
cast an apprehensive eye over the passengers in the back, and then wave
the driver on. You have to be quick to see the bribe changing hands.

I have also sat in a parked vehicle close to a checkpoint and watched
the other side of the transaction; sometimes the money is slipped surreptitiously through the window, and at other times a 100 Ksh (80 pence) note

is rolled into a tiny ball and dropped outside onto the road, to be collected after the *matatu* has driven off and the policeman can have a quick look around before picking up his sweetener. A *matatu* driver often charges only 50 or 100 Ksh (40 to 80 pence) for a short trip, so the regular bribes taken by the police can sometimes account for as much as 50 per cent of his daily takings. The police target almost all the vehicles – *matatus*, trucks and private cars, but whenever my own vehicle was stopped and they realised there was a *mzungu* inside, they would give me a broad smile, a salute and wish me a good *safari* (the word means a journey in Swahili, and only in English has it been narrowed to mean an expedition in search of wild game).

Police corruption is a fact of life in Kenya, and it has been going on for decades; yet little, if anything, is ever done about it. In 2008 a Kenya Television Network (KTN) television crew covertly videoed police road-blocks in and around Nairobi. They calculated that the police were making at least 15,000 to 18,000 Ksh (£125–£150) a day at each roadblock; each of the manned positions had a senior officer in charge who took the bulk of the bribes, and he made 30,000 Ksh (£2,500) a month or more from the scam. When the report was shown on television, the police authorities and politicians swept the scandal under the carpet; the worst that happened to the officers who were recognisable on the KTN video was that they were transferred to a remote police post. Their illicit earnings were a huge sum of money in a country where the average income is just £460 ($680) a year. Yet corruption by people in positions of power is not a simple issue; constable-level policemen in Kenya earn no more than 10,000 Ksh (£80) a month, and there is a tacit understanding that they are expected to make up their paltry salary by other means, although this will be vehemently denied by the authorities.

It would be unjust to single out police corruption in a country where bribery is common at every level, but the roadblocks are a very public display of a problem which goes right to the top of government. In 2004 a confidential government report was commissioned about ex-President Moi's illegal activities. It was believed to be part of a commitment by President Kibaki to eradicate high-level corruption, following Moi's twenty-four-year rule. The report alleged that President Moi and his two sons were involved in drug dealing, money laundering, and kickbacks; it estimated that Gideon Moi was worth some £550 million (in 2002), while his brother Philip was worth about £384 million.[1] Unfortunately, President Kibaki had a reputation for being spineless, and the joke going around Kenya a few

years ago was that he never saw a fence without wanting to sit on it. So
the report on Moi was never acted upon, and the ex-President and his sons
retained their wealth and they still remain a very influential family in Kenya.
A government spokesman, Alfred Mutua, called the release of the report
on the internet in 2007 a 'political gimmick' ahead of the elections, claiming:
'The government of Kenya believes that the leaking of this report is meant
to score political points against Kibaki.' Today Daniel arap Moi lives in a
vast mansion outside of Eldoret in western Kenya, and is lauded as the
grand old man of Kenyan politics.

With fraud occurring at the highest level, it is not surprising that the
problem runs through government at both national and local level. Even
in Kisumu, public land and buildings have been mysteriously misappro-
priated by senior local government employees, and the money from the
sales has disappeared into private bank accounts. The national newspapers
run stories literally every week of the year which identify alleged embezzlement running into billions of Kenyan shillings a year; yet very little ever
seems to change.

The biggest and longest-running case of corruption in Kenya's history
was the Goldenberg International scandal, which occurred between 1991
and 1993. Like many countries, Kenya encourages international trade by
granting tax-free status to companies who export goods, and it sometimes
subsidises the goods which are sold overseas. It is a way of encouraging
trade and earning much-needed hard currency. Goldenberg International
developed a scheme in which they smuggled gold into Kenya from the
Democratic Republic of the Congo (DRC), and then exported it as Kenyan
gold; this earned the company a 20 per cent subsidy from the government.
Huge sums of money were involved – at least $600 million – which suggests
that at least some senior government officials were involved. At one time
or another, almost all of the politicians in Moi's government were accused
of being involved, as well as many still in positions of power in the current
Kibaki administration. Senior Kenyan judges were also associated with the
scandal, and twenty-three resigned after evidence was presented which impli-
cated them. It is estimated that the Goldenberg embezzlement cost the
country more than 10 per cent of its annual gross domestic product, and
it almost certainly helped finance the brutal war that raged in the DRC
between 1997 and 2002.

Nor is the Goldenberg scandal a thing of the past. As recently as
January 2009 the *East African* ran a headline which announced a new
referral to the Kenya Anti Corruption Commission: 'KACC asked to

probe $98.7 million Triton oil theft at Kenya Pipeline.' Today, most Kenyans acknowledge that corruption is one of the biggest problems facing their country; it has been estimated the average urban Kenyan pays sixteen bribes every month, and that corruption robs local companies of 6 per cent of their revenues.

Kenyans use elaborate euphemisms when they talk about bribery and corruption, and they will frequently talk about somebody who 'eats' or who 'drinks tea'. Another vernacular term is 'TKK' – *towa kitu kidogo* – which means to 'take something small', although more recently cynics claim that it means *towa kila kitu*, which translated from the original Swahili, means 'take everything'. Corruption is endemic in Kenyan society, and it is a problem about which the new US President is acutely aware.

In August 2006 Barack Obama made his third visit to Kenya, but this time it was in an official capacity. He was now a Senator from Illinois, and as part of a two-week whistle-stop tour around Africa he delivered a speech at the University of Nairobi called 'An Honest Government, a Hopeful Future'. He opened his speech by talking of 'the warmth and sense of community that the people of Kenya possess – their sense of hopefulness even in the face of great difficulty'. He also spoke of the difficulties which his father had faced when he returned to work in Nairobi, of problems which 'put him at odds with the politics of tribe and patronage'. He acknowledged the special hurdles that Kenya faced, along with most other African countries, including the legacy of colonialism and national boundaries that were drawn 'without regard to the political and tribal alignments of indigenous peoples, and that therefore fed conflict and tribal strife'.

Then Obama hardened his message, and he became more critical of the path that Kenya was following. He pointed out that when the country gained its independence in the early 1960s, its gross national product was not very different from that of South Korea; yet today, the economy of the Asian country is forty times bigger than Kenya's. Part of the problem, Obama claimed, was that:

'Kenya is failing in its ability to create a government that is transparent and accountable. One that serves its people and is free from corruption. . . . the reason I speak of the freedom that you fought so hard to win is because today that freedom is in jeopardy. It is being threatened by corruption . . .

But while corruption is a problem we all share, here in Kenya it is a crisis – a crisis that's robbing an honest people of the opportunities they have fought for – the opportunity they deserve.'

In his speech, Obama used the word 'corruption' no fewer than twenty times. It was a tough, uncompromising message, but one that had been highlighted before by visiting dignitaries from abroad. But this time, hearing it from Obama was different, for many people see him not only as a fellow Kenyan, but more significantly as a Luo. At the time, Raila Odinga's Luo-based Orange Democratic Party was in opposition and it was proving to be an irritating thorn in the side of President Kibaki's Kikuyu-dominated government. The Kenyan President's spokesman, Alfred Mutua, was very quick to play the tribalism card when he announced that: 'It is very clear that the senator has been used as a puppet to perpetuate opposition politics.'[2] It is probably a declaration that he has since lived to regret.

Yet tribalism marches hand-in-hand with corruption – both problems represent an abuse of power by the strong over the weak and defenceless. It is impossible to count the number of people who have died in tribal-related violence since 1963. In 1992, the Kalenjin targeted Kikuyus and other 'foreigners' in the Rift Valley, and 3,000 people were killed or injured; in 1997, the Coast province was the scene of more aggression towards 'outsiders' – this time it was the Kikuyu, Luo, Luhya and Kamba people.[3] Leaflets were distributed throughout the region, inciting tribal hostility: 'The time has come for us original inhabitants of the coast to claim what is rightfully ours. We must remove these invaders from our land.'[4] Then in the early weeks of 2008, the post-electoral violence resulted in more than a thousand deaths, and the displacement of half a million people.

Richard Richburg is a respected and experienced black American journalist who has been the *Washington Post*'s bureau chief in New York since 2007. Between 1991 and 1995 he was the *Post*'s bureau chief in Nairobi; when he moved on, he wrote a candid book about his experiences called *Out of America: A Black Man Confronts Africa*, in which he admitted:

If there was one thing that I learned traveling around Africa, it was that the tribe remains the defining feature of almost every African society. Old tribal mistrusts and stereotypes linger, and the potential for a violent implosion is never very far from the surface.

Even in the supposedly more sophisticated or developed countries like Kenya, thirty years of independence and 'nation building' had still failed to create any real sense of national identity that could transcend the tribe.

In Kenya, the Kikuyu still think the Luo are inferior and that they, the Kikuyu, have the right to rule. The Luo don't trust the Kikuyu, who they think look down on them. And both tribes look down on the Luhya. It goes on and on.[5]

Although tribalism is rife throughout Africa, it is not universal. On 19 December 1961 the British colony of Tanganyika achieved independence from Britain, and under its first president, Julius Kambarage Nyerere, it ploughed a very different furrow from its northern neighbour. Nyerere was not without his faults, nor Tanzania without its problems; like his contemporary Kenyatta, Nyerere ran his nation for decades with an iron fist and repressed any political opposition, years of *ujamaa* – a dogmatic, inflexible form of socialism – together with rampant corruption left the country impoverished and underdeveloped. Yet as a nation, Tanzania achieved something which has always eluded Kenya; Nyerere was able to mould nearly 130 different ethnic groups and racial minorities into a single, relatively peaceful nation, which gave Tanzania a distinctive national character. Although a rare achievement, it is not unique on the continent. In 1957 the West African state of Ghana achieved independence from Britain under an equally charismatic leader, Kwame Nkrumah. Nkrumah fought tribalism and regionalism, and left Ghana with the enduring legacy of a well-defined regional character and a clear national identity. Yet Ghana is very different from its neighbour Nigeria, another ex-British colony; in Nigeria, an individual will most likely claim to be Hausa or Fulani before they will acknowledge being Nigerian. The reason these nations have developed in different ways is complex, but both Tanzania and Ghana have shown that it is not inevitable for an African state to resort to tribalism after independence.

It was no coincidence then, that when Barack Obama paid his first visit to Africa as President of the United States in July 2009, he chose to visit Ghana and not Kenya. The snub to the government was made all too clear to the ordinary citizens of Kenya when an article in the country's *Daily Nation* reminded its readers:

US President Barack Obama has strongly criticised Kenya's leadership, expressing concern about the country's political and economic direction. Explaining why Ghana was chosen as his first official destination in black

Africa, President Obama singled out the slow pace of reforms as a key impediment in Kenya.

In his most pointed comments on the country of his father's birth, the US President tore into Kenya's leadership saying that 'political parties do not seem to be moving into a permanent reconciliation that would allow the country to move forward.'[6]

In his speech to the Ghanaian Parliament in Accra on 11 July, Obama came back to his theme of tribalism and corruption:

'In my father's life, it was partly tribalism and patronage in an independent Kenya that for a long stretch derailed his career, and we know that this kind of corruption is a daily fact of life for far too many.

'Of course, we also know that is not the whole story. Here in Ghana, you show us a face of Africa that is too often overlooked by a world that sees only tragedy or the need for charity. The people of Ghana have worked hard to put democracy on a firmer footing, with peaceful transfers of power even in the wake of closely contested elections.'[7]

His message was heard very clearly 4,200km away in Nairobi.

It is true that the image of Africa is all too often shaped by short, two-minute features on the evening television news, or in a few words in a headline on the front page of a newspaper; these snippets of news can so easily distort the true image of a nation. Despite the poverty, corruption, poor governance and tribal animosity in Kenya, there is also much that the people should celebrate. If you visit any school in the country, you cannot but be impressed with the eagerness and commitment to learning that practically every child displays. Often they walk miles, barefoot, to the classroom, yet they are always immaculately turned out in their school uniform, well behaved, and eager to work. Often the teacher is without books and the classroom without windows, yet these school children – most of whom can speak three languages before they are ten – consider themselves to be blessed, and they are determined to make the most of their good fortune to be enrolled in a school.

Nor does their eagerness to learn stop when they leave school. I soon realised in my travels in Kenya that you should never throw away a newspaper. Although many people cannot spare even a few shillings to buy a paper for themselves, a donated copy will be eagerly read and passed on a dozen times before eventually being used as wrapping or fuel. Surprisingly, for a country where corruption and bad governance are rife, the press is remarkably free, and every day of the week there is open and candid criticism of politicians and leaders, from the President and Prime Minister down to the local administrator. If you talk with any waiter, street hawker or taxi driver they will eagerly engage you in a discussion about the latest scandal in government. Kenyans always like to keep informed of the news; they may lack power, but they never lack an opinion.

Nor will Barack Obama ever turn his back on Kenya. Although he is President to the American people and will, quite rightly, always put their interests first, he will always be conscious that he has a large and extended family back in Kenya who are subjected to all the challenges of a hand-to-mouth existence in Africa on a daily basis. He will carry on reminding the people of Kenya of the problems and frustrations, the tribalism and the patronage, which prevented his own father from realising his true potential; and Obama's ambassador to Kenya, Michael Ranneberger, will continue to speak out against these issues, openly and bluntly on his behalf.

President Obama's willingness to be direct, open and honest is something which he seems to have inherited from his grandfather Onyango who, for all his faults, would never tolerate deceit or dishonesty. Barack Jnr is a very different man from either his father or his grandfather, but there are family characteristics which seem to flow from his African bloodline; intelligence, resourcefulness, motivation and ambition are all personal qualities which can be traced back several generations, perhaps even as far back as the President's (11) great-grandfather Owiny, who led his people in the second wave of migration into Kenya. Owiny's son Kisodhi, and his grandson Ogelo, are also remembered by the Luo as great leaders. Barack Obama's (3) great-grandfather Obong'o was a pioneer, and he took a huge gamble by leaving his ancestral homeland in Alego and moving south across Winam Gulf to establish a new Obama settlement in Kendu Bay. The President's father and grandfather were also inspirational and highly motivated men in their own right, yet their intrinsic personalities developed in a different place and at a very different time. Many of their behavioural characteristics would be considered entirely inappropriate by today's standards, but they were both products of a very different world, and their conduct should be judged by their standards then and not by our standards now.

President Obama has, inevitably, inherited his genetic make-up from both sides of his family. His mother studied for a PhD as a mature student, so she too was clearly both determined and motivated. In America, Barack Jnr grew up as a young disenfranchised black man in a predominantly white society, and he is well positioned to identify with minorities; he understands what it is like 'to be different'. Between the ages of six and ten he lived in Indonesia – a predominantly non-Christian, foreign society; even though he was young, these were formative years for him, and the experience gave him an insight into other cultures at an early age, which no other US President has experienced. His background is unlike that of any other leader of a major Western nation, and as the world's most powerful statesman, his actions and decisions during his time in office will ultimately affect everybody on the planet.

Inevitably, in the land of his forefathers there is huge anticipation that he will deliver something special for them, and when talking to Kenyans about Barack Obama, they seem sometimes to forget that he is the President of the USA, and not of Kenya. Obama will continue to raise the issue of corruption and tribalism, but perhaps the other contribution that he can make is simply to be his father's son. The Luo of Kenya can identify with him because they are Luo; all the other tribal groups in the country can only claim him as their own by being Kenyan. Perhaps this, more than anything else, will help the ordinary citizens of Kenya to believe in themselves as a single nation.

As the Luo, who, of course, have a proverb for everything, might say: *Kinda e teko* – Perseverance is strength.

NOTES ON METHODOLOGY

Chien kiyany'
The past is never despised

When I set out to research this book, it was my intention to weave a triple narrative: I wanted to trace President Obama's family history back as far as possible; to set this against the fascinating story of the migration of the Luo people from southern Sudan; and to place both of these stories within a greater context of the history of Kenya, as it emerged from the chrysalis of a British colony and spread its wings to become an independent nation. The history of Kenya was, by far, the easiest story to write. Whilst I have drawn on a wide variety of sources, for the most part I have tried to present the history from the perspective of the Kenyan. We are each moulded into the person we are by our upbringing, our schooling and the greater world around us; for my part, I inevitably carry with me the baggage of a white European born into a country still coming to terms with its own decline as a major global power. However, I have worked for much of my life in the developing world, and I have spent many years trying to understand the world from the perspective of others. Whilst writing this book I have talked and listened to dozens of Kenyans, and I have relied extensively on the academic writings of many Kenyan historians. It would be audacious and impudent of me to claim that I can represent the African perspective, but I have tried to present the history of Kenya in a fair, neutral and balanced fashion.

The challenge of trying to unravel the history of the Luo people in general, and the Obama family in particular, places different demands on a writer. There are two main sources of information available: first is the academic literature from historians and archaeologists, which, by its very nature, is conservative and cautious; the second is oral history, which is so often colourful, exciting and enthralling, but which is not governed by the same rules of precision and accuracy as the former. Academic sources might sometimes suffer from being over-dry and guarded in their conclusions, but oral history – despite its appealing flamboyancy – can often be confusing, contradictory, or simply incorrect.[1] So there is an inevitable tension between trying to merge academic sources with oral tradition, and academics will caution you against taking many of these ancestral tales too literally.

Many African historians, including the eminent Professor Bethwell Ogot, consider that the early historical figures such as Jok and Podho and other great Luo ancestors were not real individuals but mythical people whose names were attached to clan genealogies.[2] In support of this theory, he points out that *jok*, for example, means 'god' or 'spirit' in the early Nilotic language, and that *pohi* means 'the land of' in Shilluk.[3] He is right, as an academic, to question the veracity of some of these individuals, but if you talk to Luo elders today, they will tell you with absolute conviction that these people were very real. When I visited William Onyango in Gangu, for example, he had a wealth of information about his ancestors and the life they lived over four centuries ago in Got Ramogi. As the Luo say, *chien kiyany'* – the past is never despised. But like oral histories throughout the world, none of this information has ever been written down; instead, it has been passed down the generations from grandfather to grandson in stories and songs. In this 'personalised history' of their families, every clan and every lineage has tales and traditions which can sometimes contradict those of their neighbours.

Such are the challenges of trying to marry academic history with oral history. What nobody doubts, however, is that a Nilotic people left their cradleland in southern Sudan over six hundred years ago in one of the greatest migrations in the history of Africa. Over a period of a dozen generations or more, they moved south through Uganda and east into Kenya, to form the Luos of western Kenya and northern Tanzania. Whether their leaders were *actually* called Ringruok and Nayo, Jok or Podho, becomes secondary to the greater story to be told; what nobody doubts is that these people had leaders who guided them through their great exodus, and at the very least these names usefully represent people who must have lived hundreds of years ago.

Trying to unravel the Obama family's oral history brings different challenges. What is clear is that a family schism exists which can be traced back to the early nineteenth century. This was when Obong'o, the great-great-great-grandfather to President Obama, left the ancestral lands in K'ogelo as part of a wider movement of the Luo from the overcrowded region of Alego. He moved south across the Winam Gulf and established a new settlement near Kendu Bay, and it was here that the Obamas flourished. In the first decade of the twentieth century, missionaries came to Kendu Bay and the Obamas were baptised into the Church of the Seventh Day Adventists. The one exception was Onyango Obama, grandfather to the President, who ploughed his own furrow and converted to Islam, taking the name Hussein. He insisted that all his wives become Muslims, and likewise his children. When Hussein Onyango resettled in K'ogelo around 1943, the division in the family only widened further, for now they were separated not only by distance, but also by religion. Inevitably, the recollections of past generations of Obamas on opposite sides of Winam Gulf differ, at least in some of the detail.

The only hope of reaching a definitive agreement over the family history was to bring a group of historians and family elders together in one room, and to let them argue it out among themselves. So one morning in June 2009 I invited a dozen family members and Luo elders to Kisumu to formalise the Obama family history (see below for the full list of participants). After several hours of discussion there was a remarkably close consensus, which has allowed us to trace President Obama's lineage back more than twenty generations. However, the group was not unanimous and the one sticking point was whether Ochuo or Otondi was the (4) great-grandfather of President Obama. The choice does not affect the earlier family lineage, but despite many hours of debate, those elders living in Alego could not completely reconcile their oral tradition with those living in south Nyanza.

The other area of uncertainty goes back to the first half of the sixteenth century, with Nyandguogi (born around 1510) and his son Oriambwa (born circa 1539). These two ancestors do not always appear in the family oral history, so there must remain some ambiguity over their inclusion in the lineage. However, I could find nobody who could claim with any certainty that they should *not* be included, so their names have stayed.

The last part of the ancestry jigsaw was to place approximate dates on past generations. In trying to develop a history based primarily on oral sources, there are very few confirmed dates available, such as from carbon dating, for example. Therefore the logical approach was to work back from the oldest reliable date in the Obama family, and that was the birth year of Hussein Onyango. It is important to clarify this date because this is the earliest birth date in the family which can be reliably confirmed, and it is from this year that all the earlier generations of the family can be traced. Unfortunately even this approach is not that straightforward.

Most sources give Hussein Onyango's year of birth as 1895 and the year of his death as 1975, although President Obama claims 1979 to be the date of his grandfather's death in *Dreams from My Father*.[4] From talking to people who knew Hussein Onyango and who went to his funeral, he was clearly an old man when he died, probably in his eighties. Yet the brass plaque on his grave in Sarah Obama's compound in K'ogelo reads *Mzee Hussein Onyango Obama, 1870–1975*. I asked Sarah about the date and she was absolutely certain that the plaque was correct: 'The dates you find there are the right ones, and they were written by Barack Senior [the President's father].' If this figure is correct, then Onyango Obama was 105 years old when he died – not an impossible age, but unlikely. If he was born in 1870, he would have been forty-four years old when he joined the King's African Rifles during the First World War, and he would have been seventy when he was in Addis Ababa working as a cook for a British army officer during the Second World War. This alone suggests that Onyango could not have been born as early as 1870; however, there is more evidence which can help substantiate the correct birth date.

Onyango married Sarah, his third wife, in 1943. If Onyango had been born in 1870, then he would have been seventy-three when he married. Onyango went on to father four children with Sarah – this would have been quite an achievement for a man in his seventies. Had he been born in 1895, a date which I have always thought to be the correct one, then he would have been forty-eight years old when he married for the fifth time – still a middle-aged man, but not an unreasonable age for a Luo to take another wife. Based on all this evidence, as well as discussions with people who knew him, his birth date is much more likely to be 1895 than 1870, and 1895 is therefore the date which I have used as the basis for fixing earlier dates in the family ancestry.

The next challenge was to work out exactly when Obama's ancestors were born. African oral history generally relies on listing early generations in the correct genealogical order, but it rarely makes reference to actual dates. However in the West, our written history allows us the luxury of using precise dates: we know, for example, that King John signed the Magna Carta in 1215, that the Spanish launched their great Armada to invade

England in 1588, and that the Boston Tea Party occurred in 1773. We are used to hanging our history on exact dates. Therefore in order to work back from Hussein Obama's birth year in 1895 to give approximate birth dates to earlier generations, it is necessary to define a patrilineal generation – this is the *average* age gap between the birth of a male baby and the birth of his first-born surviving son.

In discussion with African historians, it became clear to me that this patrilineal generation can vary between twenty-six and thirty-three years for the Luo. The historian Professor Bethwell Ogot wrote his PhD thesis on the Southern Luo of Kenya, and he found that in a traditional Padhola society, the first surviving child in a family was usually born when the father was between twenty-five and twenty-eight years old, with a mean generation to be twenty-seven years.[5] However, he accepted that this figure might, if anything, be an *underestimate*, and he quotes Archdeacon W. E. Owen, who believed that the generation gap for the Luo could not be less than thirty years.[6] There are good reasons to suppose that the length of a typical generation should be longer than twenty-seven years. For example, girls are not usually recorded in a family's ancestral history, so their births would extend the date between the births of male babies. Nor does Ogot's system take into account infant mortality; in the past it was not unusual for one baby in every three or four to die before it reached the age of five, and this would extend the generation gap. Luo men also had to prove themselves as warriors and fearless hunters before they earned the right to marry, and this too would have reduced the numbers of young men who reached the age to take a wife, thereby stretching the generation gap still further.

Taking all this into account, I have settled on a patrilineal generation of twenty-nine years to use in preparing the Obama ancestry that appears at the front of this volume. Usually, children are born to a fertile mother at regular intervals of two years, and this average figure can be used to estimate the birth year of later siblings; for example, the third child can be assumed to be born roughly four years after the first. Professor Roland Oliver, who worked extensively in Uganda, calculated that plus or minus two years should be allowed as a margin of error for each generation, or approximately seven years a century.[7] So by combining these two systems, it is possible to work back from the earliest known birth date in the Obama family – that of 1895 for Onyango Hussein – and calculate, for example, that President Obama's (15) great-grandfather Podho II was born in the mid-fifteenth century, plus or minus thirty years. It is a crude system with inevitable flaws. For example, it cannot allow for the complexities of a man fathering children from several wives, nor does it allow for infertility or low fertility which might extend the interval between births. So even taking a patrilineal generation as twenty-nine years might still be an under-estimate. Nevertheless, no matter however rudimentary this method might be, it does at least give an indication of the likely period in which these ancestors lived, and these patrilineal generation ages do seem to correspond closely with the few independent dates which have been established by archaeologists using other techniques such as carbon dating and excavation.

Those attending the Obama ancestry meeting in Kisumu, June 2009, were:

Aloyce Achayo, retired teacher, respected cultural historian and a good friend of Obama Snr

James Ojwang' Adhoch, Ojuando-K'ogelo; Alego elder and historian and friend of Mama Sarah

Elly Yonga Adhiambo, Kendu Bay; distant cousin of Obama Snr

John Aguk Ndalo; K'obama elder and a good friend of Hussein Onyango

Jackob Ramogi Amolo, Ndere-K'ogelo; respected Luo cultural historian and close friend of Mama Sarah, he is frequently consulted on Luo cultural issues

Joseph Okoth Amolo, Alego-K'ogelo; Luo elder

Peter Omondi Amolo, Ndere-K'ogelo; Luo elder

Patrick Ngeyi, Alego; retired history teacher who once shared a house with Obama Snr in Nairobi

Laban Opiyo, Karachuonyo; uncle of Hussein Onyango who, as a young man, worked for Obama Opiyo on his farm in Kendu Bay

Bishop Nashon Opondo, Kanyinek-K'ogelo; Alego elder and historian and friend of Mama Sarah

Wilson Obama, Kisumu; cousin to President Obama, elder brother of Charles Oluoch and representative of the Obama family members in K'obama, Kendu Bay

Roy Samo, consultant and local councillor, Kisumu

GLOSSARY OF PEOPLE

Achayo, Aloyce (b. c. 1932)   Retired headmaster and Luo cultural historian

Aginga, Joshua (c. 1864–1935?)   Third son of Obama Opiyo

Ainsworth, John (1864–1946)   An early British settler in Kenya

Akinyi, Pamela (b. 1976)   Clinical administrator in the Centre for Disease Control in K'ogelo

Akumu Njoga   *See* Habiba Akumu

al-Mazrui, Sulaiman bin Ali (dates unknown)   Mazrui chief who asked that Mombasa become a protectorate of Britain as a defence against the threat from the Sultan of Oman

Amin, Idi (c. 1925–2003)   Military dictator and President of Uganda 1971–9

Anderson, David (b. 1957)   Professor of African Politics and Director of the African Studies Centre, University of Oxford

Aruwa (c. mid-15th century)   Brother of Podho II; of spear and bead fame

Atieno Amani, Mwanaisha (b. c. 1938)   Older sister of Kezia Obama

Baring, Sir Evelyn (1903–73)   Governor-General in Kenya 1952–9, which covered the whole of the Mau Mau emergency

Baumann, Oscar (1864–99)   Austrian explorer who wrote about the Maasai in the late nineteenth century

Bismarck, Otto (1815–98) — German statesman responsible for establishing Germany's African colonies

Blundell, Sir Michael (1907–93) — Kenyan farmer, member of parliament for the Rift Valley, and Minister without Portfolio to the Emergency War Council during the Mau Mau insurgency

Burton, Richard (1821–90) — British explorer, who travelled to the lakes region of central Africa with John Speke

Carscallen, Arthur Asa Grandville (1879–1964) — The first Seventh Day Adventist missionary in Kendu Bay; he arrived in Kisumu in November 1906

Carscallen, Helen (c. 1885–1921) — Wife of Arthur Carscallen (m. 27 July 1907 in Kendu Bay), née Helen Bruce Thompson

Chamberlain, Joseph (1863–1914) — British politician who served as Colonial Secretary 1895–1903

Chilo Were, Samson (b. 1922) — Barack Obama Snr's primary school teacher

Cholmondeley, Hugh — *See* Delamare, Lord

Crazzolara, Joseph Pasquale (1884–1976) — Catholic missionary who worked for much of his life in East Africa and who was responsible for pioneering anthropological work on the Luo

Delamare, Lord (1870–1931) — Third Baron Delamare KCMG, who moved to Kenya in 1901, where he became one of the most influential British settlers

Dunde, Onyango (c. 1885–1960?) — Luo prophet of the Mumbo spirit

Dunham, Madelyn (1922–2008) — Née Payne, mother of Ann Dunham and maternal grandmother of President Obama

Dunham, Stanley Ann — *See* Obama, Ann

Dunham, Stanley Armour (1918–92) — Father of Ann Dunham and maternal grandfather of President Obama

Eliot, Sir Charles Norton Edgecumbe (1862–1931) — British career diplomat and linguist who was made Governor of British East Africa in 1901

Elkins, Caroline (b. 1969) — Professor of History at Harvard University and author of *Imperial Reckoning: The Untold Story of Britain's Gulag in Kenya*

Gama, Vasco da (1460/69–1524) — Portuguese explorer who was the first European to round the Cape of Good Hope; he landed in Mombasa in 1498 and sailed on to Kerala in India

Gethin, Richard (1886–1950?) British trader and the first to establish a presence in Kisii in south Nyanza in the early twentieth century

Gipiir (*c*. mid-15th century) A son of Olum; also known as Nyipiir; lived in Pubungu

Grant, Jos (1874–1947) and Nellie (1885–1977) Early British settlers in Kenya and parents of Elspeth Huxley

Habiba Akumu (*c*. 1916–2006) Née Akumu Njoga, fourth wife of Onyango Obama (m. 1933), mother of Barack Obama Snr and paternal grandmother of President Obama

Halima (dates unknown) Second wife of Onyango Obama (m. c. 1930); she came from the Ugenya region of Central Nyanza

Hobley, Charles William (1867–1947) Pioneering British colonial administrator in British East Africa 1894–1921; closely involved with the early subjugation of the Luo

Huxley, Elspeth (1907–97) British-Kenyan author, journalist, broadcaster, magistrate and early environmentalist

Johnston, Sir Harry (1858–1927) Explorer and colonial administrator who was a key British player in the 'Scramble for Africa'

Jühlke, Karl Ludwig (1856–86) Colleague of Karl Peters, he was murdered in Kismayu (now Somalia) on 1 December 1886

Kalulu (*c*. 1870–87) Henry Stanley's loyal boy servant who travelled with him from 1882, before drowning in the River Congo

Kenyatta, Jomo (1894–1978) Leading Kenyan politician; arrested by the British in 1952 and imprisoned; released in 1961, he took control of the negotiations for independence and became the first President Kenya in December 1963, holding that office until his death

Kiano, Jane (dates unknown) American-born wife of Dr Julius Kiano; she was influential in Barack Obama Snr obtaining a scholarship to the University of Hawaii

Kiano, Dr Julius Gikonyo (1930–2003) An influential politician and educationalist who supported Tom Mboya's 'student airlift' in the 1960s

Kibaki, Mwai (b. 1931) — Kenyan politician and the third President of Kenya; Minister of Finance (1969–81) under Kenyatta; Minister for Home Affairs (1982–8) and Minister for Health (1988–91) under Moi

Kimathi Waciuri, Dedan (1920–57) — Mau Mau leader shot and captured in October 1956, and subsequently hanged; his death effectively brought an end to the Mau Mau emergency

Kinyole arap Turukat (b. c. 1850) — Nandi *orkoiyot* or spiritual leader who predicted that a big snake would come across their lands belching smoke and fire, widely interpreted as the Uganda Railway

Kisodhi (b. c. 1597) — Early Luo leader and (10) great-grandfather of President Obama

Kodhek, Argwings (1923–69) — Luo Kenyan Foreign Minister in Jomo Kenyatta's government, assassinated in July 1969 in what was made to look like a road accident

Koitalel arap Samoei (1860–1905) — Nandi leader who fought the British over the Uganda Railway

Krapf, Dr Johann Ludwig (1810–81) — German Protestant missionary and accomplished linguist who arrived in Zanzibar in 1844

Labong'o (b. c. 1480) — Luo leader in Pubungu in the late fifteenth century who displaced the ruling Bachwezi dynasty; also known as Nyabong'o

Lansdowne, Lord (1845–1927) — Henry Charles Keith Petty-Fitzmaurice, 5th Marquess of Lansdowne, KG, GCSI, GCMG, GCIE, PC; British politician and Irish peer; Secretary of State for Foreign Affairs 1900–5

Lettow-Vorbeck, General Von Paul (1870–1964) — Commander of the German forces in East Africa during the First World War

Livingstone, Dr David (1813–73) — Scottish medical missionary, explorer and leading anti-slavery campaigner who travelled first to South Africa in 1841, then to East Africa in 1866

Lugard, Lord Frederick (1885–1945) — British explorer and colonial administrator; High Commissioner of the Protectorate of Northern Nigeria 1899–1906

Mackinnon, William (1823–93)	Glaswegian ship owner who became chairman of the British East Africa Company
Mazrui	*See* al-Mazrui, Sulaiman bin Ali
Mboya, Paul (1902–2000)	Luo chief who governed Kendu Bay during the 1930s and 1940s; he was in regular conflict with Onyango Obama
Mboya, Tom (1930–69)	Leading Luo politician, closely involved in the foundation of the Kenya African National Union (KANU) and Minister of Economic Planning and Development at the time of his assassination in Nairobi on 5 July 1969
Meinertzhagen, Colonel Richard (1878–1967)	British officer accused of shooting dead the Nandi supreme chief, Koitalel arap Samoei, in 1905
Mitchell, Sir Philip (1890–1964)	Officer in the KAR who rose to the rank of major general; Governor of Kenya 1944–52
Moi, Daniel arap (b. 1924)	Second President of Kenya 1978–2002, but now tainted by corruption scandals; he lives in retirement near Eldoret and is largely shunned by the current political establishment
Moi, Gideon (b. 1964)	Youngest son of ex-President Moi, claimed to have amassed a fortune of £550 million by 2002
Moi, Philip (b. 1956)	Son of ex-President Moi, claimed to have amassed a fortune of £384 million by 2002
Msovero (dates unknown)	Local chief in Usagara, Kenya, who signed over his land to Karl Peters in 1884
Mutua, Alfred (b. 1970)	Official spokesman for the Kibaki government
Nabong'o Shiundu (1841–82)	Notorious African slave trader
Ndalo, John Aguk (b. 1924)	Luo elder who knew Onyango Obama well; he still lives in Kendu Bay
Ndalo, Raburu (c. 1893–1925)	Older brother of Onyango Obama; born in Kendu Bay and died (with his two wives) of smallpox in K'ogelo
Ndesandjo, David Opiyo Obama (1969?–87)	Son of Barack Obama Snr and Ruth Nidesand and half-brother of President Obama; died in a motorcycle accident
Ndesandjo, Mark Okoth Obama (b. 1966?)	Eldest son of Barack Obama and Ruth Nidesand and half-brother of President Obama; now runs

	an internet company and corporate advice company in Shenzhen, China
Ndesandjo, Ruth	*See* Nidesand, Ruth
Ngei, Patrick (b. *c.* 1934)	Friend of Barack Obama Snr, now living in Kisumu
Ng'ong'a Odima (b. *c.* 1880)	Corrupt Luo chief who governed the Alego region, north of Winam Gulf under the British
Nidesand, Ruth (b. *c.* 1940)	Teacher from Boston, Mass. who became Barack Obama Snr's third wife; divorced, she later remarried Simeon Ndesandjo; now a kindergarten teacher in Nairobi
Njenga Njoroge, Isaac (*c.* 1947–69?)	Young Kikuyu man found guilty of Tom Mboya's assassination; allegedly executed on 25 November 1969, although rumours persist that he was spirited off to Ethiopia
Nkrumah, Kwame (1909–72)	Charismatic first President of Ghana
Nyabondo, Joseph (b. *c.* 1924)	Brother of Habiba Akumu and great-uncle of President Obama
Nyabong'o	*See* Labong'o
Nyandega, Kezia	*See* Obama, Kezia
Nyaoke (*c.* 1875–1935?)	Senior wife of Obama (son of Opiyo), mother of Onyango and great-grandmother of President Obama
Nyerere, Julius Kambarage (1922–99)	First President of Tanzania who firmly suppressed political opposition, but who also created a strong national identity
Nyipiir	*See* Gipiir
Obama, Abo (b. 1968)	Alleged half-brother of President Obama, born in K'ogelo and is now the manager of a mobile phone shop in Kenya; also known as Samson
Obama, Ann (1942–95)	Née Stanley Ann Dunham; second wife of Barack Obama Snr and mother of President Obama
Obama, Dr Auma (b. 1960)	Second child of Barack Obama Snr and Kezia and half-sister of President Obama; now lives in Nairobi
Obama, Barack Jnr (b. 1961)	44th President of the United States; born in Hawaii and was called Barry as a young boy

Obama, Barack Snr (1936–82)   Father of President Obama; an economist in the Kenyan government before his death in a road accident in Nairobi in 1982

Obama, Bernard (b. 1970)   Alleged half-brother of President Obama, born in Kenya, but now lives in Bracknell, England, with his mother Kezia

Obama, Hawa Auma (b. 1942)   Aunt and closest living relative of President Obama, third child of Onyango and Akumu and the younger sister of Barack Obama Snr; lives in Oyugis in south Nyanza

Obama, Hussein Onyango (1895–1975)   Grandfather of President Obama; born in Kendu Bay but moved to K'ogelo around late 1943 or 1944; farmer and house servant

Obama, Kezia (b. c. 1940)   Barack Obama Snr's first wife, born and raised in Kendu Bay; also known as Grace, she now lives in Bracknell, England

Obama, Malik (b. 1958)   Eldest son of Barack Obama Snr and Kezia and half-brother of President Obama; now lives in Siaya (near K'ogelo) but still keeps a house opposite Sarah Obama's compound; also called Abongo or Roy

Obama, Omar (b. 1944)   Eldest son of Onyango Obama and 'Mama' Sarah and half-uncle to President Obama; born in K'ogelo and now lives in Boston, Mass.

Obama Opiyo (c. 1833–1900?)   Great-great grandfather of President Obama; farmer and Luo warrior who lived in the Kendu Bay area near Lake Victoria

Obama, Sarah (b. 1922)   Known as 'Mama' Sarah; fifth wife of Hussein Onyango Obama (m. 1941) and step-grandmother of President Obama; née Sarah Ogwel

Obama, Sarah Nyaoke (1934–2000?)   Oldest daughter of Onyango Obama and Akumu

Obama, Sayid (b. c. 1950s)   Son of Onyango Obama and 'Mama' Sarah (b. K'ogelo); half-uncle of President Obama; works in a molasses factory in Kisumu

Obama, Yusuf (b. c. 1950s)   Son of Onyango Obama and 'Mama' Sarah (b. K'ogelo); half-uncle of President Obama

Obama, Zeituni Onyango (b. 1952)   Daughter of Onyango Obama and Sarah (b. Kendu Bay); half-aunt of President Obama

Obong'o (b. c. 1802)   (3) great-grandfather of President Obama; left his ancestral home in K'ogelo and established a homestead in the Kendu Bay area around 1830

Ochieng', William R. (b. 1943)   Professor of History at Maseno University, Kisumu

Odera, Sofia (c. 1914–90?)   Third wife of Onyango Obama (m. c. 1932)

Odhiambo Ochieng', James (b. 1941)   Friend of Barack Obama Snr at Harvard

Odhiambo, Zablon (b. c. 1960)   Keeper of Got Ager

Odhiambo Mbai, Dr Crispin (1954–2003)   Senior Luo official of the Kenya constitution review commission, assassinated 14 September 2003

Odinga, Raila (b. 1945)   Current prime minister of Kenya; son of Oginga Odinga

Odonei Ojuka, Charles (b. c. 1922)   Brother of Habiba Akumu and a great-uncle of President Obama

Ogelo (b. c. 1626)   President Obama's (9) great-grandfather and the first person to settle in K'ogelo around 1660

Oginga Odinga, Jaramogi Ajuma (c. 1911–94)   Leading Luo politician, government minister and vice-president during early independence in Kenya; from Bondo, a village near K'ogelo in central Nyanza

Ogot, Bethwell A. (b. 1929)   Professor of History and incumbent chancellor of Moi University, Eldoret

Okech, Abdo Omar (b. 1933)   Younger brother of 'Mama' Sarah Obama

Okwiri, Jonathan (dates unknown)   A teacher from Nyanza who founded the Young Kavirondo Association in 1922

Oluoch, Charles (b. 1948)   Second son of Peter Oluoch, who was adopted and raised by his uncle, Onyango Obama; retired and living in Kendu Bay

Oluoch, Peter (c. 1923–2000?)   Second son of Ndalo Raburu, adopted by Onyango Obama

Oluoch, Wilson Obama (b. c. 1946)   Oldest son of Peter Oluoch; runs a general store in Kisumu; attended President Obama's inauguration in January 2009

Olum (c. 1460)   An influential Luo leader based in Pubungu in the mid- to late fifteenth century

Omolo, Leo Odera (b. 1936)   An eminent Luo journalist, now living in Kisumu

Onyango, William (b. c. 1960)   A farmer living near Got Ramogi

Onyango Mobam (b. *c.* 1713)   (6) great-grandfather of President Obama; *mobam* means 'born with a crooked back', and the name was probably corrupted to Obama

Opiyo, Laban (b. 1920)   Luo elder still living near Kendu Bay; first cousin of Onyango Obama

Otieno, James (b. *c.* 1920)   Luo elder still living in Kendu Bay

Otieno, Joseph (b. *c.* 1942)   Retired farmer and Luo elder from a remote community in Gangu in western Kenya

Otin, Magdalene (b. *c.* 1938)   School friend of Barack Obama Snr, still living in a traditional round hut in K'ogelo

Ouko, Dr Robert (1931–90)   Luo Minister of Foreign Affairs in President Moi's government, assassinated 12 February 1990

Owen, Archdeacon Walter Edwin (1879–1945)   Anglican Archdeacon in Nyanza who effectively blunted the political demands of the Young Kavirondo Association in 1922

Owen, Captain William Fitzwilliam (1774–1857)   Royal Navy captain who established British control in Mombasa in 1824

Owiny Sigoma (b. *c.* 1635)   Younger son of Kisodhi who fought his brother Ogelo over the family leadership

Owiny the Great (b. *c.* 1568)   Ancient Luo leader and warrior, and believed to be the (11) great-grandfather of President Obama

Patterson, John Henry (1865–1947)   Chief engineer on the Uganda Railway who was responsible for shooting dead the two marauding lions of Tsavo

Peters, Karl (1856–1918)   German traveller in East Africa and one of the founding members of the Gesellschaft für Deutsche Kolonisation (Society for German Colonisation)

Pfeil, Count Joachim von (1857–1924)   Colleague of Karl Peters who was also involved in establishing the Gesellschaft für Deutsche Kolonisation

Podho II (b. *c.* 1452)   Probably lived in Pubungu and linked to the spear and bead story with his brother Aruwa

Poeschel, Hans (1881–1960)   Editor of *Deutsch-Ostafrika Zeitung* during the First World War

Rando, Lando (b. *c.* 1920)   Luo elder and oral historian from the Siaya region

Ramogi Ajwang' (b. *c.* 1503)   By oral tradition, the first Luo to settle in Kenya, probably around the early sixteenth century

Rebmann, Johannes (1820–76)   Swiss Lutheran missionary who joined Johann Krapf in East Africa in 1846

Richburg, Richard B. (b. 1958)   The *Washington Post*'s bureau chief in Nairobi 1991–5 and author of *Out of America: A Black Man Confronts Africa*, a candid account of his time in Africa

Ruck, Roger, Esme and Michael (d. 1953)   Family of white settlers brutally murdered in January 1953 during the early months of the Mau Mau uprising

Salisbury, Lord (1830–1903)   Robert Arthur Talbot Gascoyne-Cecil, 3rd Marquess of Salisbury, KG, GCVO, PC; was a British Prime Minister on three occasions and presided over the partition of Africa

Samo, Roy (b. 1981)   Local councillor in Kisumu region

Seje (*c.* 1650)   A Luo leader in Nyanza

Seyyid Sa'id (1790–1856)   Ruler of Oman and a successful slave trader in the early nineteenth century

Solf, Dr Wilhelm Heinrich (1862–1926)   German Secretary of State for the Colonies during the First World War

Speke, John (1827–64)   British explorer who travelled to the lakes region of central Africa and was the first European to see Lake Victoria

Stanley, Henry Morton (1841–1904)   Welsh-born journalist and explorer who famously found Livingstone, and who later circumnavigated Lake Victoria, and then went on to traverse Africa from east to west

Thompson, Helen Bruce   *See* Carscallen, Helen

Thomson, Joseph (1858–95)   Scottish explorer who travelled extensively in Kenya in the early 1880s

Thuku, Harry (1895–1970)   Kenyan political activist and founder of the Young Kikuyu Association

Tifool (*c.* 1450)   A son of Olum; lived in Pubungu during the middle part of the fifteenth century

Zheng He (1371/75–1435?)   Chinese admiral whose fleet sailed to East Africa in 1414

GLOSSARY OF
TERMS AND
PLACE NAMES

adhula	Traditional Luo hockey game
agoro	Luo victory song chanted after battle
ajua	Popular Luo game played with small pebbles on a board with two rows of eight holes
ajuoga	Luo expert in dispensing medicine and magic
Albert, Lake	One of the African Great Lakes and part of the complex river system of the Upper Nile
arungu	Luo war club
as-Sudd	*See* Sudd
asere	Luo arrow
askari	A locally recruited East African soldier; the word is also used to denote anybody in uniform, such as a policeman
baba	Swahili word meaning 'father'
Bahr-al-Ghazāl	Arabic name for the River of Gazelles in southern Sudan
Bahr-al-Jabal	Arabic name for the White Nile
Bantu	Collection of over 400 ethnic groups in Africa who share a language group and a broad ancestral culture
BEA	British East Africa
Berlin Conference	The conference that established European spheres of

	influence in Africa, which ran from 15 November 1884 to 26 February 1885
bhang	Swahili word for marihuana
bilharzia	Parasitic fluke caught from a water snail which can cause damage to internal organs and impair a child's growth
British East Africa Company (BEAC)	Predecessor to the Imperial British East Africa Company (IBEAC), a chartered company formed in 1888
bul ker	Luo sacred drum
bware	Plant used in traditional Luo medicine
chang'aa	Traditional Kenyan 'home brew', now often supplemented with industrial alcohol to make a dangerously strong drink
chiwo	Present or payment given to a traditional Luo diviner
chola	A state of *purdah* by the wives of a deceased man, which can last several months before they are 'inherited'
Chollo	*See* Shilluk
contagious bovine pleuropneumonia (CBPP)	Also known as lung plague, a contagious bacterial infection which affects cattle, buffalo and zebu and which devastated herds in Kenya in the late nineteenth and early twentieth centuries
crocuta	Dholuo name for the spotted hyena
Deutsch-Ostafrika	German East Africa before the First World War, comprising present-day Tanzania, Rwanda and Burundi
Deutsche Ost-Afrika Gesellschaft	The German East Africa Company, founded by Karl Peters and his colleagues in 1885
Dholuo	The traditional Luo language
diero	Part of a traditional Luo wedding celebration
Dinka	A tribe of the Bahr-al-Ghazāl region of the Nile basin in southern Sudan; *see also* Jii-speakers
Dunga Beach	Fishing village on the shore of Winam Gulf, close to Kisumu
duol	Small hut of the head of a Luo family
East Africa Protectorate	*See* Imperial British East Africa Company (IBEAC)
Elgon, Mount	Dormant volcano on the border of Kenya and Uganda; at 4,320m it is the second highest mountain in Kenya
Euphorbia candelabrum	Spiky succulent which is traditionally found in many Luo homesteads
Fort Jesus	Large defensive stronghold built by the Portuguese in Mombasa in 1593 to protect the harbour

Gangu	Region in western Kenya, first settled by the Luo at the beginning of the sixteenth century; pronounced 'Gang'
gangi	Literally 'casting pebbles', a technique using small stones or cowrie shells to tell the future
Gendia	Site of the first Seventh Day Adventist mission in Kendu Bay, established in 1907
Gesellschaft für Deutsche Kolonisation	*See* Peters, Karl in Glossary of People
golo nyathi	Lit. 'removing the baby'; when a four-day-old baby is introduced to the world by leaving it outside the mother's hut
Got Ager	Traditional hill fortress of the Luo leader Ager, believed to have been inhabited during the mid-seventeenth century
Got Ramogi	Traditional hill fortress of the Luo leader, Ramogi, believed to have been inhabited from the early sixteenth century
gundni bur	Ancient Luo fortified communities
Harvard	Prestigious university in Boston, Mass.; alma mater of both Barack Obama Snr and President Obama
Homa Bay	Fishing village on the south side of Winam Gulf, about 20km west of Kendu Bay
Imatong Mountains	A mountain range on the border between Sudan and Uganda
Imperial British East Africa Company (IBEAC)	Formed in 1888 as a commercial association to develop African trade in the areas controlled by the British; as the administrative body of British East Africa, it was the forerunner of the East Africa Protectorate, later to become Kenya
jachien	Luo demonic spirit
jadak	Dholuo name for a foreigner or outsider
jagam	A 'pathfinder' or marriage maker
jago	Luo sub-chief
janak	Luo elder who traditionally removes teeth during an initiation ceremony; *see nak*
Jiaang	Another name for the Dinka
Jii-speakers	A collective name for people living in southern Sudan that include the Luo, the Jiaang (or Dinka) and the Naath (or Nuer)

jodong'	Part of a traditional Luo wedding celebration
jojuogi	Luo witch, sorcerer or magician
jo-kal	Luo chief's enclosure
Joka-Jok	The first wave of Luo migrants who entered western Kenya between 1530 and 1680
Jok'Omolo	A third wave of Luo migrants who entered Kenya in the late seventeenth century
Jok'Owiny	Luo followers of Owiny, who formed a second wave of migrants who arrived in western Kenya in the early seventeenth century
Juba	City in southern Sudan, situated on the banks of the White Nile
Kajulu	Sprawling rural village north of Kisumu
kal	Brown finger-millet flour; *see also mbare*
Kalenjin	Ethnic group of Nilotic people living mainly in the Kenyan Rift Valley; the fourth largest tribal group in Kenya
kalo nyathi	First lovemaking between a father and mother after the birth of a child, usually on the fourth day; literally, 'jumping over the child'.
Kamba	A Bantu ethnic group who live in the semi-arid Eastern province of Kenya; they were renowned as middle-men and traders
Kampala	Capital of Uganda
kanga	Famine in Luoland in 1919; also used to refer to the Administration Police in Kenya
KAR	*See* King's African Rifles
Kavirondo, Gulf	Early name for the Winam Gulf
Kavirondo region	Early name given to Nyanza by the colonial British
Kendu Bay	Small town on the southern shore of Winam Gulf; home to the majority of the Obama family
Kenya	Country in East Africa previously under the colonial rule of the British; achieved independence on 12 December 1963
Kenya, Mount	The highest mountain in Kenya; called Kirinyaga by the Kikuyu and Kirenia by the Embu
Kenya African Democratic Union (KADU)	Formed in 1960 to defend the interests of the Kalenjin, Maasai, Samburu and Turkana against the dominance of the larger Luo and Kikuyu tribes who dominated

KANU; in 1964, KADU dissolved itself voluntarily and merged with KANU

Kenya African
National Union
(KANU)

In 1960, KAU merged with the Kenya Independent Movement and the People's Congress Party to form KANU; after 1969, KANU, led by Kenyatta, remained the only political party in Kenya until 2002

Kenya African Union
(KAU)

Originally called the Kenya African Study Union, the KAU was a political organisation formed in 1944 to articulate grievances against British colonial rule; in 1946, Kenyatta returned to Kenya and became its unrivalled leader (*see* also Kenya African National Union)

Kenya Emergency

See Mau Mau

Kenya People's Union
(KPU)

A small but influential socialist party formed in 1966 by the Luo politician, Jaramogi Oginga Odinga, a former vice president; the Union was banned by Kenyatta in 1969

ker

Luo king

Kibera

Shanty town west of Nairobi and home to an estimated one million people, making it Africa's largest slum

Kikuyu

Kenya's most populous ethnic group, comprising approximately 22 per cent of the population

Kikuyu Central
Association (KCA)

Political organisation formed in 1924–5 (after the Young Kikuyu Association was banned in 1922) to represent the interests of the Kikuyu people against British colonial rule; the KCA was banned by the British in 1940 with the outbreak of war in East Africa

Kilimanjaro, Mount

Volcanic mountain in Tanzania, at 4,600m the highest in East Africa; in 1848 Johannes Rebmann became the first European to identify it

King's African Rifles

A British multi-battalion colonial regiment which operated in East Africa from 1902 until independence in 1963

kipande

Small steel cylinder containing identity papers, which every African labourer had to wear, and without which he could not find employment; taken from the Swahili word meaning 'a piece', or 'a part of something'

kiru

A traditional hut made from branches and leaves

Kisii

A major town in central south Nyanza; also a name for the Kisii people or Kisii tribe

Kismayo	City on the Indian Ocean (now in southern Somalia), used as a detention camp by the colonial British
Kisumu	Kenya's third largest city and capital of the Nyanza province; a port on the shores of Winam Gulf; founded in 1901 when the Uganda Railway reached Lake Victoria, and originally called Port Florence
Kiswahili	The Swahili word for the Swahili language, also sometimes used in English
Kit Mikayi	A dramatic rock formation outside of Kisumu, literally 'stones of the first wife'
Kitara	Ancient kingdom in Uganda which plays an important role in the oral tradition of the great lakes region of East Africa; it was at the height of its power in the fourteenth and fifteenth centuries, until invaded by the Luo
K'obama	Village in Kendu Bay and home to the majority of the Obama family
K'ogelo	Village in Siaya district in central Nyanza which is home to 'Mama' Sarah Obama and the burial site of Onyango Obama and Barack Obama Snr; its full name is Nyang'oma K'ogelo
kom ker	Luo royal three-legged stool
kom nyaluo	Luo elder's three-legged stool
kuon	Dholuo word for *ugali*
kuot	Large, strong Luo shield made from layers of buffalo skin
kwer	Traditional shaving of the head at a funeral as a mark of respect
Kyoga, Lake	Large, shallow lake in eastern Uganda which was on the migration route of the Luo from Sudan to Kenya
Lari	Small town in Central province about 30km north of Nairobi; in March 1953 it was the location of one of the worst atrocities of the Mau Mau emergency
lielo fwada	First shaving of a baby, usually several weeks after birth
loko ot	Literally 'changing hut', when the huts of a deceased man are destroyed and new ones built in their place
Luhya	Bantu ethnic group in Kenya (and also Uganda and Tanzania); they form the second largest tribe in Kenya comprising 14 per cent of the population
Lunatic Line	Nickname given to the Uganda Railway
Luo	Nilotic ethnic group in Kenya, Tanzania and Uganda;

	the third largest tribe in Kenya comprising 13 per cent of the population and has a reputation for supplying many academics and doctors in Kenya, as well as radical politicians; also the tribe of the Obama family
lwak or *luak*	Traditional name given to ordinary Luo subjects
Lwoo	Archaic name for the Luo
Maasai	Semi-nomadic tribe from central Kenya and northern Tanzania, renowned for their distinctive dress and warrior tradition; also spelt Masai
Madi	Tribal group which lived around Pubungu before the Luo arrived in the fifteenth century
magenga	Large fire lit at a traditional Luo funeral
majimbo	Swahili name meaning 'group of regions' or regional governments; a system designed to minimise the problem of tribalism in Kenya
Maseno school	Prestigious boys' boarding school near Kisumu, opened in 1906 and the alma mater of Barack Obama Snr
matatu	Kenyan mini buses which provide most of the public transport in the country; they have a reputation for being driven dangerously
Mau Mau	Violent uprising by Kenyan farmers (mainly Kikuyu) against the British colonialists from 1952 to 1960; known as the Kenya Emergency in British official documents
mbare	Traditional Luo beer made from brown finger-millet flour (*kal*)
mbofwa	Wooden board used in divining
modhno	A type of grass used in a traditional blessing of a new Luo home
Mombasa	Kenya's second city and a major port on the Indian Ocean, originally called Kisiwa M'vita, meaning Island of War
Muhimu	Group of Nairobi-based urban militants, active in the early 1950s and who predated the Mau Mau
Mumbo cult, Mumboism	Religious cult in western Kenya in the early twentieth century, based on the teaching of a giant serpent which lived in Lake Victoria; the cult rejected European customs and advocated a return to traditional ways
Mumias	A town in Central Nyanza which was a headquarters for the British colonial administration

muruich	A piece of sharpened corn husk traditionally used to cut the umbilical cord of a newborn infant
mzungu	Swahili name for a white man; plural *wazungu*
Naath	Another name for the Nuer
Nairobi	Capital of Kenya, which takes its name from the Maasai name En Kare Nyirobi, meaning 'the place of cool waters'
Naivasha	Kenyan town in the Rift Valley about 95km north of Nairobi
Naivasha, Lake	Large lake in the Kenyan Rift Valley
nak	Traditional Luo ceremony to remove teeth; *see also janak*
Nam Lolwe	The Dholuo name for Lake Victoria
Nandi	Pastoralists of the Rift Valley and a sub-group of the Kalenjin who organised strong resistance against the construction of the Uganda Railway in the early 1900s
nduru	High-pitched howling cry at a Luo funeral
ngero	A traditional Luo riddle; plural *ngeche*
nindo liel	Literally 'stepping over the grave'; an act of remembrance for the deceased
North Ugenya	Region in western Kenya through which the early Luo are believed to have migrated
Nuer	Nilotic tribe which originated in Southern Sudan; *see also* Jii-speakers
nyalolwe	Dholuo name for sleeping sickness
Nyang'oma K'ogelo	*See* K'ogelo
Nyanza province	Administrative region in western Kenya on the shores of Lake Victoria, predominantly inhabited by the Luo; one of seven provinces in Kenya outside of Nairobi; Nyanza is the Bantu word for a large body of water
Nyasaye	Traditional god of the Luo
nyatiti	Eight-stringed wooden lyre
ohangla	Traditional drum made from the skin of a monitor lizard
okumba	Luo shield
olengo	Luo village wrestling match
oluwo aora	Dholuo for 'the people who follow the river'
omieri	A large python believed to possess spiritual powers
omower	The night of consummation of a marriage

ondiek	Duluo for hyena, but also used colloquially to describe a new mother who eats well
ong'ong'a famine	Widespread famine in Luoland in 1889
oporo	Horn from a bull or a buffalo, which gives a low-pitched booming sound; used to sound an attack
orkoiyot	Spiritual leader of the Nandi tribe
orundu	Traditional Luo kitchen garden
oseke	Large communal pot from which elders sip with a long wooden straw
otia	The best quality traditional Luo beer, brewed from sorghum flour
Pakwach	*See* Pubungu
panga	Broad-bladed machete
Port Florence	Early name given to the town on the shores of Lake Victoria now called Kisumu; named after Florence Preston, wife of the Uganda Railway's chief foreman platelayer Ronald Preston
powo	Tree with a very smooth surface used as a door post in a traditional Luo house
Pubungu	A large military encampment established by the Luo in the mid-fifteenth century, located near Pakwach in Uganda
Rift Valley	A large geographical feature running north–south through Kenya; the Rift Valley province is one of Kenya's seven administrative provinces outside of Nairobi
rinderpest	Also known as cattle plague, a contagious viral infection which affects cattle, buffalo and some wildlife and which devastated large numbers of animals in Kenya during the late nineteenth and early twentieth centuries
River-Lake Nilotes	Ethnic group from southern Sudan; a breakaway group migrated to Kenya and became known as the Luo
romo	Alternative name for *nindo liel*
Rumbek	Capital of the State of Lakes in southern Sudan, and situated close to the 'cradleland' of the Luo
ruoth	Luo chief
Seventh Day Adventists	Often known as the 'Adventists' or the SDAs; a Christian denomination which observes Saturday as the Sabbath and which established a mission in Kendu Bay in 1904

Shilluk	Third largest Nilotic tribe in Southern Sudan, also called the Chollo
Siaya district	One of twelve administrative districts which make up the Nyanza province of western Kenya
simba	Traditional Luo hut of a young man, located inside his father's compound
Simbi Kolonde	Small village near Kendu bay and birthplace of Akumu, paternal grandmother of President Obama
simsim	Arabic word for sesame
singo	Form of traditional Luo barter
siwindhe	Traditional Luo hut of a grandmother
'slug map'	An ambitious but ultimately misleading representation of East Africa by Johannes Rebmann, which shows a single huge lake in the centre of Kenya; dated c. 1855
smallpox	Infectious viral disease which results in a rash and blisters on the body, with a 30 per cent mortality rate unless treated
south Nyanza	The part of Nyanza province which lies to the south of Winam Gulf
southern Sudan	The mainly Christian region in the south of Sudan which experienced a protracted conflict from 1983 to 2005 between the Muslim government forces in the north and the Sudanese People's Liberation Army in the south
'spear-and-bead' story	Mythical story about a conflict between two brothers over the loss of a spear and a bead; the story is retold by a large number of East African ethnic groups, including the Luo
Sudd	Vast swamp in southern Sudan formed by the flooding of the White Nile; the word Sudd comes from the Arabic word *sadd*, which means 'block' or 'barrier'
Swahili	Comes from the Arabic *sawāhīl*, meaning 'of the coast'; a Bantu language widely used throughout East Africa (*see also* Kiswahili)
Tanganyika	East African territory lying between the Indian Ocean and Lake Victoria; originally called Deutsch-Ostafrika or German East Africa before the First World War, and then known as Tanganyika under British colonial rule; *see also* Tanzania

Tanzania	A republic comprising twenty-six *mikoa* or regions; it became independent from British rule in 1961 and when the country merged with Zanzibar in 1964, the new nation took the name Tanzania
tero buru	Literally, 'taking the dust'; a traditional Luo funeral ceremony to scare away the dead spirits
Thika	A small town about 30km north-east of Nairobi, on the route 'up country' towards the popular farming land around the foothills of Mount Kenya; childhood home to Elspeth Huxley
thimlich	Dholuo word meaning 'frightening dense forest'
Thimlich Ohinga	Fortified Luo settlement in south Nyanza dating from before the 1700s
tipo	The invisible part of a person of 'shadow', which when combined with the visible part creates life
tong'	Dholuo word for a spear
tong' ker	A royal spear
Tororo	Town in eastern Uganda which was an important staging post during the Luo migration in the fifteenth century
tung'	A small sheep's horn which makes a high-pitched wailing sound audible over a long distance
trypanosomiasis	Sleeping sickness
ugali	The Swahili name for a dough made from hot water and maize; a staple food in East Africa
Uganda	A landlocked ex-British colony in central Africa which takes its name from the ancient kingdom of Buganda; it became independent of British rule in October 1962
Uganda Railway	The railway system which links Mombasa on the Indian Ocean with the interior; the railway was completed in 1901 when it reached Port Florence (now called Kisumu), but it was subsequently extended between 1913 and 1964
ujamaa	A dogmatic and inflexible form of socialism in Tanzania introduced by Julius Nyerere
University of Hawaii	Alma mater of Barack Obama Snr, where he studied economics between 1959 and 1962
uyoma	Luo witch doctor or shaman
Victoria, Lake	The second largest freshwater lake in the world, bordered by Uganda to the west, and Kenya and Tanzania to the east

Wanandi	Early name for the Nandi people
Wau	City in southern Sudan on the banks of the River Jur; it is the capital of the Bahr-al-Ghazāl region, the historic cradleland of the Luo
wazungu	*See mzungu*
Western Nilotes	*See* River-Lake Nilotes
White Nile	One of two main tributaries of the River Nile (the other being the Blue Nile); the White Nile has its source in the mountains of Burundi, and is over 3,700km long
Winam Gulf	A large enclosed bay in the north-eastern corner of Lake Victoria, formerly known as the Kavirondo Gulf
Young Kavirondo Association	Political organisation formed by the Luo in 1921 to represent their grievances against what they considered to be unjust British colonial rule; it later became known as the Kavirondo Taxpayers' Welfare Association with a greatly reduced influence
yweyo liel	Literally the 'cleansing of the grave', when the family compound is cleaned after the death of the husband
Zanzibar	An island off the east coast of Africa, originally under British control from around 1890; now a semi-autonomous region of the United Republic of Tanzania

TIMELINE

<u>PRE-HISTORY</u>

2.4 million BC   A man-like ape or hominid called *Australopithecus africanus* lives in East Africa

2 million BC   There is evidence that *Homo habilis* lived around Lake Turkana in northern Kenya; known as 'Handy Man', the first tool-maker

1.6 million BC   *Homo erectus* makes hand axes and cleavers, and spreads throughout East Africa

300,000 BC   *Homo sapiens* lives in the Lake Baringo region

5,000 BC   Kenya is populated by hunter-gatherers

500 BC to
    AD 500   Bantu migrants arrive in Kenya, bringing with them metal-working skills. The people enter the Iron Age

AD 43   *Romans invade Britain*

c. AD 410   *Romans leave Britain*

<u>EARLY HISTORY</u>

c. 600   Arab traders begin to settle in Mombasa and other ports

1066   *King Harold killed at the Battle of Hastings*

1095–1291   *Europe fights the Crusades to restore control in the Holy Land*

1215	*King John signs the Magna Carta*
1348	*The Black Death arrives in Britain and ultimately kills about one third of the population*
c. 1400	The Luo-speakers of southern Sudan begin their migration south into Uganda
1414	A fleet of sixty-two Chinese trading galleons and over a hundred support ships under the command of Zheng He crosses the Indian Ocean and lands on the African coast
c. 1450	The first Luo are thought to establish the Pubungu military encampment and begin to dominate Uganda
c. 1480	Podho II may have left Pubungu around this time and moved his people eastwards, towards Kenya
1492	*Christopher Columbus lands on an island in the Bahamas and 'discovers' the New World for Spain*
8 July 1497	Vasco da Gama sets sail from Lisbon in search of a sea route to the Orient
1498	Da Gama arrives in Mombasa but is repulsed; he sails on to Malindi
1500	The Portuguese sack Mombasa
1500-1700	The Portuguese establish a series of trading posts and forts along the Kenyan coast
c. 1500	The three sons of Olum, Labong'o (or Nyabong'o), Gipiir (or Nyipiir) and Tifool, establish Luo dominance in Uganda and the Congo
1502	*The Atlantic slave trade begins in earnest with West African slaves taken to Spanish and Portuguese colonies in the New World; later English, French and Dutch traders supplied the Caribbean islands with slaves*
1509	*Henry VIII is crowned king of England*
c. 1530	Ramogi Ajwang' is thought to have arrived with his people in western Kenya around this time
1558	*Elizabeth I accedes to the English throne*
1587	*Sir Walter Raleigh founds Roanoke Colony, the first British settlement in the New World*
c. 1590	The second wave of Luo arrive in Kenya, the Jok'Owiny, led by President Obama's (11) great-grandfather Owiny
1593	The Portuguese begin the construction of Fort Jesus in Mombasa
c. 1600	Luo establish a settlement in Gang, in western Kenya

1603	*James VI of Scotland is crowned King James I of England*
1607	*Jamestown Settlement is founded in what would become Virginia*
Nov. 1620	*The* Mayflower *lands in Plymouth, New England*
1624	*New York City is founded, originally as New Amsterdam*
1642–51	*English Civil Wars*
c. 1660	The Luo leader Kisodhi dies and his succession leads to a major dispute between his eldest son Ogelo, and two of his other sons, Ager and Owiny Sigoma
c. 1670	Ogelo, President Obama's (9) great-grandfather, settles in Nyang'oma K'ogelo
1698	After a siege lasting nearly three years, the Arabs and their allies take Fort Jesus
c. 1700	The Luo occupy Thimlich Ohinga and build up the defences
1720	The Portuguese withdraw from Kenya permanently
1760–1820	A third wave of Luo migrants enter Nyanza, called the Jok'Omolo, which puts increased pressure on land and resources in the region, and feuding begins among the Luo sub-clans
1822	Seyyid Sa'id, the new ruler in Oman, sends a fleet of warships to subdue the querulous Swahili coastal towns
27 Feb 1824	The British Royal Navy hoists their flag over Fort Jesus
c. 1825	Obong'o, (3) great-grandfather to President Obama, leaves his ancestral home in K'ogelo and establishes a new homestead in south Nyanza
1773	*The Americans revolt against the British at the Boston Tea Party*
1782	*The British government informally, but officially, recognises American independence*
1789	*George Washington becomes the first President of the USA*
22 Feb 1807	*Britain bans the slave trade, but not slavery itself*
Jan. 1808	*USA bans the importation of slaves*
1817	The first American trading vessel reaches Zanzibar
1822	The Mazrui chief Sulaiman bin Ali asks for British protection against Seyyid Sa'id of Oman
1824	The British warship HMS *Leven* arrives in Mombasa and Captain William Owen declares the town a British protectorate

1827	The British government withdraws the protectorate from Mombasa
1830–80	The East African slave trade flourishes under Seyyid Sa'id
1833	The USA exchanges 'most favoured nation' status with Zanzibar and establishes the first US trade-consul in 1835
c. 1833	Opiyo, great-great-grandfather to President Obama, is born in Kendu Bay, south Nyanza
1 Aug. 1833	*Britain finally abolishes slavery*
1841	Britain establishes a trade consul in Zanzibar

EXPLORATION

Early 1844	Dr Johann Ludwig Krapf, a German Protestant missionary and accomplished linguist, arrives in Zanzibar
1846	Krapf and his countryman Johannes Rebmann begin their evangelical journeys inland
1848	Johannes Rebmann becomes the first European to see Mount Kilimanjaro
1849	Johann Krapf becomes the first European to see Mount Kenya
1854	Johannes Rebmann produces the 'slug map' of central Africa, showing a large inland lake – possibly Lake Victoria
1856	Richard Burton and John Hanning Speke explore inland to determine if this 'inland sea' is the source of the Nile
1858	Speke becomes the first European to see Lake Victoria; in Egypt, work starts on the Suez Canal
1860	British Roman Catholic missionaries arrive in Zanzibar
1861-65	*The American Civil War*
c. 1864	Obama, great-grandfather to President Obama, is born in Kendu Bay, south Nyanza
Jan. 1866	Dr David Livingstone first arrives in East Africa with the intention of finding the source of the Nile
Nov. 1869	The Suez Canal opens to shipping
March 1871	Henry Stanley sent out to find Livingstone
10 Nov. 1871	Stanley meets Livingstone in Ujiji, in present-day Tanzania
1873	The British force the ruler of Zanzibar to close his slave market, but with only limited success
1 May 1873	David Livingstone dies in the village of Ilala, Zambia

12 Nov. 1874	Henry Stanley leaves Zanzibar on a second expedition to cross Africa from east to west
24 Mar. 1875	Henry Stanley sails north up the eastern coastline of Lake Victoria and becomes the first European to enter Luoland
1883	Joseph Thomson explores inland from Mombasa and makes contact with the Maasai
4 Nov. 1884	Karl Peters and two companions arrive in Zanzibar to establish a German colonial presence in East Africa
15 Nov. 1884	Berlin Conference opens
12 Feb. 1885	Karl Peters establishes the Deutsche Ost-Afrika Gesellschaft, the German East Africa Company, to which he cedes all his territorial gains in Africa
17 Feb. 1885	Bismarck agrees to issue an imperial charter, which gives the protection of the Emperor to all the territories acquired by the German East Africa Company
26 Feb. 1885	Berlin Conference closes with an agreement to carve up Africa among the European nations
1885	More than 300 Europeans are now living in East Africa, mostly Anglican or Catholic missionaries
1886	The Anglo-German Agreement defines the spheres of influence in East Africa of Britain and Germany
1888	The British East Africa Company is granted a royal charter and is renamed the Imperial British East Africa Company (IBEAC); it establishes its headquarters in Mombasa and creates its own currency and stamps
1890	The Treaty of Berlin brings all of Uganda and Kenya under British jurisdiction, and Tanzania under German control; Charles William Hobley arrives in Mombasa and works for the IBEAC as a transport superintendent
1891	Karl Peters is made Imperial High Commissioner to German East Africa (later to be Tanzania)
1892	Johnstone Kamau, later known as Jomo Kenyatta, is born in the Kikuyu highland region north of Nairobi

BRITISH EAST AFRICA

1880–92	Luoland is hit by a series of natural disasters, including contagious bovine pleuropneumonia, locust invasions, the *ong'ong'a* famine, great rinderpest, anthrax, and smallpox, resulting in virtual civil war between the Luo

1 July 1895	The British government takes control of the assets of the IBEAC in order to maintain strategic control in the region
1895	Onyango Obama, grandfather to President Obama, is born in Kendu Bay, western Kenya; Charles Hobley is made the new regional colonial administrator in Luoland (Nyanza)
30 May 1896	The construction of the Uganda Railway begins
1896–1900	The British mount a series of 'punitive raids' to suppress the Luo
1899	The railway headquarters are established at Nyrobi, later to be renamed Nairobi
1901	Sir Charles Eliot is appointed the new governor of the IBEAC; there are thirteen white farmers resident in Kenya
19 Dec. 1901	The railway reaches Port Florence (later to be called Kisumu) on Lake Victoria
1902–8	The tsetse fly returns to Luoland and at least 250,000 people die from sleeping sickness
1903	Large grants of land are made available to white farmers around the Lake Naivasha region in the Rift Valley
1905	There are 700 Afrikaner farmers and more than 250 European settlers established in the Rift Valley
Oct. 1905	Col Richard Meinertzhagen shoots Kiotalel, the Nandi leader, which breaks the resistance of the Nandi to the construction of the Uganda Railway
Nov. 1906	Arthur Carscallen establishes the first Seventh Day Adventist mission in Kendu Bay
c. 1910	Onyango Obama leaves home and lives with white missionaries
1912	There are now 3,175 white settlers in Kenya and 11,886 Asians
1914–18	First World War, and members of the King's African Rifles (KAR) fight in East Africa; Onyango Obama is drafted into the KAR
1915	The government increase the land tenure of white farmers from 99 years to 999
1916	The British increase the hut and poll tax payable by Africans
1918	British East Africa is formally annexed by Britain and made a colony, called Kenya; the British government offers veterans of the Great War land in the Kenyan Highlands

1919	The Treaty of Versailles creates 'mandates' in Africa, under the administration of the League of Nations; Luoland is struck by the *Kanga* famine
c. 1920	Onyango Obama returns from the war having lived in Zanzibar for two years; he has converted to Islam and takes the name Hussein
1920	Onyango's older brother Ndalo returns to the family's ancestral lands in K'ogelo
1921	There are now 9,651 white farmers in Kenya; Harry Thuku establishes the Young Kikuyu Association (YKA), Kenya's first nationalist organisation
23 Dec. 1921	The Young Kavirondo Association is formed in Nyanza
21 Mar. 1922	Harry Thuku is arrested and exiled without charge
c. 1922	Having built his hut in Kendu Bay, Hussein Onyango goes to seek employment in Nairobi
1924	The Kikuyu Central Association (KCA) evolves from the YKA, with Jomo Kenyatta as its secretary
c. 1925	Ndalo and his two wives die in K'ogelo from smallpox; Onyango takes their three children, Odero, Peter and Judy into his care
1926	22,000 Africans are working in domestic service in Kenya
c. 1927	Hussein Onyango marries a woman (name unknown) from Kawango in Mumias; she becomes his first wife
c. 1929	Hussein Onyango marries Helima, his second wife
1929	Kenyatta goes to London to make the case for Kenyan independence
c. 1930	Obama, President Obama's great-grandfather, dies in Kendu Bay
c. 1931	Hussein Onyango marries Sophia Odera, his third wife
1933	Hussein Onyango abducts and then marries Akumu Njoga, his fourth wife; she converts to Islam and takes the name Habiba
1934	Sarah Nyoke Obama is born in Kendu Bay, the first child of Hussein Onyango and Habiba Akumu
1936	Barack Hussein Obama Snr is born in Kendu Bay
1939–45	The Second World War, and members of the King's African Rifles fight in Ethiopia, India and Burma; Hussein Onyango is posted to Ethiopia and Burma
1940	The KCA and other African organisations are banned

1941	Hussein Onyango returns from the war and marries Sarah Ogwel, his fifth wife
7 Dec. 1941	*The Japanese attack Pearl Harbor in Hawaii, and the USA enters the Second World War*
1942	Barack Obama Snr starts his schooling at Gendia Primary School, near Kendu Bay; Hawa Auma Obama is born in Kendu Bay, the third child of Hussein Onyango and Habiba Akumu
29 Nov. 1942	*Stanley (Ann) Dunham is born in Wichita, Kansas*
1943	Onyango, his two wives and three children move to K'ogelo
1944	The Kenyan African Union (KAU) is formed to campaign for African independence. The first African appointment is made to the legislative council.
June 1944	Omar, Hussein Onyango's second son, born to Sarah
1944/5	Habiba Akumu attacked by Hussein Onyango; she flees K'ogelo and returns to Kendu Bay
1945	Sarah and her younger brother Barack Snr run away from home in K'ogelo; Barack Snr moves to Ng'iya Intermediate School
1946	Jomo Kenyatta returns from Britain and becomes chairman of the newly formed Kenya African Union (KAU)
Late 1940s	The General Council of the banned Kikuyu Central Association begin a campaign of civil disobedience
1948	Rumours circulate of secret oathing ceremonies in the forests of the White Highlands and in the Rift Valley
1949	Hussein Onyango arrested by the British authorities and detained for six months; no charges are proven
1950	Nairobi-based militants organise mass oathings throughout central Kenya; the Mau Mau insurrection begins in earnest; Barack Obama Snr goes to Maseno school aged fourteen
Early 1952	Mau Mau make arson attacks on white farms in the highlands
1952	Zeituni is born to Hussein Onyango and Sarah
Oct. 1952	A state of emergency is declared in Kenya and war is declared on Mau Mau
18 Nov. 1952	Jomo Kenyatta arrested and charged with being a supporter of Mau Mau
24 Jan. 1953	Roger and Esme Ruck and their six-year-old son Michael are attacked and killed on their isolated farm

26 Mar. 1953	Mau Mau massacre over 120 residents at Lari
April 1953	Kenyatta found guilty and given seven years' hard labour
1953	KAU declared illegal; Barack Obama Snr leaves Maseno at the age of seventeen and works in Mombasa, before moving to Nairobi
1955	Barack Obama Snr works for the Kenya Railway; he is arrested during the Mau Mau emergency; Tom Mboya wins a scholarship to Ruskin College, Oxford, to study industrial management
1956	First elected Kenyan representatives join the Legislative Council
21 Oct. 1956	Dedan Kimathi captured and Mau Mau emergency is effectively over
25 Dec. 1956	Barack Snr meets Kezia at a party in Kendu Bay
Jan. 1957	Barack Snr sets up home with Kezia in Jericho, a residential section of Nairobi for government employees
c. Mar. 1958	Roy Obong'o Malik born, first son of Obama Snr and Kezia
1959	*Stanley Dunham moves to Hawaii with his wife Madelyn and seventeen-year-old daughter Ann*
21 Aug. 1959	*Hawaii becomes the fiftieth state of the USA*
1959	Jomo Kenyatta is released from prison but is put under house arrest; Kezia becomes pregnant with Auma; she is three months' pregnant when Obama Snr leaves Kenya; Tom Mboya returns from a fund-raising visit to the USA and announces that he has scholarships for young Kenyans to study there; Barack Obama Snr leaves Nairobi for university in Hawaii
Jan. 1960	Auma born, second child of Obama Snr and Kezia
Feb. 1960	The first Lancaster House conference is held in London and the ban on African political parties is lifted
11 June 1960	Tom Mboya and Oginga Odinga form the Kenya African National Union (KANU)
Summer 1960	Barack Obama Snr meets Ann Dunham in a Russian language class at the University of Hawaii and they start dating
Nov. 1960	Ann Dunham becomes pregnant
2 Feb. 1961	Barack Obama Snr marries Ann Dunham in Maui, Hawaii

Feb. 1961	KANU and the Kenya African Democratic Union (KADU) contest Kenya's first election
4 Aug. 1961	Barack Jnr born at 7.24 p.m. local time, at the Kapi'olani Medical Center for Women & Children, Honolulu
21 Aug. 1961	Jomo Kenyatta released from detention
Summer 1962	James Odhiambo goes to Harvard
May 1963	First full national elections held in Kenya
1 June 1963	Jomo Kenyatta becomes Prime Minister of the autonomous Kenyan government
Summer 1963	Barack Obama Snr goes to Harvard to study for a PhD; Ann Obama returns to college; her parents help to raise her young baby, Barack Obama
22 Nov. 1963	*US President John F. Kennedy is assassinated in Dallas*

INDEPENDENT KENYA

12 Dec. 1963	Kenya becomes a fully independent nation
Jan. 1964	Ann Obama files for divorce from Barack Snr in Honolulu
2 July 1964	*The Civil Rights Act of 1964 in the USA makes racial discrimination and segregation illegal*
12 Dec. 1964	Kenya becomes a republic with Jomo Kenyatta as president and Oginga Odinga as vice-president
Mid-1965	Barack Obama Snr returns to Kenya and is followed by Ruth Nidesand; Obama first works for Kenya Shell
July 1965	Barack Obama Snr writes article for *East Africa Journal* which criticises the government's approach to economic planning
Late 1965	Barack Obama Snr joins Kenya Central Bank as an economist
1966	Oginga Odinga leaves KANU after an ideological split and forms the rival Kenya People's Union (KPU)
1967	Ann Dunham marries Lolo Soetoro and the couple move to Jakarta, Indonesia; Barack Obama Jnr is six years old
4 April 1968	*Martin Luther King Jnr is assassinated in Memphis, Tennessee*
6 June 1968	*US presidential candidate, Robert F. Kennedy, is assassinated in Los Angeles, California*
1968	Rumours that President Kenyatta has suffered a heart attack; Barack Obama Snr gets a new job at the Ministry

	of Economic Planning and Development; Abo born to Kezia Obama, her third child and second son
5 July 1969	Tom Mboya assassinated in Nairobi, which sparks ethnic unrest and riots
25 Oct. 1969	Jomo Kenyatta makes a speech in Kisumu which results in riots and forty-three people are killed by police
25 Nov. 1969	The Kenya Prison Service announces that Tom Mboya's killer, Isaac Njenga Njoroge, has been hanged
1970	Bernard born, Kezia Obama's fourth child and third son
15 Aug. 1970	Barack Obama Jnr's half sister, Maya Kassandra Soetoro-Ng is born in Jakarta; Ann Dunham's second marriage begins to disintegrate
1970?	Barack Obama Snr fired from his government job; later takes job at the Kenya Tourist Development Corporation (KTDC)
1971	Ann Dunham sends Barack Obama Jnr back to Honolulu to live with his white grandparents, where he gets a scholarship to Punahou, a prestigious prep school
Dec. 1971	Barack Obama Snr makes a pre-Christmas visit to see his son in Hawaii
1972?	Barack Obama Snr loses his job at the KTDC
1972	Ann Dunham leaves her husband Lolo Soetoro and returns from Indonesia to Hawaii with two-year-old Maya to join Barack, now eleven; she studies for a PhD in anthropology
1974	Kenyatta re-elected President of Kenya
1975?	Barack Obama Snr is given a job in the Kenyan Treasury
22 Aug. 1978	Jomo Kenyatta dies in Mombasa aged eighty-nine; and is succeeded by his vice-president, Daniel arap Moi
1978	Former Kisumu deputy Mayor Benjamin Okang' Tolo hosts party for Barack Obama Snr, which he attends with Jael Otiene; Barack Obama Jnr begins his first year at Occidental College in Los Angeles; at the end of his second year he transfers to Columbia University in New York
1980	Ann Dunham files for divorce from her second husband, Lolo Soetoro
1981	Barack Obama Snr marries Jael Otieno, his fourth wife
Mid-1982	Kenya is officially declared a one-party state by the National Assembly; Jael gives birth to a son, George; he is Obama

	Snr's eighth child; a coup by the Kenyan Air Force is suppressed and the leaders executed
24 Nov. 1982	Barack Obama Snr dies in a car crash in Nairobi; Barack Obama Jnr, now twenty-one, is told about his father's death by telephone when he is living in New York
1983	Barack Obama Jnr graduates from Columbia University and works for a year at the Business International Corporation, a small newsletter-publishing company that printed features relating to global business; he later worked for the New York Public Interest Research Group
1985–8	Barack Obama Jnr takes a job with a Chicago based group called Developing Communities Project, where he begins working to improve the conditions of a public housing project
1987	Opposition groups in Kenya are suppressed and there is international criticism of political arrests and human rights abuses in Moi's government; Barack Obama Jnr is accepted to Harvard Law School, but he first visits his father's family in Kenya
1989	Political prisoners in Kenya are freed
1990	Foreign minister Robert Ouko is brutally assassinated, which leads to increased dissent against government
5 Feb. 1990	Barack Obama Jnr becomes the first African-American president of the *Harvard Law Review*
1991	Barack Obama Jnr graduates from Harvard with a Juris Doctor magna cum laude and signs with a publisher to write his autobiography, *Dreams from My Father*
Dec. 1991	A special conference of KANU agrees to introduce a multi-party political system in Kenya
1992	Approximately 2,000 people killed in tribal conflict in western Kenya
1992	Barack Obama Jnr returns to Chicago to work as a junior lawyer with Davis, Miner, Barnhill & Gallard; he visits his family in K'ogelo with his girlfriend, Michelle Robinson, to seek his step-grandmother's approval before getting married
10 Oct. 1992	Barack Obama Jnr and Michelle Robinson are married
1995	Barack Obama Jnr's memoir, *Dreams from My Father*, is published to positive reviews

7 Nov. 1995	Barack Obama Jnr's mother Ann dies of ovarian cancer, aged fifty-three
1996	Barack Obama Jnr is elected to the Illinois State Senate
1998	Barack and Michelle Obama's first daughter is born, and is named Malia Ann
Dec. 1999	Daniel arap Moi wins a further presidential term in an election which is widely criticised. His main opponents are former vice-president Mwai Kibaki and Raila Odinga, son of Oginga Odinga
2001	Barack and Michelle's second daughter is born, and is named Natasha (and often called Sasha)
Dec. 2001	Ethnic tensions continue and thousands of people flee Nairobi's Kibera slum over rent battles between Nubian and Luo communities
Dec. 2002	Daniel arap Moi's twenty-four-year rule ends when opposition candidate Mwai Kibaki wins a landslide victory over KANU rival Uhuru Kenyatta (son of Jomo)
Dec. 2003	The government grants former president Daniel arap Moi immunity from prosecution on corruption charges
7 July 2004	Barack Obama Jnr is chosen to deliver the keynote speech at the Democratic National Convention in Boston, Mass.; the speech is viewed as a defining moment in his political career and it earns him worldwide recognition
2 Nov. 2004	Barack Obama Jnr, now forty-three, is elected to the US Senate with an unprecedented 70 per cent of the vote
4 Jan. 2005	Barack Obama Jnr is sworn in as a US senator
Aug. 2006	Barack Obama Jnr visits Kenya and gives a speech at the University of Nairobi which is critical of the government
10 Feb. 2007	Barack Obama Jnr announces his candidacy for the 2008 presidential election
Dec. 2007	President Kibaki claims victory and a second term in office; the opposition claims the polls were rigged, and more than 1,500 die in the post-election violence
Feb. 2008	Former UN chief Kofi Annan brokers talks between President Kibaki and opposition leader Raila Odinga, which lead to a power-sharing agreement
April 2008	President Kibaki and Prime Minister Odinga agree a forty-member cabinet; it is Kenya's biggest and costliest ever

3 Nov. 2008	Barack Obama Jnr's grandmother Madelyn Dunham dies of cancer at the age of eighty-six
5 Nov. 2008	The Democratic Senator Barack Hussein Obama is elected President of the United States of America
20 Jan. 2009	Barack Obama is sworn-in as the 44th President of the USA, the country's first black president
July 2009	The Kenyan government announces that it will not establish a special tribunal to examine the post-election violence, but will use the local courts instead
Aug. 2009	US Secretary of State Hillary Clinton visits Kenya and criticises the government for failing to investigate the violence which followed the 2007 election

NOTES

Prologue

[1] Barack Obama, *Dreams from My Father*, Three Rivers, 1995, pp. 429–430.

[2] Ibid., p. 302.

[3] Barack Obama, *The Audacity of Hope*, Three Rivers, 2006, p. 2

[4] Ibid., p. 10.

[5] Ibid., p. 3.

Chapter 1: Two Elections, Two Presidents

[1] Korwa G. Adar and Isaac M. Munyae, 'Human Rights Abuse in Kenya under Daniel arap Moi, 1978–2001', *African Studies Quarterly*, vol. 5, no. 1 (2001).

[2] Amnesty International Report, 'Kenya', 2000.

[3] International Centre for Settlement of Investment Disputes (ICSID), *World Duty Free Company Ltd. v. Kenya*, 4 October 2006.

[4] The CIA World Factbook, www.cia.gov/library/publications/the-world-factbook/geos/ke.html.

[5] World Health Organization, 'Male Circumcision: Africa's Unprecedented Opportunity', WHO, August 2007.

[6] 'Strange Reversal in Kogelo', *East African*, 23 January 2009.

[7] United Nations Children's Fund, 'The State of Africa's Children', UNICEF, May 2008, p. 12.

Chapter 2: Meet the Ancestors

1 W. R. Ochieng, *A History of Kenya*, Macmillan, 1985, p. 17.

2 Andrew Goudie, *Environmental Change* (3rd edn), Oxford University Press, 1992.

3 Roland A. Oliver and Anthony Atmore, *Medieval Africa, 1250–1800* (2nd edn), Cambridge University Press, 2001, p. 137.

4 Elizabeth Isichei, *A History of African Societies to 1870*, Cambridge University Press, 1997, p. 138.

5 D. W. Cohen, 'The River-Lake Nilotes from the Fifteenth to the Nineteenth Century', in B. A. Ogot (ed.), *Zamani: A Survey of East African History*, East African Publishing House, 1968, pp. 135–49.

6 Ibid., p. 140.

7 Oliver and Atmore, *Medieval Africa*.

8 J. P. Crazzolara, *The Lwoo*, part I, Verona, 1950, p. 47.

9 B. A. Ogot, *A History of the Luo-Speaking Peoples of Eastern Africa*, Anyange Press, 2009, p. 27.

10 Oliver and Atmore, *Medieval Africa*, p. 144.

11 Cohen, 'The River-Lake Nilotes', p. 142.

12 Oliver and Atmore, *Medieval Africa*, p. 143.

13 Cohen, 'The River-Lake Nilotes', p. 142.

14 Richard Nunoo, 'The Preservation and Presentation of the Monuments and Sites of Koobi Fora, Lamu, Ishakani and Thimlich Ohinga', UNESCO Restricted Technical Report RP/1984–1985/XI, 1, 4, 1985.

15 Oliver and Atmore, *Medieval Africa*, p. 141.

16 Okumba Miruka, *Oral Literature of the Luo*, East African Educational Publishers, 2001.

17 Ibid.

18 Cohen, 'The River-Lake Nilotes', p. 144.

19 Oliver and Atmore, *Medieval Africa*, p. 148.

20 Ogot, *A History of the Luo-Speaking Peoples of Eastern Africa*, p. 28.

21 Cohen, 'The River-Lake Nilotes', p. 147.

22 Ogot, *A History of the Luo-Speaking Peoples of Eastern Africa*, p. 488.

23 W. R. Ochieng', 'The Transformation of a Bantu Settlement into a Luo "Ruothdom": A Case Study of the Evolution of the Yimbo Community in Nyanza up to AD 1900', in B. A. Ogot (ed.), *History and Social Change in East Africa*, Hadith 6, Nairobi: East African Literature Bureau, 1976, p. 49.

24 Ogot, *A History of the Luo-Speaking Peoples of Eastern Africa*, p. 158.

25 D. W. Cohen and E. S. Atieno Odhiambo, *The Historical Anthropology of an African Landscape*, Eastern African Studies, James Currey, 1989.

26 Cohen, 'The River-Lake Nilotes', p. 144.

27 Ogot, A *History of the Luo-Speaking Peoples of Eastern Africa*, p. 159.

28 Cohen, 'The River-Lake Nilotes', p. 148.

29 Ogot, A *History of the Luo-Speaking Peoples of Eastern Africa*, p. 519.

Chapter 3: The Life and Death of Opiyo Obama

1 Okumba Miruka, *Oral Literature of the Luo*, East African Educational Publishers, 2001.

2 Ibid.

3 S. H. Ominde, *The Luo Girl; From Infancy to Marriage*, Macmillan, 1952.

Chapter 4: The *Wazungu* Arrive

1 Louis Levather, *When China Ruled the Seas: The Treasure Fleet of the Dragon Throne, 1405–1433*, Oxford University Press, 1997.

2 Richard Hall, *Empires of the Monsoon*, HarperCollins, 1996, p. 168.

3 Ibid., pp. 382–7.

4 Johannes Rebmann, *The Church Missionary Intelligencer*, vol. 1, no. 1 (May 1849).

5 Roland Oliver, *The Missionary Factor in East Africa*, Longmans, Green, 1952, p. 6.

6 Harry H. Johnston, 'Livingstone as an Explorer', *Geographical Journal*, vol. 41, no. 5 (May 1913), pp. 423–446.

7 Hall, *Empires of the Monsoon*, p. 15.

8 Elikia M'bokolo, 'The Impact of the Slave Trade on Africa,' *Le Monde diplomatique* (English edn), April 1998.

9 C. Magbaily Fyle, *Introduction to the History of African Civilization: Precolonial Africa*. University Press of America, 1999, p. 146.

10 Assa Okoth, A *History of Africa*, vol. 1: *1800–1914*, East African Educational Publishers, 2006, p. 58.

11 Arnold Talbot Wilson, *The Suez Canal: Its Past, Present and Future*, Oxford University Press, 1933.

12 *New York Herald*, July, 1871.

13 H. M. Stanley, 'The Search for Livingstone', *New York Times*, 2 July 1872.

14 H. M. Stanley, *Through the Dark Continent*, vol. 1, Dover, 1988.

15 Ibid., p. 63.

16 Ibid., p. 217.

17 H. M. Stanley, *My Kalulu, Prince, King, and Slave: A Story of Central Africa*, Sampson Low, 1873.

18 Norman Robert Bennett, A *History of the Arab State of Zanzibar*, Routledge, 1978, p. 32.

[19] Oliver, *The Missionary Factor in East Africa*, p. 1.

[20] W. P. Johnson, *My African Reminiscences, 1875–1895*, Universities' Mission to Central Africa, 1924, p. 126.

[21] Okoth, *A History of Africa*, vol. 1, p. 118.

[22] Ibid., p. 96.

Chapter 5: The New Imperialism

[1] W. O. Henderson, *Studies in German Colonial History*, Routledge, 1962, p. 13.

[2] Ibid., p. 4.

[3] Ibid., p. 13.

[4] Assa Okoth, *A History of Africa*, vol. 1: *1800–1914*, East African Educational Publishers, 2006, p. 124.

[5] Kolonial-Politische Korrespondenz (Colonial-Political Correspondence), 1st Year, Berlin, 16 May 1885.

[6] Henderson, *Studies in German Colonial History*, p. 87.

[7] Okoth, *A History of Africa*, vol. 1, p. 138.

[8] C. W. Hobley, *Kenya: From Chartered Company to Crown Colony*, Witherby, 1929, pp. 24–5.

[9] Okoth, *A History of Africa*, vol. 1, p. 138.

[10] J. L. Krapf, *Travels, Researches, and Missionary Labours during an Eighteen Years Residence in Eastern Africa*, London, Trübner, 1860, p. 292.

[11] Oscar Baumann, *Durch Massailand zur Nilquelle* (Through the lands of the Maasai to the Source of the Nile), Dietrich Reimer, 1894.

[12] *The Times*, 28 September 1891, p. 60.

[13] Lawrence H. Officer, 'What Were the UK Earnings and Prices Then?', MeasuringWorth, 2009, www.measuringworth.org/ukearncpi/.

[14] 'Uganda Railway (Cost of Construction)', Hansard, House of Commons Debates, 19 Oct. 1909, vol. 12, cols. 123–4.

[15] Okoth, *A History of Africa*, vol. 1, p. 351.

[16] Thomas R. Metcalf, *Imperial Connections: India in the Indian Ocean Area, 1860–1920*, University of California Press, 2008, p. 188.

[17] Sir Harry Johnston, F.O. 2/204, Johnston to Salisbury, 13 Oct. 1899, quoted in J. S. Mangat, *A History of the Asians in East Africa: 1886–1945*, Oxford University Press, 1969, p. 40.

[18] Joseph Thomson, *Through Masai Land*, Sampson Low, 1885, pp. 72–3

[19] Bruce D. Patterson, *The Lions of Tsavo: Exploring the Legacy of Africa's Notorious Man-Eaters*, McGraw-Hill, 2004.

[20] 'Murder that Shaped the Future of Kenya', *East African*, 5 December 2008.

[21] William Ochieng', *A History of Kenya*, Macmillan, 1985, p. 94.

[22] David Anderson and Douglas H. Johnson, *Revealing Prophets: Prophesy in Eastern African History*, James Currey, 1995, p. 188.

[23] B. A. Ogot, *A History of the Luo-Speaking Peoples of Eastern Africa*, Anyange Press, 2009, p. 645.

[24] C. W. Hobley, *Kenya: From Chartered Company to Crown Colony* (2nd edn), Frank Cass, 1970, pp. 217–18.

[25] Luise White, Stephen E. Miescher and David William Cohen (eds), *African Words, African Voices: Critical Practices in Oral History*, Indiana University Press, 2001, p. 37.

[26] Ogot, *A History of the Luo-Speaking Peoples of Eastern Africa*, p. 670.

[27] Ibid., p. 666.

[28] Osaak A. Olumwullah, *Dis-ease in the Colonial State*, Praeger, 2002, p. 131.

[29] Elspeth Huxley, *White Man's Country: Lord Delamere and the Making of Kenya*, vol. 1: 1870–1914, Macmillan, 1935.

[30] B. A. Ogot and W. R. Ochieng', *Decolonization and Independence in Kenya, 1940–93*, Ohio University Press, 1995, p. 10.

[31] Ochieng', *A History of Kenya*, p. 103.

[32] Ogot, *A History of the Luo-Speaking Peoples of Eastern Africa*, p. 678.

[33] Neil Sobania, *Culture and Customs of Kenya*, Greenwood, 2003, p. 19.

[34] Okoth, *A History of Africa*, p. 353.

[35] Philip Wayland Porter and Eric S. Sheppard, *A World of Difference: Society, Nature, Development*, Guildford, 1998, p. 357.

[36] Ibid.

[37] Elspeth Huxley, *The Flame Trees of Thika*, Chatto & Windus, 1959, p. 7.

[38] C. S. Nicholls, *Elspeth Huxley: A Biography*, Thomas Dunne, 2002, p. 5.

[39] *Seventh-Day Adventist Encyclopedia*, Review and Herald Publishing Association, 1976.

[40] Jack Mahon, 'What Happened in 1906?' *The Messenger*, vol. 111 (1996): 100 Years of Mission, 1906–1996, p. 8.

[41] Richard Gethin, *Private Memoirs*, pp. 35–6, quoted in Ogot, *A History of the Luo-Speaking Peoples of Eastern Africa*, p. 683.

[42] Barack Obama, *Dreams from my Father* (revised edn), Three Rivers, 2004, pp. 397–8.

[43] Ogot, *A History of the Luo-Speaking Peoples of Eastern Africa*, p. 678.

[44] Brett L. Shadle, 'Patronage, Millennialism and the Serpent God Mumbo in South-west Kenya, 1912–34', *Africa*, vol. 72, no. 1 (2002), pp. 29–54.

[45] George F. Pickens, *African Christian God-Talk*, University Press of America, 2004, p. 134.

[46] B. A. Ogot, 'Kenya Under the British, 1895 to 1963', in B. A. Ogot (ed.),

Zamani: A Survey of East African History, East African Publishing House, 1968, p. 264.

[47] C. S. Nicholls, *Red Strangers: The White Tribe of Kenya*, Timewell, 2005, p. 119.

Chapter 6: Five Wives and Two World Wars

[1] P. H. S. Hatton, 'The Search for an Anglo-German Understanding through Africa, 1912–14', *European Studies Review*, vol. 1, no. 2 (1971), p. 125.

[2] John Iliffe, *Honour in African History*, African Studies no. 107, Cambridge University Press, 2005, p. 235.

[3] A. Davis and H. J. Robertson, *Chronicles of Kenya*, Cecil Palmer, 1928, pp. 97–8.

[4] Lawrence H. Officer, 'What Were the UK Earnings and Prices Then?', MeasuringWorth, 2009, www.measuringworth.org/ukearncpi/.

[5] W. E. Burghardt DuBois, 'The African Roots of War', *Atlantic Monthly*, vol. 115, no. 5 (May 1915), p. 714.

[6] Iliffe, *Honour in African History*, p. 234.

[7] Edward Paice, *Tip and Run: The Untold Tragedy of the Great War in Africa*, Phoenix, 2007, p. 159.

[8] Robert O. Collins and James McDonald Burns, A *History of Sub-Saharan Africa*, Cambridge University Press, 2007, p. 278.

[9] Hans Poeschel, *The Voice of German East Africa: The English in the Judgement of the Natives*, Naburu, 2010, p. 27.

[10] Barack Obama, *Dreams from My Father* (revised edn), Three Rivers, 2004, p. 400.

[11] Sir Phillip Mitchell, *African Afterthoughts*, Hutchinson, 1954, p. 40.

[12] Ibid., p. 34.

[13] John Dawson Ainsworth and F. H. Goldsmith, *John Ainsworth – Pioneer Kenya Administrator, 1864–1946*, Macmillan, 1955, p. 94.

[14] John Buchan, A *History of the Great War*, vol. 1, Houghton & Mifflin, 1922, p. 429.

[15] Paul von Lettow-Vorbeck, *My Reminiscences of East Africa*, Battery Press, 1990, p. 318.

[16] Edward Paice, *Tip and Run: The Untold Tragedy of the Great War in Africa*, Weidenfeld and Nicolson, 2007, p. 400.

[17] Brian Digre, *Imperialism's New Clothes: The Repartition of Tropical Africa 1914–1919*, Peter Lang, 1990, p. 156.

[18] League of Nations Covenant, Article 22, para 1.

[19] Digre, *Imperialism's New Clothes*.

[20] Anthony Clayton and Donald C. Savage, *Government and Labour in Kenya 1895–1963*, Routledge, 1974, p. 88.

[21] H. R. A. Philp, *A New Day in Kenya*, World Dominion Press, 1936, pp. 32–3.

[22] Harry Thuku, *An Autobiography*, Oxford University Press (Nairobi), 1970.

[23] Obama, *Dreams from My Father*, p. 403.

[24] Clayton and Savage, *Government and Labour in Kenya 1895–1963*, p. 125.

[25] Obama, *Dreams from My Father*, pp. 425–6.

[26] Iliffe, *Honour in African History*, p. 230.

[27] Obama, *Dreams from My Father*, p. 411.

[28] Ibid., pp. 370–1.

Chapter 7: A State of Emergency

[1] Barack Obama, *Dreams from My Father* (revised edition), Three Rivers, 2004, p. 415.

[2] Ibid., p. 419.

[3] A. Adu Boahen, *General History of Africa*, vol. VII: *Africa under Colonial Domination 1880–1935*, James Currey/UNESCO, 1990, p. 281.

[4] David Anderson, *Histories of the Hanged*, Weidenfeld and Nicolson, 2005, p. 10.

[5] Charles Abiodun Alao, *Mau-Mau Warrior*, Osprey, 2006, p. 6.

[6] George Bennett and Carl G. Rosberg, *The Kenyatta Election: Kenya 1960–1961*, Oxford University Press, 1961, p. 7.

[7] Alao, *Mau-Mau Warrior*, p. 5.

[8] Obama, *Dreams from My Father*, p. 417.

[9] Ben Macintyre and Paul Orengoh, 'Beatings and Abuse Made Barack Obama's Grandfather Loathe the British', *The Times*, 2 December 2008.

[10] Anderson, *Histories of the Hanged*, p. 50.

[11] Ibid., p. 69.

[12] Ibid., p. 1.

[13] Michael Blundell, *So Rough a Wind*, Weidenfeld and Nicolson, 1964, pp. 123–4.

[14] Caroline Elkins, *Imperial Reckoning: The Untold Story of Britain's Gulag in Kenya*, Henry Holt, 2004, p. xiii.

[15] Ibid., p. 70.

[16] Ibid., p. 71.

[17] Anderson, *Histories of the Hanged*, p. 4.

[18] Elkins, *Imperial Reckoning*, p. 66.

[19] Ibid., p. 87.

[20] Anderson, *Histories of the Hanged*, p. 300.

[21] John Blacker, 'The Demography of Mau Mau: Fertility and Mortality in Kenya in the 1950s: A Demographer's Viewpoint', *African Affairs*, vol. 106, no. 423 (2007), pp. 205–27.

Chapter 8: Mr 'Double-Double'

[1] Elizabeth Sanderson, 'Barack Obama's Stepmother Living in Bracknell', *Daily Mail*, 6 January 2008.

[2] Ibid.

[3] Speech given by President Obama from the pulpit of the historic Brown Chapel in Selma, Alabama, 4 March 2007.

[4] Tom Shachtman, *Airlift to America: How Barack Obama, Sr., John F. Kennedy, Tom Mboya, and 800 East African Students Changed Their World and Ours*, St Martin's Press, 2009.

[5] Jonathan Martin, 'Obama's Mother Known Here as "Uncommon"', *Seattle Times*, 8 April 2008.

[6] Amanda Ripley, 'The Story of Barack Obama's Mother', *Time*, 9 April 2008.

[7] Barack Obama, *Dreams from My Father*, Three Rivers, 2004, pp. 7–8.

[8] George Bennett and Carl G. Rosberg, *The Kenyatta Election: Kenya 1960–1961*, Oxford University Press, 1961, pp. 176–180.

[9] Barack H. Obama, 'Problems Facing Our Socialism', *East Africa Journal*, July 1965, pp. 26–33.

[10] B. A. Ogot and William Ochieng', *Decolonization and Independence in Kenya, 1940–1993*, Ohio University Press, 1995, p. 98.

[11] Godfrey Mwakikagile, *Kenya: Identity of A Nation*, New Africa Press, 2007, p. 37.

[12] Sally Jacobs, 'A Father's Charm', *Boston Globe*, 21 September 2008.

[13] *East African Standard*, 7 July 1969.

[14] D. Goldworth, *The Man Kenya Wanted to Forget*, Holmes & Meier, 1982, p. 281.

[15] Ibid.

[16] Jacobs, 'A Father's Charm'.

[17] E. S. Atieno Odhiambo, 'Ethnic Cleansing and Civil Society in Kenya, 1969–1992', *Journal of Contemporary African Studies*, vol. 22, no. 1 (2004), pp. 29–42. The speech, which was given in Swahili, was translated into English for the paper.

[18] Tania Branigan, 'Barack Obama's Half-Brother Writes Book "Inspired by Father's Abuse"', *Guardian*, 4 November 2009.

[19] Barack Obama, 'My Spiritual Journey', *Times* 16 October 2006.

[20] Obama, *Dreams from My Father*, p. 5.

[21] Ibid., p. 430.

Epilogue

[1] Nick Wadhams, 'Kenyan President Moi's "Corruption" Laid Bare', *Daily Telegraph*, 1 September 2007.

[2] Ellis Cose, 'Walking the World Stage', *Newsweek*, 11 September 2006.

[3] Godfrey Mwakikagile, *Kenya: Identity of a Nation*, New Africa Press, 2007.

[4] James C. McKinley, 'Political Violence Taking A Toll on Kenya Tourism', *New York Times*, 31 August 1997.

[5] Richard B. Richburg, *Out of America: A Black Man Confronts Africa*, Basic Books, 1997, pp. 104–5.

[6] Oliver Mathenge, 'Obama Scolds Kenya', *Daily Nation*, 3 July 2009.

[7] Barack Obama, 'A New Moment of Promise', speech given in Accra, Ghana, 11 July 2009.

Notes on Methodology

[1] Luise White et al. (eds), *African Words, African Voices: Critical Practices in Oral History*, Indiana University Press, 2001.

[2] B. A. Ogot, *History of the Southern Luo*, vol. 1, East African Publishing House, 1967, pp. 142–3.

[3] B. A Ogot, 'The Concept of Jok', *African Studies*, vol. 20, no. 2 (1961), pp. 123–30.

[4] Barack Obama, *Dreams from My Father*, Three Rivers, 2004, p. 376.

[5] Ogot, *History of the Southern Luo*, p. 27.

[6] Cited ibid., p. 27n.

[7] Cited ibid.

BIBLIOGRAPHY

Ainsworth, John Dawson and F. H. Goldsmith, *John Ainsworth – Pioneer Kenya Administrator, 1864–1946*, Macmillan, 1955

Alao, Charles Abiodun, *Mau-Mau Warrior*, Osprey, 2006

Anderson, David, *Histories of the Hanged*, Phoenix, 2006

Anderson, David and Douglas H. Johnson, *Revealing Prophets: Prophesy in Eastern African History*, James Currey, 1995

Ayodo, Awuor, *Luo* (The Heritage Library of African peoples), Rosen Publishing, 1995

Baumann, Oscar, *Durch Massailand zur Nilquelle* (Through the lands of the Maasai to the source of the Nile), Dietrich Reimer, 1894

Bennett, George and Carl G. Rosberg, *The Kenyatta Election: Kenya 1960–1961*, Oxford University Press, 1961

Bennett, Norman Robert, *A History of the Arab State of Zanzibar*, Routledge, 1978.

Blacker, John, 'The Demography of Mau Mau: Fertility and Mortality in Kenya in the 1950s: A Demographer's Viewpoint, *African Affairs*, vol. 106, no. 423, 2007

Blundell, Michael, *So Rough a Wind*, Weidenfeld & Nicolson, 1964

Boahen, A. Adu, *General History of Africa*, vol. VII: *Africa under colonial domination 1880-1935*, James Currey/UNESCO, 1990

Branigan, Tania, 'Barack Obama's half-brother writes book "inspired by father's abuse"', *Guardian*, 4 November 2009

Buchan, John, A *History of the Great War*, vol. 1, Houghton & Mifflin, 1922

Clayton, Anthony and Donald C. Savage, *Government and Labour in Kenya 1895–1963*, Routledge, 1974

Cohen, D. W., 'The River-Lake Nilotes from the Fifteenth to the Nineteenth Century', in B A Ogot (ed.), *Zamani: A Survey of East African History*, East African Publishing House, 1968

Cohen, D. W. and E. S. Atieno Odhiambo, *The Historical Anthropology of an African Landscape*, Eastern African Studies, James Currey, 1989

Collins, Robert O. and James McDonald Burns, A *History of Sub-Saharan Africa*, Cambridge University Press, 2007

Cose, Ellis, 'Walking the World Stage', *Newsweek*, 11 September 2006

Crazzolara, J. P., *The Lwoo*, part I, Verona, 1950

Davis, A. and H. J. Robertson, *Chronicles of Kenya*, Cecil Palmer, 1928

Digre, Brian, *Imperialism's New Clothes: The Repartition of Tropical Africa 1914–1919*, Peter Lang, 1990

DuBois, W. E. Burghardt, 'The African Roots of War', *Atlantic Monthly*, vol. 115, no. 5, May 1915

Dugard, Martin, *Into Africa: The Epic Adventures of Stanley and Livingstone*, Doubleday, 2003

East African, 'Murder that Shaped the Future of Kenya', 5 December 2008

East African Standard, 7 July 1969

Elkins, Caroline, *Imperial Reckoning: the Untold Story of Britain's Gulag in Kenya*, Henry Holt, 2004

Farwell, Byron, *The Great War in Africa: 1914–1918*, Norton, 1989

Fyle, C. Magbaily, *Introduction to the History of African Civilization: Precolonial Africa*, University Press of America, 1999

Goldworth, D., *The Man Kenya Wanted to Forget*, Holmes & Meier, 1982

Goudie, Andrew, *Environmental Change*, (3rd edition), Oxford University Press, 1992.

Hall, Richard, *Empires of the Monsoon*, Harper Collins, 1996

Hatton, P. H. S., 'The Search for an Anglo-German Understanding through Africa, 1912-14', *European Studies Review*, vol. 1, no. 2, (1971)

Henderson, W. O., *Studies in German Colonial History*, Routledge, 1962

Hobley, C. W., *Kenya: from Chartered Company to Crown Colony*, Witherby, 1929

Huxley, Elspeth, *White Man's Country: Lord Delamere and the Making of Kenya*, vol. 1: 1870–1914, Macmillan, 1935

Huxley, Elspeth, *The Flame Trees of Thika*, Chatto & Windus, 1959

Iliffe, John, *Honour in Africa History*, African Studies no. 107, Cambridge University Press, 2004

Isichei, Elizabeth, *A History of African Societies to 1870*, Cambridge University Press, 1997

Jacobs, Sally, 'A Father's Charm', *Boston Globe*, 21 September 2008

Johnson, W. P., *My African Reminiscences, 1875–1895*, Universities' Mission to Central Africa, 1924

Johnston, Harry H., 'Livingstone as an Explorer', *Geographical Journal*, vol. 41, no. 5, (May 1913)

Kenyatta, Jomo, *Facing Mount Kenya: The Tribal Life of the Gikuyu*, Secker & Warburg, 1938

Kenyatta, Jomo, *Harambee! – The Prime Minister of Kenya's Speeches 1963–64*, Oxford University Press, Nairobi, 1964

Kolonial-Politische Korrespondenz (Colonial-Political Correspondence), 1st Year, Berlin, 16 May 1885

Lamb, Hubert H, *Climate, History and the Modern World*, (2nd edn), Routledge, 1995

League of Nations Covenant, Article 22

Lettow-Vorbeck, Paul von, *My Reminiscences of East Africa*, Battery Press, 1990.

Luthuli, Albert et al, *Africa's Freedom*, Unwin, 1964

Macintyre, Ben and Paul Orengoh, 'Beatings and Abuse made Barack Obama's Grandfather Loathe the British, *The Times*, 2 December 2008.

Mahon, Jack, 'What happened in 1906?' *The Messenger*, vol. 111 (1996): 100 Years of Mission, 1906–1996

Martin, Jonathan, 'Obama's Mother Known Here as "Uncommon"'. *Seattle Times*, 8 April 2008

Mathenge, Oliver, 'Obama scolds Kenya', *Daily Nation*, 3 July 2009

Maxon, Robert M, in Kevin Shillington (ed.), *Encyclopedia of African History*. Routledge, 2004

M'bokolo, Elikia, 'The Impact of the Slave Trade on Africa,' *Le Monde diplomatique* (English edn), April 1998

Mboya, Tom, *Freedom and After*, Andre Deutsch, 1963

Mboya, Tom, *The Challenge of Nationhood: A Collection of Speeches and Writings*, Andre Deutsch, 1970

McKinley, James C., 'Political Violence Taking A Toll on Kenya Tourism', *New York Times*, 31 August 1997

Metcalf, Thomas R., *Imperial Connections: India in the Indian Ocean Area, 1860–1920*, University of California Press, 2008

Miruka, Okumba, *Oral Literature of the Luo*, East African Educational Publishers, 2001

Mitchell, Sir Phillip, *African Afterthoughts*, Hutchinson, 1954

Mwakikagail, Godfrey, *Kenya: Identity of A Nation*, New Africa Press, 2007

Newman, James L., *Imperial Footprints: Henry Morton Stanley's African Journeys*, Brassey's, 2005

Nicholls, C. S., *Elspeth Huxley: A Biography*, Thomas Dunne, 2002

Nicholls, C. S., *Red Strangers: The White Tribe of Kenya*, Timewell, 2005

Nunoo, Richard, 'The Preservation and Presentation of the Monuments and Sites of Koobi Fora, Lamu, lshakani and Thimlich Ohinga' UNESCO Restricted Technical Report RP/1984-1985/XI,1,4, 1985

Obama, Barack, *Dreams from My Father*, Three Rivers, 1995

Obama, Barack, *The Audacity of Hope*, Three Rivers, 2006

Obama, Barack, 'My Spiritual Journey', *Time*, 16 October 2006

Obama, Barack, 'Selma Voting Rights March Commemoration', speech given in Brown Chapel, Selma, Alabama, 4 March 2007

Obama, Barack, 'A New Moment of Promise', speech given in Accra, Ghana, 11 July 2009

Obama, Barak H., 'Problems Facing Our Socialism', *East Africa Journal*, July 1965

Ochieng', W. R., 'The Transformation of a Bantu Settlement into a Luo "Ruothdom"': A Case Study of the Evolution of the Yimbo Community in Nyanza up to AD 1900', in B. A. Ogot (ed.), *History and Social Change in East Africa*, Hadith 6. Nairobi: East African Literature Bureau, 1976

Ochieng', W. R., *A History of Kenya*, Macmillan, Kenya, 1985

Odhiambo, E S Atieno, 'Ethnic Cleansing and Civil Society in Kenya, 1969–1992', *Journal of Contemporary African Studies*, vol. 22, no. 1 (2004)

Odinga, Oginga, *Not yet Uhuru*, Heinemann, 1968

Officer, Lawrence H., 'What Were the UK Earnings and Prices Then?', MeasuringWorth, 2009, www.measuringworth.org/ukearncpi/

Ogot, B. A., 'The Concept of Jok', *African Studies*, vol. 20, no. 2 (1961

Ogot, B. A., *History of the Southern Luo*, vol. I, East African Publishing House, 1967

Ogot, B. A., (ed.), *Zamani: A Survey of East African History*, East African Publishing House, 1968

Ogot, B. A., (ed.), *History and Social Change in East Africa*, Hadith 6, Nairobi: East African Literature Bureau, 1976

Ogot, B. A., *A History of the Luo-Speaking Peoples of Eastern Africa*, Anyange Press, 2009

Ogot, B. A. and W. R. Ochieng' (eds) *Decolonization & Independence in Kenya 1940-93*, Ohio University Press, 1995

Okoth, Assa, *A History of Africa, vol. 1: 1800–1914*, East African Educational Publishers, 2006

Oliver, Roland, *The Missionary Factor in East Africa*, Longmans, 1952

Oliver, Roland A. and Anthony Atmore, *Medieval Africa, 1250–1800*. (2nd edition), Cambridge University Press, 2001

Olumwullah, Osaak A., *Dis-ease in the Colonial State*, Praeger, 2002

Ominde, S. H., *The Luo Girl; From Infancy to Marriage*, Macmillan, 1952

Paice, Edward, *Tip and Run: The Untold Tragedy of the Great War in Africa*, Phoenix, 2007

Patterson, Bruce D., *The Lions of Tsavo: Exploring the Legacy of Africa's Notorious Man-Eaters*, McGraw-Hill, 2004

Philp, H. R. A., *A New Day in Kenya*, World Dominion Press, 1936

Pickens, George F., *African Christian God-talk*, University Press of America, 2004

Poeschel, Hans, *The Voice of German East Africa: The English in the Judgement of the Natives*, Naburu, 2010

Porter, Philip Wayland and Eric S. Sheppard, *A World of Difference: Society, Nature, Development*, Guildford, 1998

Rebmann, Johannes, *The Church Missionary Intelligencer*, vol. 1, no. 1, (May 1849)

Richburg, B. Richard, *Out of America: A Black Man confronts Africa*, Basic Books, 1997

Ripley, Amanda, 'The Story of Barack Obama's Mother'. *Time*, 9 April 2008

Sanderson, Elizabeth, 'Barack Obama's stepmother living in Bracknell'. *Daily Mail*, 6 January 2008

Seventh-Day Adventist Encyclopedia, Review and Herald Publishing Association, 1976

Shachtman, Tom, *Airlift to America: How Barack Obama, Sr., John F. Kennedy, Tom Mboya, and 800 East African Students Changed Their World and Ours*, St Martin's Press, 2009

Shadle, Brett L., 'Patronage, Millennialism and the Serpent God Mumbo in south-west Kenya, 1912-34', *Africa*, vol. 72, no.1 (2002)

Sobania, Neil, *Culture and Customs of Kenya*, Greenwood, 2003

Stanley, H. M., writing in the *New York Herald*, July 1871

Stanley, H. M., 'The Search for Livingstone', *New York Times*, 2 July 1872

Stanley, H. M., *My Kalulu, Prince, King, and Slave: A Story of Central Africa*, Sampson Low, 1873

Stanley, H. M., *Through the Dark Continent*: vol. 1. Dover, 1988

Taylor, A. J. P., *Germany's First Bid for Colonies*, Macmillan, 1938

The Times, 28 September 1891.

Thomson, Joseph, *Through Masai Land*, Sampson Low, 1885.

Thuku, Harry, *An Autobiography*, Oxford University Press, Nairobi, 1970.

Wadhams, Nick, 'Kenyan President Moi's "Corruption" Laid Bare'. *Daily Telegraph*, 1 September 2007.

White, Luise et al. (eds), *African Words, African Voices: Critical Practices in Oral History*, Indiana University Press, 2001.

Wilson, Arnold Talbot, *The Suez Canal: It's Past, Present and Future*, Oxford University Press, 1933.

INDEX

NOTE ON
THE AUTHOR

Peter Firstbrook worked for the BBC for twenty-five years before developing a successful freelance writing and film-making career in 2002, specialising in making history and international documentaries. He has published three bestselling books. During 2008–9 Peter spent several months in Kenya tracing Barack Obama's roots from the present day back more than twenty generations, thanks to the Luo tribe's remarkable oral tradition. In June 2009 he convened a committee made up of members of the Obama family in Kisumu, Kenya, which approved his Obama family tree.